Raspberry Pi Blueprints

Design and build your own hardware projects that interact with the real world using the Raspberry Pi

Dan Nixon

[PACKT] open source*
PUBLISHING   community experience distilled

BIRMINGHAM - MUMBAI

Raspberry Pi Blueprints

First published: March 2015

Production reference: 1200315

Published by Packt Publishing Ltd.
Livery Place
35 Livery Street
Birmingham B3 2PB, UK.

ISBN 978-1-78439-290-1

www.packtpub.com

Credits

Author
Dan Nixon

Reviewers
Soumen Chandra Laha

Maryala Srinivas

Commissioning Editor
Akram Hussain

Acquisition Editor
Meeta Rajani

Content Development Editor
Shubhangi Dhamgaye

Technical Editor
Siddhi Rane

Copy Editor
Neha Vyas

Project Coordinator
Harshal Ved

Proofreaders
Simran Bhogal

Maria Gould

Paul Hindle

Indexer
Mariammal Chettiyar

Production Coordinator
Manu Joseph

Cover Work
Manu Joseph

About the Author

Dan Nixon lives in England and is a 20-year old software engineering student who is currently studying at Newcastle University and is in his third year. He has long had an interest in electronics and embedded computing projects.

Previously, Dan has worked on a 360-degree camera system for the Raspberry Pi and this is where his interest in the platform started.

Currently, he is on a year-long work placement and is working on neutron data analysis software at the Rutherford Appleton Laboratory in Oxford, UK.

I would like to thank my mother and father for their support while writing this book. I would also like to thank the members of Maker Space, Newcastle, for providing the facilities to prototype the projects and allowing me to use some of their projects in this book.

About the Reviewers

Soumen Chandra Laha has been working as a senior embedded design engineer at Wine Yard Technologies since 2008. He started his career as a quality control engineer and gradually became an embedded design engineer. He has been working in the field of embedded systems and has industry experience of more than 6 years in various domains, including automotive, consumer electronics, healthcare, and so on. He has hands-on experience in various microcontrollers and microprocessors, such as 8051, PIC, AVR, PSoC, ARM Cortex, ARM7, ARM9, ARM11, and the TI-DSP microcontroller. He has development exposure to embedded Linux and Windows CE and knows how to port real-time operating systems on various ARM platforms.

He is an electronic hobbyist and designer and believes in continuous learning. His strengths lie in developing, maintaining, integrating, and debugging large sized C code of applications and system-level embedded software designs.

Maryala Srinivas is the founder and managing director of Wine Yard Technologies, which was founded in 2006. He has over 10 years of experience in the field of advanced embedded systems design and development. He is a passionate and enthusiastic entrepreneur. His passion to become an entrepreneur made him reject a great job offer from Delhi Metro Rail Corporation (DMRC), where he was to work for the signaling department in the R&D Division. He is associated with Junior Chamber International, India and Hyderabad Directors/CEO's Forum (HDCF). He received the Indira Gandhi Sadbhavana Award in 2012 for outstanding services, achievements, and contributions to the nation in the field of science and technology.

Many of his articles are published in national and international journals and technical magazines. He has addressed several technical conferences and seminars in the field of embedded systems and RTOS design. He was recognized as the star speaker at EFY Design Engineers' Conference, held at New Delhi in March 2012. Many of the faculty members from universities such as NITs, JNTU, AU, and OU and other private engineering colleges benefited immensely by the technology talent transformation workshops conducted by him at Wine Yard Technologies. The Wine Yard team led by him has achieved many milestones. More than 100,000 students and over 400 professionals, including the teaching faculty from universities and many working engineers, have immensely benefited from the talent transformation programs.

www.PacktPub.com

Support files, eBooks, discount offers, and more

For support files and downloads related to your book, please visit www.PacktPub.com.

Did you know that Packt offers eBook versions of every book published, with PDF and ePub files available? You can upgrade to the eBook version at www.PacktPub.com and as a print book customer, you are entitled to a discount on the eBook copy. Get in touch with us at service@packtpub.com for more details.

At www.PacktPub.com, you can also read a collection of free technical articles, sign up for a range of free newsletters and receive exclusive discounts and offers on Packt books and eBooks.

PACKTLIB

https://www2.packtpub.com/books/subscription/packtlib

Do you need instant solutions to your IT questions? PacktLib is Packt's online digital book library. Here, you can search, access, and read Packt's entire library of books.

Why subscribe?

- Fully searchable across every book published by Packt
- Copy and paste, print, and bookmark content
- On demand and accessible via a web browser

Free access for Packt account holders

If you have an account with Packt at www.PacktPub.com, you can use this to access PacktLib today and view 9 entirely free books. Simply use your login credentials for immediate access.

Table of Contents

Preface

The Raspberry Pi is a small form factor, single board, ARM-based computer. It is capable of running on many desktop applications that can be run on a standard Linux computer. While the Pi is only slightly larger than a credit card, it uses very little power. As such, it has become very popular among the hacker and maker community, which uses the Pi to integrate more computing power in their projects.

The Pi is very easy to set up and in less than 20 minutes, you can run it on a modified version of popular, Linux-based operating systems. It will function just like you would expect a desktop PC to. Thanks to its small form factor, many people have used it as an alternative to a traditional PC for fast access to applications and the Internet. Since the Pi draws very little power, it can be left running.

Where the Pi really excels is that it brings more computing power to hardware and electronics projects. This is made possible by a wide range of interfaces on the Pi that are typically not found on conventional computers.

This has led to a rise in new projects that are made using the Pi, which otherwise would have been considerably more difficult or expensive to make.

What this book covers

Chapter 1, *Raspberry Pi Pirate Radio*, introduces the Pi and gives an overview of its setup and configuration procedure and some fundamental Linux concepts. This chapter then demonstrates the basic use of the GPIO header and Python scripting.

Chapter 2, *Portable Speaker System*, explores how to use the Pi as a portable, battery-powered speaker system with a self-contained media server that can be used without any ties to a power supply or home network.

Chapter 3, Mini Retro Arcade Cabinet, demonstrates how the Pi can be used to create a mini arcade cabinet complete with a traditional joystick and button controls and how it can be used to play a range of classic arcade and console games.

Chapter 4, GPS-enabled Time-lapse Recorder, covers how to use the Pi as a time lapse recorder that can also capture the location of each image and trigger the image capture based on the current position of and distance traveled by the camera.

Chapter 5, Home Theater PC, explores the way in which the Pi can be used as a home theater PC using the popular XBMC media center software and a custom, purpose-built enclosure.

Chapter 6, Outdoor Weather Station, delves into the topic of interfacing hardware to the Pi using intermediate devices, in this case, Arduino. We also take a look at Python web applications running on the Pi.

Chapter 7, Home Security System, explores how to use the Pi as a hub for a wireless network of sensors and how this data can be used and displayed on a web application.

Chapter 8, Remote-operated Robotic Arm, focuses on how to use the Pi to control and monitor devices remotely in the form of a robotic arm that can be controlled through a web application.

Chapter 9, Magic Mirror, expands your knowledge of woodworking and designing, which will prove to be important skills for any further projects that you do in the field of electronics and physical computing.

Chapter 10, Bottle Xylophone, covers how the Pi, several servos, and some empty bottles can be turned into a musical instrument driven by MIDI files.

What you need for this book

This book assumes that you are familiar with the basics of the Raspberry Pi and Linux. Most of the code in this book is in Python with some C++. However, the source code for each of the projects is available alongside the book that can be used straight on the Pi.

Several of the projects will also deal with some basic electronics, and as such, some basic tools will be needed for the completion of some projects. However, note that at the start of each chapter, the procedure to build the electronics side of the project is explained step by step.

Some projects will also require access to woodworking tools in order to construct cases and enclosures. Usually, you will require just the common "garden shed" tools. However, there is information in the relevant chapters on what you can do if not having the correct tools causes an issue in the relevant chapters.

Who this book is for

This book is aimed at those are just getting started with the Raspberry Pi, already have a few small projects under their belt, and are looking to get into the world of hardware and physical computing projects.

Conventions

In this book, you will find a number of text styles that distinguish between different kinds of information. Here are some examples of these styles and an explanation of their meaning.

Code words in text, database table names, folder names, filenames, file extensions, pathnames dummy URLs and user input are shown as follows: "Where `path/to/raspbian_image.img` is the extracted image file and `sdX` is the path to your SD card."

A block of code is set as follows:

```
#!/bin/bash
sleep 20
cd /home/pi
python player.py -d music --random -f 99.9 &
```

Any command-line input or output is written as follows:

```
ffmpeg -i file.mp3 -f s16le -ar 22.05k -ac 2 - | sudo ./pifm - freq 22050 stereo
```

New terms and **important words** are shown in bold. Words that you see on the screen, for example, in menus or dialog boxes, appear in the text like this: "Files can be uploaded by right-clicking on them and selecting **Upload**."

> Warnings or important notes appear in a box like this.

[💡   Tips and tricks appear like this.   ]

Reader feedback

Feedback from our readers is always welcome. Let us know what you think about this book—what you liked or disliked. Reader feedback is important for us as it helps us develop titles that you will really get the most out of.

To send us general feedback, simply e-mail `feedback@packtpub.com`, and mention the book's title in the subject of your message.

If there is a topic that you have expertise in and you are interested in either writing or contributing to a book, see our author guide at `www.packtpub.com/authors`.

Customer support

Now that you are the proud owner of a Packt book, we have a number of things to help you to get the most from your purchase.

Downloading the example code

You can download the example code files from your account at `http://www.packtpub.com` for all the Packt Publishing books you have purchased. If you purchased this book elsewhere, you can visit `http://www.packtpub.com/support` and register to have the files e-mailed directly to you.

Downloading the color images of this book

We also provide you with a PDF file that has color images of the screenshots/diagrams used in this book. The color images will help you better understand the changes in the output. You can download this file from `https://www.packtpub.com/sites/default/files/downloads/2901OS_ColoredImages.pdf`.

Errata

Although we have taken every care to ensure the accuracy of our content, mistakes do happen. If you find a mistake in one of our books—maybe a mistake in the text or the code—we would be grateful if you could report this to us. By doing so, you can save other readers from frustration and help us improve subsequent versions of this book. If you find any errata, please report them by visiting http://www.packtpub.com/submit-errata, selecting your book, clicking on the **Errata Submission Form** link, and entering the details of your errata. Once your errata are verified, your submission will be accepted and the errata will be uploaded to our website or added to any list of existing errata under the Errata section of that title.

To view the previously submitted errata, go to https://www.packtpub.com/books/content/support and enter the name of the book in the search field. The required information will appear under the **Errata** section.

Piracy

Piracy of copyrighted material on the Internet is an ongoing problem across all media. At Packt, we take the protection of our copyright and licenses very seriously. If you come across any illegal copies of our works in any form on the Internet, please provide us with the location address or website name immediately so that we can pursue a remedy.

Please contact us at copyright@packtpub.com with a link to the suspected pirated material.

We appreciate your help in protecting our authors and our ability to bring you valuable content.

Questions

If you have a problem with any aspect of this book, you can contact us at questions@packtpub.com, and we will do our best to address the problem.

1
Raspberry Pi Pirate Radio

In this chapter, we will take a quick look at the Raspberry Pi hardware and some of the software that will be used both in this project and the majority of others throughout this book.

As the Pi was based on hardware that was to be included in embedded or portable electronics (such as smartphones and tablets), it has a few extra hardware features that are not found on a typical desktop or laptop PC, one of which is the **General Purpose Input and Output (GPIO)** header. This is a set of pins (26 on the model A and B, and 40 on the model B+) that allows you to communicate with external hardware such as GPS sensors, accelerometers, and motors through programming languages such as Python, C, and C++. When we get further in this chapter, we will take a look at a little trick that can be done to turn one of these pins into an FM radio transmitter.

What you will need

You will need the following:

- The Raspberry Pi and power supply
- An SD card with at least 4 GB memory (16 GB is recommended as it holds a good amount of music)
- A thick wire or FM radio antenna
- Male to male 0.1 inch pin jumper wires

Setting up the Pi

In order to get the Pi up and running, the bare minimum you will need is a USB power supply, micro USB cable, an Ethernet cable to connect the Pi to your network, and an SD card that has at least 4 GB memory. Although, later on, some projects will need a larger capacity of the SD card.

While a monitor, mouse, and keyboard can also be used for a lot of the projects in this book, they are not actually required assuming that you have a network that runs a DHCP server, which you can connect with the Pi in order to set it up over SSH.

It is worth mentioning now that for a USB-powered device, the Pi is quite power-hungry (drawing around 600-700 mA), therefore, while the Pi can be powered from a USB port, which is usually rated for around 500 mA, it is recommended that you use a mains powered adapter. Without this, the Pi can become unstable when additional devices are connected that draw more power, for example, a USB Wi-Fi dongle or camera module.

Choosing a Linux distribution

There are a wide range of Linux distributions available for the Pi, some of which are very general purpose while others are built for specific purposes (a couple of which will be used in the later projects of this chapter). For now, we will use the most standard distribution, Raspbian, which as the name suggests is based on the Debian distribution.

> The Raspberry Pi downloads page (http://www.raspberrypi.org/downloads) has a good selection of general purpose distributions.

Another relatively new distribution that is worth mentioning is Minibian (http://minibianpi.wordpress.com), a distribution based on Raspbian, which has the majority of its default software removed. While this may not seem that helpful, it means that the Pi boots in a useable OS in around 25 seconds and saves the SD card space. This type of OS is more suited to a project that has finished being developed and is going into a more natural usage environment. You usually would not expect a Wi-Fi router to take 3 minutes to boot, so why should your Pi-based Internet radio?

Writing an SD card

When you have all the relevant hardware, head over to `http://www.raspberrypi.org/downloads` and download the ZIP archive for Raspbian and extract it.

The next steps vary depending on your operating system.

Windows

Windows does not natively include a tool used to write disk images, therefore, the Win32 Disk Imager (`http://sourceforge.net/projects/win32diskimager`) application is used to write images to an SD card.

First, go to the download link mentioned in the preceding paragraph, download, and install Win32 Disk Imager. As writing images to drives requires administrator permissions, you will need to run Win32 Disk Imager by right-clicking on its entry in the Start menu, and selecting **Run as administrator**:

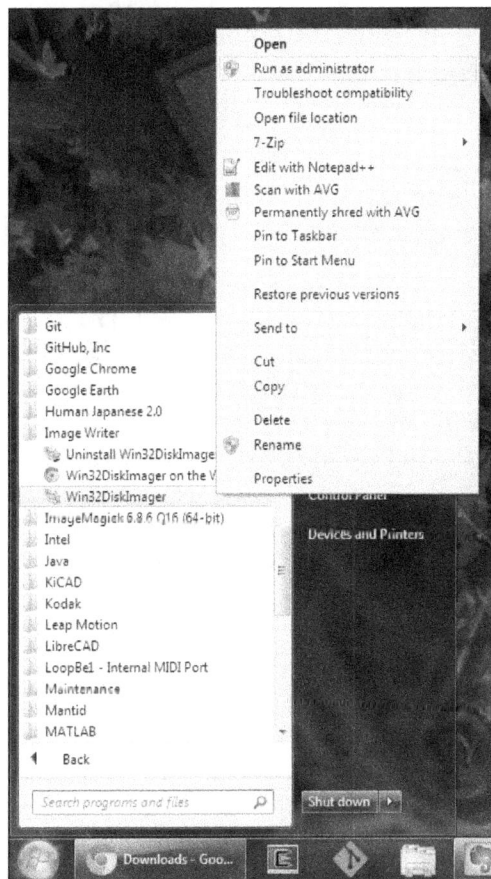

Next, select the `.img` file that was extracted from the Raspbian ZIP file using the folder icon under **Image File** and the drive letter of the SD card from the drop-down box:

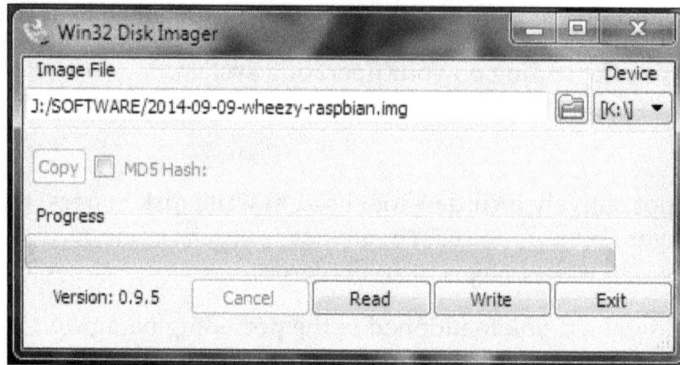

> Ensure that the correct drive letter is selected, and the SD card does not contain any data that has not been backed up, as this operation will destroy all of the data already present in the card.

Finally, click on **Write** to write the image to the SD card.

Linux and Mac OS

Unix and Unix-like operating systems already have a tool to read and write images to external storage—dd.

First, you will need to find the path for your SD card. The easiest way to do this is to use the udev management tool, udevadm, to monitor the udev log, which logs activity from various devices on the system, including the SD card being inserted and will allow you to see the device path that was assigned to it and the partitions already existing on it. This can be done by running the following command:

```
udevadm monitor --udev
```

Then, insert the SD card, at which point, you should see a set of log messages similar to the ones shown in the following screenshot:

```
dan@dannixon-envy-ubuntu -> udevadm monitor --udev
monitor will print the received events for:
UDEV - the event which udev sends out after rule processing

UDEV  [435.546548] add      /devices/pci0000:00/0000:00:14.0/usb2/2-4 (usb)
UDEV  [435.547730] add      /devices/pci0000:00/0000:00:14.0/usb2/2-4/2-4:1.0 (usb)
UDEV  [435.548896] add      /devices/pci0000:00/0000:00:14.0/usb2/2-4/2-4:1.0/host8 (scsi)
UDEV  [435.550318] add      /devices/pci0000:00/0000:00:14.0/usb2/2-4/2-4:1.0/host8/scsi_host/host8 (scsi_host)
UDEV  [436.542079] add      /devices/pci0000:00/0000:00:14.0/usb2/2-4/2-4:1.0/host8/target8:0:0 (scsi)
UDEV  [436.542673] add      /devices/pci0000:00/0000:00:14.0/usb2/2-4/2-4:1.0/host8/target8:0:0/8:0:0:0 (scsi)
UDEV  [436.543387] add      /devices/pci0000:00/0000:00:14.0/usb2/2-4/2-4:1.0/host8/target8:0:0/8:0:0:0/scsi_disk/8:0:0:0 (scsi_disk)
UDEV  [436.543987] add      /devices/pci0000:00/0000:00:14.0/usb2/2-4/2-4:1.0/host8/target8:0:0/8:0:0:0/scsi_device/8:0:0:0 (scsi_device)
UDEV  [436.545361] add      /devices/pci0000:00/0000:00:14.0/usb2/2-4/2-4:1.0/host8/target8:0:0/8:0:0:0/bsg/8:0:0:0 (bsg)
UDEV  [436.545433] add      /devices/pci0000:00/0000:00:14.0/usb2/2-4/2-4:1.0/host8/target8:0:0/8:0:0:0/scsi_generic/sg1 (scsi_generic)
UDEV  [436.732587] add      /devices/virtual/bdi/8:16 (bdi)
UDEV  [436.917684] add      /devices/pci0000:00/0000:00:14.0/usb2/2-4/2-4:1.0/host8/target8:0:0/8:0:0:0/block/sdb (block)
UDEV  [437.064569] add      /devices/pci0000:00/0000:00:14.0/usb2/2-4/2-4:1.0/host8/target8:0:0/8:0:0:0/block/sdb/sdb1 (block)
UDEV  [437.323475] add      /devices/pci0000:00/0000:00:14.0/usb2/2-4/2-4:1.0/host8/target8:0:0/8:0:0:0/block/sdb/sdb2 (block)
```

Here, the important information can be seen on the last three lines, which tells us that in this case, the path for the entire card is /dev/sdb, with two partitions at /dev/sdb1 and /dev/sdb2.

We must now ensure that none of these partitions on the SD card are currently mounted, as some desktop managers (such as GNOME, the default desktop manager on Ubuntu) will try to automatically mount partitions when they are detected.

To do this, we will run the following command for every partition (that is, in my case, /dev/sdb1 and /dev/sdb2), where PATH is the path to the partition:

```
umount PATH
```

If the partition was mounted, you will not see any output from the command; however, if the partition was not mounted, you will get the following message:

```
dan@dannixon-envy-ubuntu -> umount /dev/sdb1
umount: /dev/sdb1 is not mounted (according to mtab)
dan@dannixon-envy-ubuntu -> 
```

Once you know the path for your SD card and have ensured that no existing partitions are mounted, you can then write the Raspbian image to your SD card using the following command, where PATH is the path to the SD card (/dev/sdb in my case):

```
sudo dd if=path/to/raspbian_image.img of=PATH
```

> Be certain that the path to the SD card is correct, and the card does not contain any data that has not been backed up as this operation will destroy all of the data already present on the card.

Where `path/to/raspbian_image.img` is the extracted image file and `sdX` is the path to your SD card. Note that this step can take up to 5-8 minutes, since no output is given on the screen, the SD card reader's busy/data LED is a good indication that the image is being written.

> Since the GNU Coreutils (which include commands such as `cp`, `mv`, `dd`, and so on) do not provide much (or any) output to indicate the progress, you may want to take a look at the Coreutils Viewer tool (`https://github.com/Xfennec/cv`), which shows the progress of the Coreutils commands.

Booting the Pi for the first time

Once you have the image written to the card, it is time to boot the Pi and perform the initial setup. The most common way to do this is by using a keyboard, mouse, and monitor; however, if you have access to a network that provides DHCP (as most home networks do), then the setup can be done entirely over **Secure Shell (SSH)**.

First, set up the hardware and boot the Pi by inserting the SD card, connecting the power, and the Ethernet cable. Within a few seconds, you will see that the ACT LED starts to flicker. If it flashes for very short pulses or does not light at all, then this indicates an issue with either the SD image, the connection between the card and the Pi (a common issue for the models A and B), or the card itself.

Once the Pi has booted (indicated by less frequent flashing of the ACT LED), you will need to determine its IP address. There are two main ways to do this: by accessing the DHCP allocations via your router or by scanning the local network.

Network scanning

The cross-platform tool, the Nmap utility (`http://nmap.org`) can be used to scan a network.

To do so, you will need to find the IP address of your PC (in order to find the subnet on your local network to search for the Pi in). On Windows, this can be done by opening the Command Prompt and executing this command:

```
ipconfig
```

This should give you the information about your network interfaces similar to the following:

On Unix, this can be done by using the following command:

```
ifconfig
```

This command gives output similar to the following:

The search IP range that is given to Nmap is obtained by replacing the last number of IPv4 or InetAddress with `*`. In our case, it will be `192.168.0.*`.

Now that we know the address range in which we will be looking, we can open a terminal and run the following command:

```
nmap --open 192.168.0.*
```

Replacing the IP range with your search range will try to make contact with every host in the given IP address range and will return with a list of every host that is up, with a list of their open ports, and what services they correspond to. In our case, we are looking for any hosts that have an open SSH port:

```
Starting Nmap 5.21 ( http://nmap.org ) at 2014-09-21 11:58 BST
Nmap scan report for 192.168.0.8
Host is up (0.0064s latency).
Not shown: 999 closed ports
PORT    STATE SERVICE
22/tcp open  ssh
Nmap done: 256 IP addresses (5 hosts up) scanned in 5.84 seconds
```

Here, I have only shown the report for the Pi. Usually, after the first boot, SSH will be the only service that is started, so it is usually given away as the device that only provides SSH.

Connecting to the Pi via SSH

On Unix, accessing the Pi via SSH is as simple as executing the following:

```
ssh pi@[Pi IP]
```

Here, `Pi IP` is the IP address of the Pi. You may get a warning similar to this the first time you run the command:

```
The authenticity of host '192.168.0.8 (192.168.0.8)' can't be
established.
ECDSA key fingerprint is 32:4c:46:1b:dd:7e:8b:52:a0:31:c3:f5:9f:73:d1:c6.
Are you sure you want to continue connecting (yes/no)?
```

This can safely be ignored by typing yes and pressing *Enter*. You will then be asked for a password, and as this is the first boot, the default is `raspberry`.

On Windows, PuTTY (`http://www.putty.org`) can be used to SSH into the Pi. Once downloaded, run PuTTY and enter the IP address of the Pi and the **Host Name** field, ensuring that **Port** is set to 22 and **SSH** is selected. Then, click on **Open**:

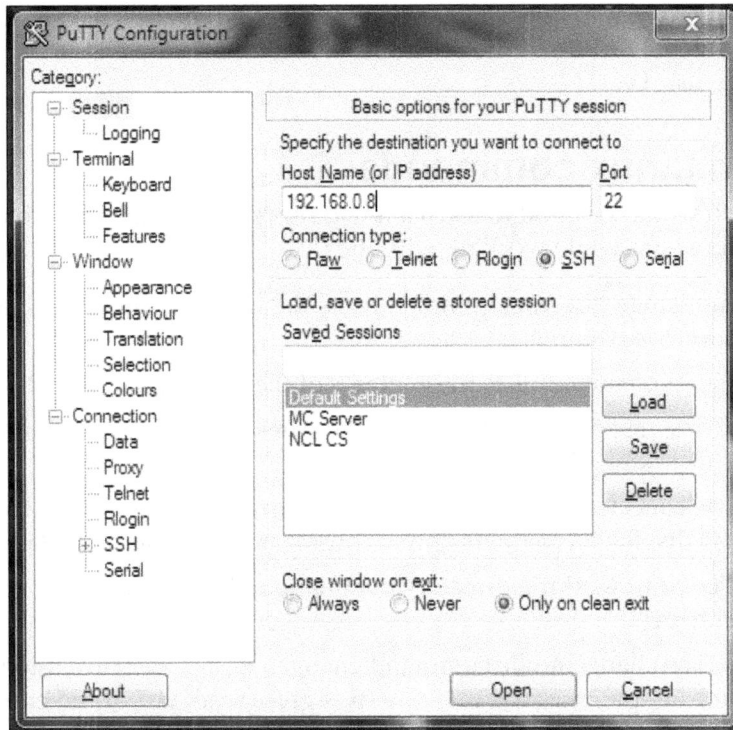

You will see a warning message similar to the following about the identity of the host:

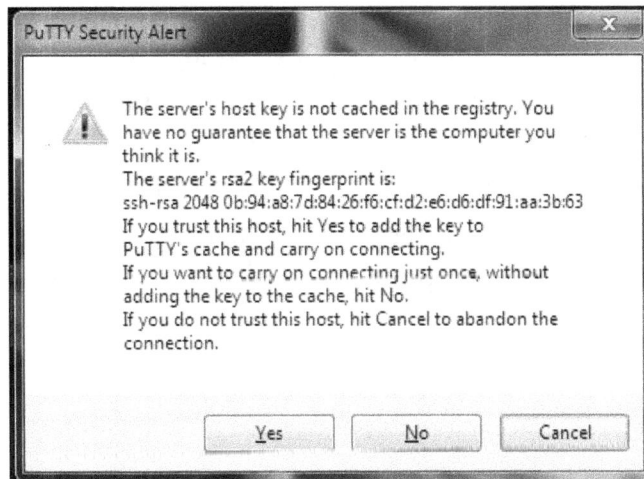

Again, this can be ignored by clicking on **Yes**. You will then be asked for a username and password in the PuTTY terminal window. Since this is the first boot, the defaults are `pi` and `raspberry`.

Common Linux commands

At this point, it would be good to learn a few Linux shell commands, which you will no doubt come across while working with the Pi:

- `cd`: The change directory command sets the working directory to a given directory, for example, `cd /home/pi`

- `ls`: The list command lists the contents of the current working directory

- `mkdir`: The make directory command creates a new directory within the current working directory, for example, `mkdir code`

- `cat`: The concatenate command can perform operations on text files, and it can also display its contents on the console, for example, `cat /etc/passwd`

- `pwd`: The print working directory command tells you the directory you are currently in

- `chmod`: The change mode command changes the access permission to a file, for example, `chmod 744 file` (this gives read, write, and execute permissions to the owner, and read-only permission to everyone else)

- `sudo`: The super user do command executes the following commands as root, for example, `sudo apt-get upgrade`

- `mv`: The move command moves the file or directory in the first argument to the second, for example, `mv file.txt misc_files`

- `cp`: The copy command creates a copy of a file or directory in another directory, for example, `cp file.txt misc_files/file2.txt`

- `rm`: The remove command deletes a file, for example, `rm file.txt`

More information can be obtained about a given command via its man page, which can be accessed using the following command, where `command` is the command you wish to know more about:

```
man command
```

The initial setup

Once you are able to SSH in the Pi, run the configuration utility using the following command:

```
sudo raspi-config
```

This utility allows you to configure the Pi hardware and perform useful configuration tasks such as changing passwords and resizing the root partition on the SD card, both of which, we will do now.

First, select the **Expand Filesystem** option and press *Enter*. The utility will modify the partition table and report that it has completed, and that the changes made will only affect the filesystem after the next reboot. Press *Enter* again to return to the main menu.

Now, select **Change User Password** and hit *Enter* twice. You will be taken back to the shell and prompted to enter a new password, which has to be entered twice. Once done, a confirmation box will notify you that the password was changed successfully; press *Enter* to return to the menu.

As this is all that needs to be done in `raspi-config` for now, press the left arrow key twice to select **Finish** and *Enter* to confirm. You will be asked whether you want to reboot now; select **Yes** and press *Enter*. Once the Pi is rebooted, SSH back into it using your new password.

Once you have access again, check whether you now have access to the full storage space on the SD card using:

```
df -h
```

The command should report the size of `rootfs` much closer to the SD card capacity:

```
rootfs  16G  2.5G  13G  17%  /
```

All that is left to do now is to make sure that the software on the Pi is up to date. Since we are using an image that was just downloaded, it is not likely that there will be a large number of updates; however, it is a good practice to keep an installation up to date.

Running the following commands will first update the list of available packages then update any installed packages with newer versions than what was installed:

```
sudo apt-get update
sudo apt-get upgrade
```

Note that this process can take up to 10 minutes depending on the number of updates, and usually takes longer than a desktop PC or laptop as this process is writing to an SD card rather than a traditional hard drive.

Setting up the pirate radio

It's now time to download and set up the PiFM software, which will allow you to use the GPIO header as an FM transmitter. First, we'll need to download the software using the following commands:

```
wget http://omattos.com/pifm.tar.gz
tar -xzvf pifm.tar.gz
```

This will get the gzipped archive that contains the PiFM software, the Python library, and some test files and uncompress them.

For now, a single male to male 0.1 inch pin jumper will suffice as an antenna; this should be connected to GPIO 4 (pin number 7) on the GPIO header and made to stand as upright as possible to ensure the best range (refer to the following image):

You are now ready to test the setup with an FM radio; firstly, you will need to choose a frequency that will not overlap with any licensed broadcasts in your area and is within the FM radio transmission range in your area (usually between 88 Mhz and 108 Mhz). A lot of radios that do automatic tuning also tend to prefer frequencies that are a multiple of 0.1 MHz (for example, 99.9, 101.3, and so on).

Once you have chosen your frequency, tune your radio in to it, and run the following command on the Pi, where freq is the frequency you wish to broadcast on:

```
sudo ./pifm left_right.wav freq 22050 stereo
```

You should now hear a sample auto clip demonstrating the ability to broadcast stereo audio.

Transferring MP3 files to the Pi

For our media player, we are going to need a selection of MP3 files on the Pi SD card. There are two main ways to do this, either by moving the card back to your PC and mounting it like a regular SD card, or by using the **Secure File Transfer Protocol (SFTP)**.

In this case, since the Pi is already running, I have opted to use SFTP. This can be done using the FileZilla (https://filezilla-project.org) FTP client. Once installed and opened, enter the same details that you used to connect to the Pi over SSH in the fields at the top of the window (using **22** for **Port**), and click on **Quickconnect**.

You should now be able to browse the filesystems of both your computer and the Pi, as shown in the following screenshot. Files can be uploaded by right-clicking on them and selecting **Upload**.

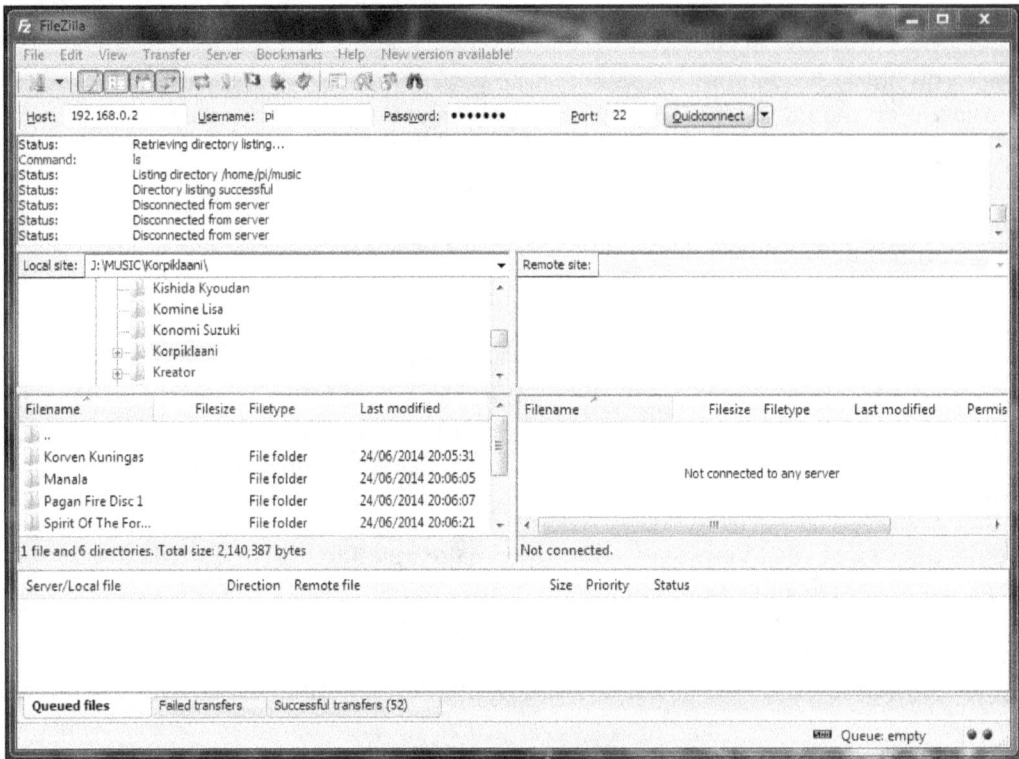

In order to play the music you have just transferred to the Pi, you will need to install the `ffmpeg` utility, which is a tool that is commonly used to transcode media files and can be installed using the following command:

```
sudo apt-get install ffmpeg
```

Now that you have some of your own music on the Pi, you can try playing it by piping the output of `ffmpeg` to PiFM:

```
ffmpeg -i file.mp3 -f s16le -ar 22.05k -ac 2 - | sudo ./pifm - freq 22050
stereo
```

Here, `file` is the MP3 file to be broadcasted and `freq` is the frequency to broadcast it on. Since we are telling `ffmpeg` to provide output for two audio channels (`-ac 2`) and giving the stereo option to PiFM, this should give a stereo audio broadcast.

Scripting a media player

Now that the FM transmitter is working, we can make it do something a little more useful; in this case, we will use it to broadcast a personalized radio station with a collection of your own music.

To do this, we will write a Python script that manages to search for MP3 files and calls PiFM to broadcast them.

Calling PiFM from Python

In the PiFM download and on the PiFM website, you may have noticed that there is a Python library that can be used to control PiFM. Although, looking at the source code for it, you can see that all the library can do is call the `pifm` executable with the minimum number of commands, and therefore will not allow us to play MP3 files.

However, it is a simple process to create our own function that will allow us to pass the filename of an MP3, a frequency, and that will allow Python to call `ffmpeg` and PiFM in order to broadcast the audio in the file for us:

```
def play_file(filename, frequency):
  command = 'ffmpeg -i "%s" -f s16le -ar 22.05k -ac 2 - | sudo ./pifm
- %f 22050 stereo' % (filename, frequency)
  subprocess.call(command, shell=True)
```

This code is an extract from the `player.py` file; all we are doing here is taking the shell commands used to play an MP3 file and replacing the filename and broadcast frequency with values that are passed to the function as parameters. Then, we are using the Python subprocess module to execute the command as if it was typed into a shell.

Searching for MP3 files

For our script to play any MP3 files, it needs to be able to find them first. Finding an MP3 file involves taking a look at each file in a starting directory to check whether a file is an MP3 file, and then repeating this process for every directory within the start directory. Thankfully, Python makes this very easy:

```
mp3_files = list()
for root, dirs, files in os.walk(directory):
  for filename in files:
    if filename.endswith(".mp3"):
      mp3_files.append(os.path.join(root, filename))
```

Here, `directory` is the directory we want to search for files media in. The `os.walk` function returns a tuple; the first element (`root`) is a string that contains the absolute path to the search directory, `dirs` is a list of directories within the search directory and its subdirectories, and `files` is a list of all the files within the search directory and its subdirectories.

The `if` statement is a simple way to check whether a file is an MP3 file based solely on its file extension. If it has the `.mp3` extension, it is added to the `mp3_files` list, which is then passed to the playlist code.

Getting input from a command line

In order to set various settings for our player script, for example, the directory in which you can search for files, we need a way to get input from the user via a command line, and in this case, from the arguments passed to the script when it is started. To do this, we will use the `argparse` Python module:

```
parser = argparse.ArgumentParser(description='Broadcast a set of MP3s
over FM')
parser.add_argument(
  '-f', '--frequency',
  default=101.1,
  type=float,
  help='Frequency on which to broadcast')
params = parser.parse_args()
```

The `argparse` Python module allows you to define a set of arguments that can be passed to a Python program, it allows you to parse the arguments when the script is run, and it automatically allows you to generate a help page (accessed by passing `-h` to the script).

In this case, we will add an argument for the broadcast frequency, which is set using either -f or --frequency; type is used to validate input from the user, default is what is read by the program if the user does not set a value, and help is what is shown for this argument on the help page.

Queuing the media files to be played

Our media player will also need a way to manage which file should be played next. We will implement this in two ways: linear playback in the order the files were discovered and randomized playback:

```
file_number = -1
while True:
  if params.random:
    file_number = random.randint(0, len(filenames) - 1)
  else:
    file_number += 1
    if file_number >= len(filenames):
      return
play_file(filenames[file_number], params.frequency)
```

Here, if the --random parameter has been passed to our script, whenever we are about to play a file, the file to be played will be selected at random using the randint function in the random Python module. This number is then used to get a certain file from the list of filenames that were previously discovered.

Using the media player script

The player.py script can be invoked using the following command:

python player.py -d music -f 99.9 --random

This will search for all MP3 files under the music directory and broadcast them at 99.9 MHz in a random order. A full list of commands will be available to you if you run:

python player.py -h

Since the radio is not much of use when you have to SSH into it to start playing the music, we will add a cron job that will start the player.py script when the Pi boots up.

To do this, we will use a shell script to start the Python script (`start_player.sh`):

```
#!/bin/bash
sleep 20
cd /home/pi
python player.py -d music --random -f 99.9 &
```

This will ensure that the player script is executed in the correct folder, in this case, `/home/pi`, as this is where our PiFM executables and music directories are.

Next, we will add an entry in the crontab, which is where cron jobs are defined. This can be edited with the following command:

```
sudo crontab -e
```

This command will open the default command-line text edit on the Pi, `nano`, which will allow you to add entries to the crontab. To start our media player script, we will need to add the following line to the end of the crontab that is opened:

```
@reboot /home/pi/start_player.sh
```

In our case, we will use the `@reboot` cron rule instead of specifying a time for the command to be run, and as the name suggests, this will run the given command when the OS starts.

Press *Ctrl + X* followed by *Y* and *Enter* to save the changes to the crontab, then use the following command to reboot the Pi, and if all goes as planned, start your personalized radio station:

```
sudo reboot
```

Summary

In this chapter, we covered the basic setup of the Pi hardware and Raspbian OS. You learned how to discover the IP address of the Pi in order to allow remote access to it over SSH; this process will be used in the majority of the projects later in this book.

We also took a quick look at the GPIO expansion header, and how it is typically used to interface with external hardware. We also used this as a crude FM transmitter through which we wrote a single Python script to broadcast music.

In the next chapter, we will go into further details regarding how to set up various software packages in order to run them on the Pi, as well as you will learn the various ways to configure networking when we make a portable speaker system that runs the Logitech Media Server.

2
Portable Speaker System

In this chapter, we will build a wireless, battery-powered speaker system that can be controlled using a web browser or smartphone.

To provide the music for the speaker system, we will use the Logitech Media Server software, which is a piece of software that can be used to stream music, videos, and photos from one computer on a network to multiple other devices. It also allows us to control the playback from any computer or smartphone on the same network.

Initially, we will set up the Pi to connect it to an existing server (the one running on a laptop for instance), which is suitable for use around your home or garden. Later, we will look at how to make the system truly portable by removing the need for an existing server and network.

The system will be self contained within a standard flight case with the speakers exposed when the lid is opened as it is possible to run Logitech Media Server on the Pi itself. It is not necessary that you have any controls on the system itself other than a power switch.

This project is based on a similar project made by Iain Yarnall at Maker Space, Newcastle.

What you will need

This is a list of the parts that you will need for this project; specific parts have a link of where they can be purchased (it is recommended that you use these specific parts as other similar parts may need an assembly that differs from the instructions given here), and all other parts can be purchased from an electronics components store:

- The Raspberry Pi

- A USB storage device to store a media library (it is possible to use a hard drive; however, to keep the wiring simple, it is advisable that you use a memory stick)
- A Wi-Fi adapter (uk.rs-online.com/web/p/product/7603621/)
- A flight case (http://www.maplin.co.uk/p/flight-case-triple-pack-with-dividers-n50ju)
- A length of 26 AWG wire
- A length of 32 AWG wire
- A 3.5 mm stereo audio connector
- A strip of terminal blocks
- A fuse holder and 1 Amp fuse
- Eight 20 mm M3 screws, washers, and nuts
- Two full-range speakers (http://cpc.farnell.com/visaton/2133/speaker-full-range-5-60w-black/dp/LS02184)
- Two mono amplifier modules (http://cpc.farnell.com/1/1/85173-amplifier-module-18w-m033n-kemo-electronic.html)
- A variable switch mode voltage regulator (http://imall.iteadstudio.com/im130731002.html)
- A power switch (http://cpc.farnell.com/arcolectric-switches/c1300abaaa/switch-spst-16a-250vac-black-i/dp/SW05094)
- Volume control (stereo potentiometer) (http://cpc.farnell.com/_/lp-200-8/speaker-l-pad-stereo/dp/LS00544)
- A battery (http://www.hobbyking.com/hobbyking/store/__11945__Turnigy_nano_tech_2200mah_4S_35_70C_Lipo_Pack.html)

Tools you will need

This is a list of tools that you will need for this chapter; they can all be purchased from either an electronics components store or a tool/hardware store:

- Drill and drill bits ranging from 3 mm to 10 mm
- A jigsaw
- A try square (optional)
- A soldering iron and solder
- A multimeter
- A small, flat screwdriver
- A small Posidrive screwdriver

Setting up Logitech Media Server

We will first start by downloading and installing Logitech Media Server, which is the server backend that manages the media library and controls the players based on the commands from devices that can control the server (known as controllers). Examples of controllers include the web interface and smartphone applications.

The players are devices that actually output audio (also known as Squeezebox clients), our Pi, for example. It is possible to have several controllers and players running from the same server.

To get started, go to `http://www.mysqueezebox.com/download`, and download the correct version for your OS. In most of the cases, the download is an executable or a package file that can be installed in the same way as any other piece of software.

Once Logitech Media Server is installed, open a web browser on the same PC and navigate to `localhost:9000`; you should see the Logitech Media Server web interface, as shown in the following screenshot. This allows you to browse the media library and stream media to players connected to that server.

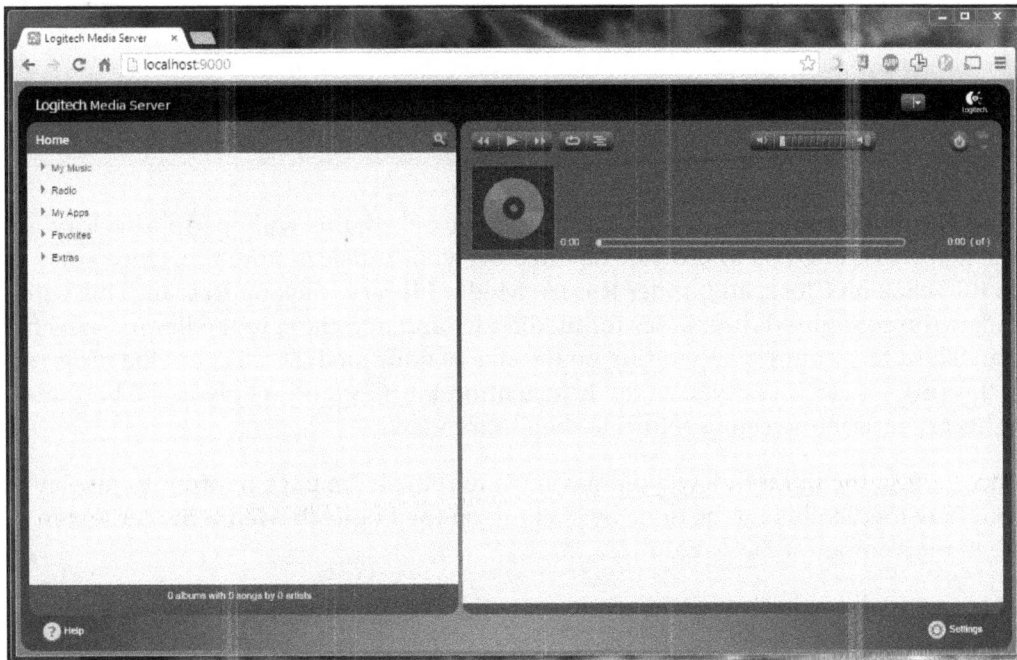

In order to make your media available in Logitech Media Server, you may need to change the search path and perform a library rescan; this can be done by clicking on the **Settings** link in the bottom-right corner of the **Basic Settings** page:

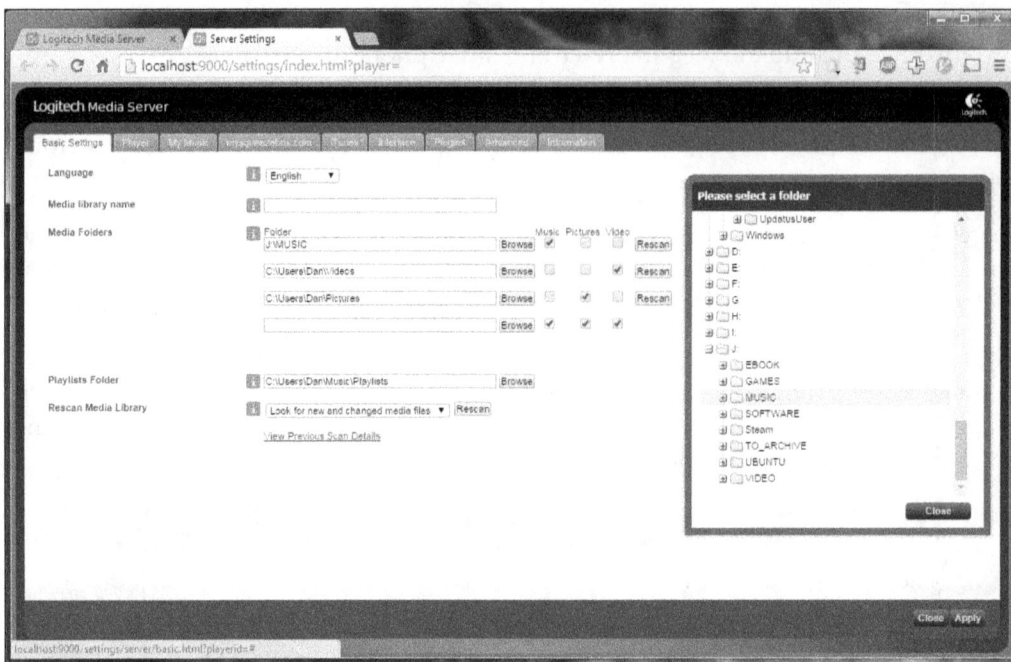

Next, select **Browse** on the folder that has **Music** ticked; this will open a directory tree that will allow you to browse the directory your music is stored in. Once you do this, click on **Close**, and under **Rescan Media Library**, click on **Rescan**. This will look in the configured directories for media files and add them to the library, which may take a few minutes depending on the size of your media collection; the progress of this process can be viewed in the **Information** tab. Click on **Apply** in the bottom-right corner of the screen to return to the library view.

Once back to the library view, you may have to refresh the page in order to display your new media; this can be done by clicking on the **Logitech Media Server** text in the top-left corner of the page.

Since this is all Logitech Media Server can without a player, we will now set up the Pi as a Squeezebox client.

Setting up the Pi as a Squeezebox client

In order to use the Pi as a Squeezebox client, we will use the open source software, squeezelite (`https://code.google.com/p/squeezelite`).

First, we need to install some prerequisites on the Pi which are required to run the squeezelite software, which can be done using the following command:

```
sudo apt-get install -y libflac-dev libfaad2 libmad0
```

Next, we will download the precompiled squeezelite binary from the Google Code page using `wget`. We will give it execute permissions to it and move it into the binary directory, allowing it to be executed like any other command-line application:

```
wget http://squeezelite-downloads.googlecode.com/git/squeezelite-armv6hf
sudo chmod a+x squeezelite-armv6hf
sudo mv squeezelite-armv6hf /usr/bin
```

Now that the client application is installed, we will do a little bit of testing to be sure that the setup is working properly. We will do this to determine the parameters that need to be passed to the client to get the best audio quality and performance.

To start, execute the following command:

```
squeezelite-armv6hf -n Pi -a 160
```

This command will start squeezelite in an auto-discovery mode in which it will search the network for a Logitech Media Server instance and connect to the first one it finds. If you have more than one instance and want to specify the server to connect to, then you can use the `-s` parameter:

```
squeezelite-armv6hf -s server_ip:port -n Pi -a 160
```

The `-n` parameter defines the name of the client and subsequently, what it will be called in Logitech Media Server; this is useful for identification when you are using more than one client on the same server. The `-a` parameter is used to specify additional ALSA parameters that are to be used while opening the output audio device; in this case, we will increase the default buffer size, which will help us to rectify some audio quality issues that may occur with the Pi.

Once squeezelite is running on the Pi, go back to the Logitech Media Server web interface and select the player from the drop-down list in the top-right corner of the page (you may need to refresh the page to display the player).

You can then browse your media library and queue the music to be played on the Pi using the add and play buttons, which can be seen when each media item is highlighted, as shown in the following screenshot:

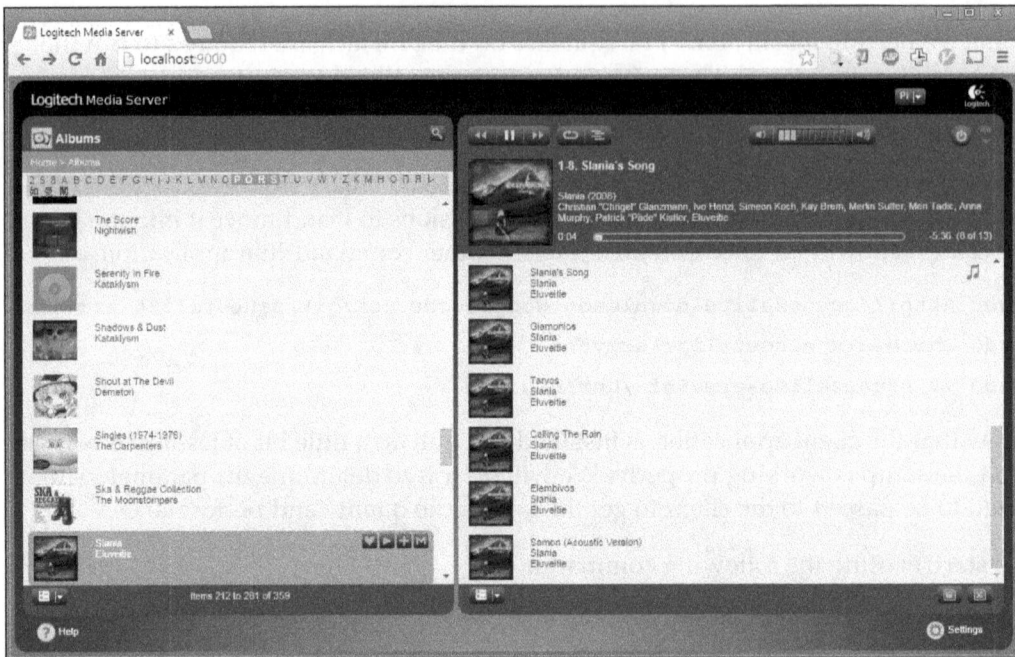

Setting up Wi-Fi on the Pi

Running an Ethernet cable through the Pi is a little bit unrealistic for this use. Hence, we will connect the Pi to a wireless network. Since not all Wi-Fi adapters work well with the Pi, it is a good idea to check the list of the supported devices (http://elinux.org/RPi_USB_Wi-Fi_Adapters) before purchasing one specifically for this project.

Firstly, we will make sure that we have all the Wi-Fi tools installed using the following command:

```
sudo apt-get install wpasupplicant wireless-tools
```

There is a good chance that these packages will already be installed on Raspbian, but it is a simple step to check beforehand.

It is likely that you already know the **service set identifier (SSID)** or name of the wireless network you want to connect to, but if not, or just to check whether it is being picked up by the Wi-Fi adapter, use the following command to get a list of all the Wi-Fi networks available in the range:

```
sudo iwlist wlan0 scan | grep ESSID
```

You will get output similar to the following:

```
pi@raspberrypi ~ $ sudo iwlist wlan0 scan | grep ESSID
                   ESSID:"VM543181-2G"
                   ESSID:"VM201955-2G"
pi@raspberrypi ~ $ 
```

Now that we know the name of the network we want to connect to, we can go ahead and add an entry in the wpa_supplicant configuration file, which contains the connection details for the network. This can be edited by the nano text editor, using the following command:

```
sudo nano /etc/wpa_supplicant/wpa_supplicant.conf
```

At the end of the file, add the following lines and replace SSID and PASSWORD with SSID and the password for your wireless network:

```
network={
    ssid="SSID"
    psk="PASSWORD"
    key_mgmt=WPA-PSK
}
```

Once the lines have been added to the file, save the changes, exit nano, and reboot the Pi using the following command:

```
sudo reboot
```

Once the Pi has booted, SSH back into it and make sure that the Pi has a Wi-Fi connection, using the following command:

```
ifconfig
```

If the configuration is successful, you will see output similar to this, which shows an active Ethernet (on 192.168.0.2) and a Wi-Fi (on 192.168.0.18) connection:

```
pi@raspberrypi ~ $ ifconfig
eth0      Link encap:Ethernet  HWaddr b8:27:eb:26:56:b3
          inet addr:192.168.0.2  Bcast:192.168.0.255  Mask:255.255.255.0
          UP BROADCAST RUNNING MULTICAST  MTU:1500  Metric:1
          RX packets:121 errors:0 dropped:2 overruns:0 frame:0
          TX packets:85 errors:0 dropped:0 overruns:0 carrier:0
          collisions:0 txqueuelen:1000
          RX bytes:12232 (11.9 KiB)  TX bytes:10625 (10.3 KiB)

lo        Link encap:Local Loopback
          inet addr:127.0.0.1  Mask:255.0.0.0
          UP LOOPBACK RUNNING  MTU:65536  Metric:1
          RX packets:0 errors:0 dropped:0 overruns:0 frame:0
          TX packets:0 errors:0 dropped:0 overruns:0 carrier:0
          collisions:0 txqueuelen:0
          RX bytes:0 (0.0 B)  TX bytes:0 (0.0 B)

wlan0     Link encap:Ethernet  HWaddr 80:1f:02:f7:3e:08
          inet addr:192.168.0.18  Bcast:192.168.0.255  Mask:255.255.255.0
          UP BROADCAST RUNNING MULTICAST  MTU:1500  Metric:1
          RX packets:35 errors:0 dropped:2 overruns:0 frame:0
          TX packets:8 errors:0 dropped:0 overruns:0 carrier:0
          collisions:0 txqueuelen:1000
          RX bytes:5223 (5.1 KiB)  TX bytes:1608 (1.5 KiB)

pi@raspberrypi ~ $
```

After this, you should be able to SSH in the Pi via its Wi-Fi IP address and disconnect the Ethernet cable.

Running squeezelite as a daemon

Since we want the Pi to be ready to stream music without having to do anything other than apply power to it, we need a way to launch squeezelite when the Pi boots; this time, we will look at another way of doing this, using a **daemon**.

A daemon is a program that runs in the background and is not directly visible to the user; because of this, it is often used for applications such as servers.

In our case, we will use the start-stop-daemon utility to create a daemon that will start squeezelite on boot. We will do this by writing a shell script and placing it in the /etc/inti.d directory:

```
#!/bin/bash

### BEGIN INIT INFO
# Provides:          squeezelite
```

```
# Required-Start:
# Required-Stop:
# Default-Start:    2 3 4 5
# Default-Stop:     0 1 6
# Short-Description: Squeezelite client
# Description:       Logitech media server client
### END INIT INFO

DAEMON_USER=pi
PIDFILE=/var/run/squeezelite.pid
DAEMON=/usr/bin/squeezelite-armv6hf

DAEMON_OPTS="-n Pi -a 160"

do_start()
{
  start-stop-daemon --start --background --pidfile $PIDFILE --
  make-pidfile --user $DAEMON_USER --chuid $DAEMON_USER --startas
  $DAEMON -- $DAEMON_OPTS
}

do_stop()
{
  start-stop-daemon --stop --pidfile $PIDFILE --retry 10
}

case $1 in
  start)
    do_start
    ;;
  stop)
    do_stop
    ;;
  restart)
    do_stop
    do_start
    ;;
  *)
    ;;
esac
```

Make the script executable and move it to the /etc/init/d directory:

```
sudo chmod a+x squeezelite
sudo mv squeezelite /etc/init.d/squeezelite
```

Finally, use the following command to update the list of daemons:

```
sudo update-rc.d squeezelite defaults
```

To ensure that the daemon is working properly, try to start squeezelite by executing:

```
sudo service squeezelite start
```

Check whether the process is running:

```
ps aux | grep squeeze
```

This should give you output similar to the following:

```
pi@raspberrypi ~ $ ps aux | grep squeeze
pi        2456  0.0  0.2   4268  1212 pts/0    S    10:35   0:00 /bin/bash /usr/bin/squeez
lite-armv6hf -n Pi -a 160
pi        2467  0.0  0.1   3548   808 pts/0    S+   10:36   0:00 grep --color=auto squeeze
pi@raspberrypi ~ $
```

The preceding output shows that the squeezelite process is running; this can also be verified if you attempt to stream music in the player.

Building the electronics

The electronics for the speaker system can be split into two main sections – the power circuit and the audio circuit.

The circuit structure of the electronics is shown in the following diagram:

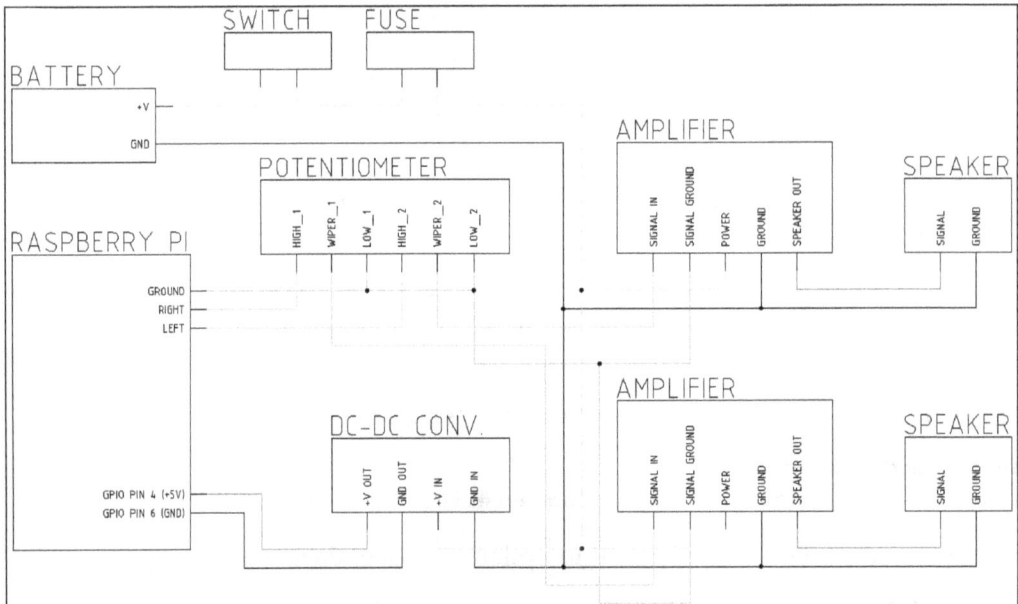

The speaker system block diagram

Note the color coding of the wiring. Here, black shows the power ground, gray shows the audio ground, cyan shows the unamplified audio, blue shows the amplified audio, yellow represents the battery voltage, and red shows 5 V.

Note the color coding of the wiring. This is important as it is the most common way in which different signals and power supplies are identified within an electronic product. There are a few common conventions that, while are not used here, are good to know; black is always ground, red and yellow usually indicate a power supply (5 V and 12 V, respectively), and yellow and green stripes usually represent a mains earth.

For small projects, such as this, following a standard color code for wiring is not as important. Different signals have a colored wire of their own to make identification and troubleshooting easier.

> Unless otherwise stated, a 26 AWG wire should be used. The wire color you choose to use does not have to match the ones shown in the preceding diagrams; however, it is preferable that you follow it to make identification easier.

The amplifier circuit

Firstly, we will wire the two mono amplifier modules to a strip of terminal blocks to make a stereo amplifier module. This is done by connecting the common connections from each amplifier together and keeping the signal and output connections separate, as shown in the following diagram:

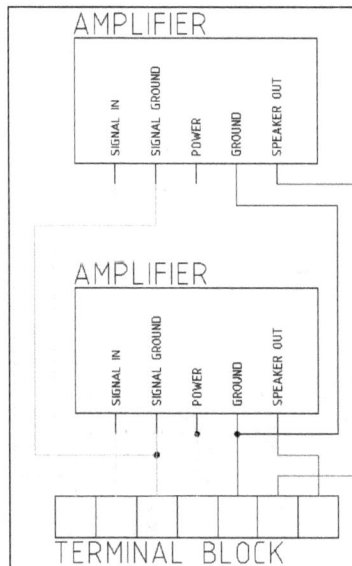

Next, take the volume control and solder the wires onto it in the configuration, as shown in the following diagram:

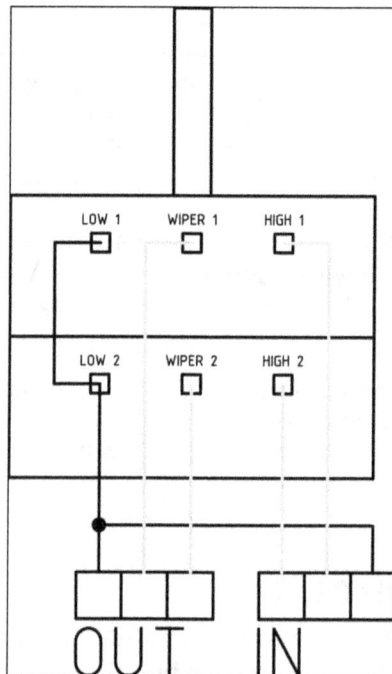

The audio input wires should be relatively short (around 50 mm) and connected to a strip of three terminal blocks; the output should have enough wire to reach the amplifier module (around 150-200 mm). This volume control is essentially comprised of two potential dividers with their wipers fixed together such that each potential divider is always at the same position.

Now, we can solder wires to the 3.5 mm audio jack; since this is a bit smaller and it will only carry the unamplified audio signal, we can use a 32 AWG wire for this:

The audio connector can now be connected to the terminal block on the volume control; at this stage, the orientation of the left and right channels is not important.

Then, connect the output from the volume control to the first three connections on the amplifier terminal blocks; again, the orientation is not important at this stage.

Since the power ground connection on the amplifier will have to be connected to both the speakers, the battery and the DC-DC converter to power the Pi will be best to extend the speakers connections to their own strip of terminal blocks. This will reduce the number of connects that have to be made in the same connection.

This is simply a case of adding a short length of wire (around 50-100 mm) to the two speaker outputs and power ground from the amplifier terminal blocks and connecting them to a strip of three terminal blocks:

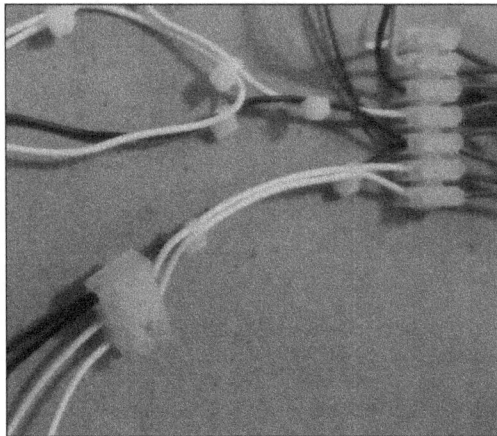

Next, we need to solder a wire (around 300 mm) to the two speakers. Note that the speaker will have markings that show the correct polarity it is to be wired in:

Now, connect each speaker to the strip of three terminal blocks coming from the amplifier modules. Once again, the correct speaker orientation is not important at this stage.

This is all with respect to the wiring for the audio section of the speaker system.

Running the speaker system on battery power

Since the battery we will use is rated at 14.4 V, we are able to power the amplifier directly from the battery. However, the Pi must be powered with 5 V. So, we will need a power converter to be able to power the Pi using the battery.

The power converter we will use is a DC-DC switch mode converter, which will accept input voltage from the set output voltage up to 35 V. Therefore, we will continue to power the Pi as the battery voltage drops while under heavier load (for example, when playing at higher volumes) or as the battery starts to drain.

As lithium polymer batteries can be very dangerous if used incorrectly, it is vital that a fuse is used in line with the power switch to protect the battery just in case there's a fault in the speaker system. A rating of around 0.8 to 1.5 A will be suitable for this purpose.

We will start with powering just the amplifiers. This is a fairly simple task as all it involves is connecting the battery positive terminal to the power connector on the amplifier terminal blocks via the switch and fuse. The ground is connected directly, as shown in the earlier diagram. Perform the following steps to connect the circuit:

1. Take the connector for your battery, and assuming that it has leads presoldered onto it, connect them to a strip of two terminal blocks. If they do not have leads soldered onto them, then this should be done first using a short length of wire (around 50 mm).

2. Solder a 100 mm length of wire onto one pole of the power switch and connect the other end to the positive terminal on the battery terminal block.

3. Solder a 50 mm length of wire from the other switch pole to one contact of the fuse.

4. Solder a 50 mm length of wire from the other fuse contact and connect the other end to the positive power connection on the amplifier terminal blocks.

5. Connect the grounds of the battery terminal block and the amplifier terminal blocks with a 100 mm length of wire.

Once these steps have been completed, the setup should look like what is shown in the following image:

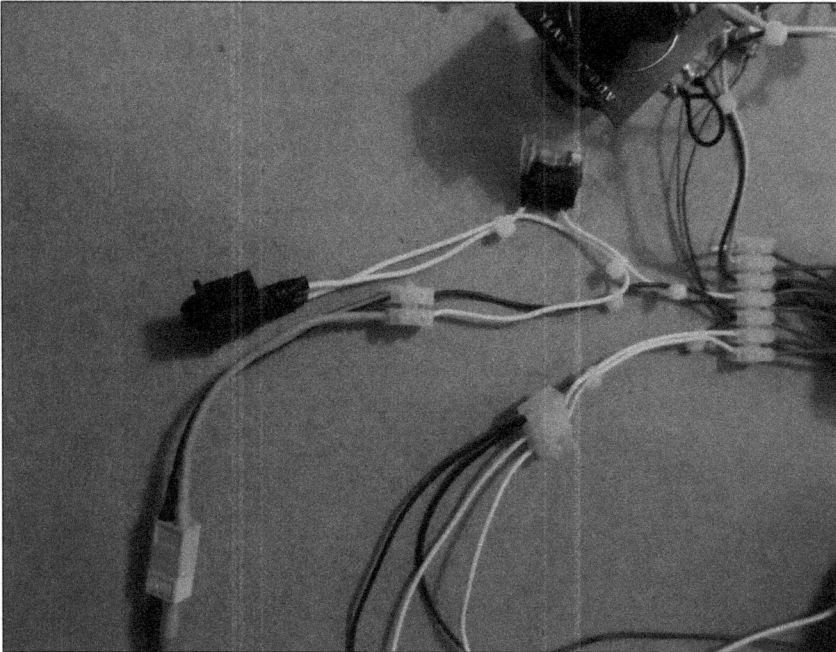

Now would be a good time to give the audio electronics a test by connecting the battery and powering on the amplifiers. You can either use the Pi powered from a USB or any other media player as the audio source. It is best to have the volume control set to its lowest setting and gradually increase it.

Next, we want to power the Pi from the battery using the DC-DC converter. There are two main ways of doing this: either by applying power to the GPIO header or by back-powering the Pi using a powered USB hub. In this case, I will be powering via the GPIO header, which will likely be sufficient for what we are doing here. Powering using a powered USB hub will only be needed if you are using an external hard drive to store the music library.

First, we need to solder wires to each of the terminals of the DC-DC converter and note the polarity of the connections to ensure that the color coding of the wiring is consistent. A length of around 100 mm is sufficient for each connection.

Next, connect the positive and ground connections on the power input side of the converter to the positive and ground connections on the amplifier terminal blocks, and connect the two leads from the output terminals of the DC-DC converter to a strip of two terminal blocks.

Now that we have the DC-DC converter connected, we need to set it to the correct output voltage before we connect it to the Pi. To do this, set a multimeter to the voltage mode and place the probes across the two connections on the terminal blocks connected to the DC-DC converter's output (if possible, screw the tips of the probes into the terminal blocks to avoid having to hold them in place). Turn the power on, and if needed, adjust the range on the multimeter.

Usually, I find that these converters come preset to the output just below the input voltage, which would be far too high for the Pi, which is designed to operate at 5 V. In order to adjust the voltage, use a small, flat-head screwdriver to adjust the square blue potentiometer. This is a multiple turn potentiometer, so do not be surprised if it takes a few rotations of the potentiometer for the voltage to change. A reasonable voltage to aim for is 5.1 V, as under load, the voltage is expected to drop slightly.

Once the voltage is corrected, turn the power off, remove the multimeter from the output of the DC-DC converter, remove one end of two 0.1 inch jumper leads, and connect them to the terminal block on the output of the DC-DC converter. Connect the positive lead to pin 4 of the GPIO headers on the Pi and the ground lead to pin 6.

By now, the setup should look similar to the following:

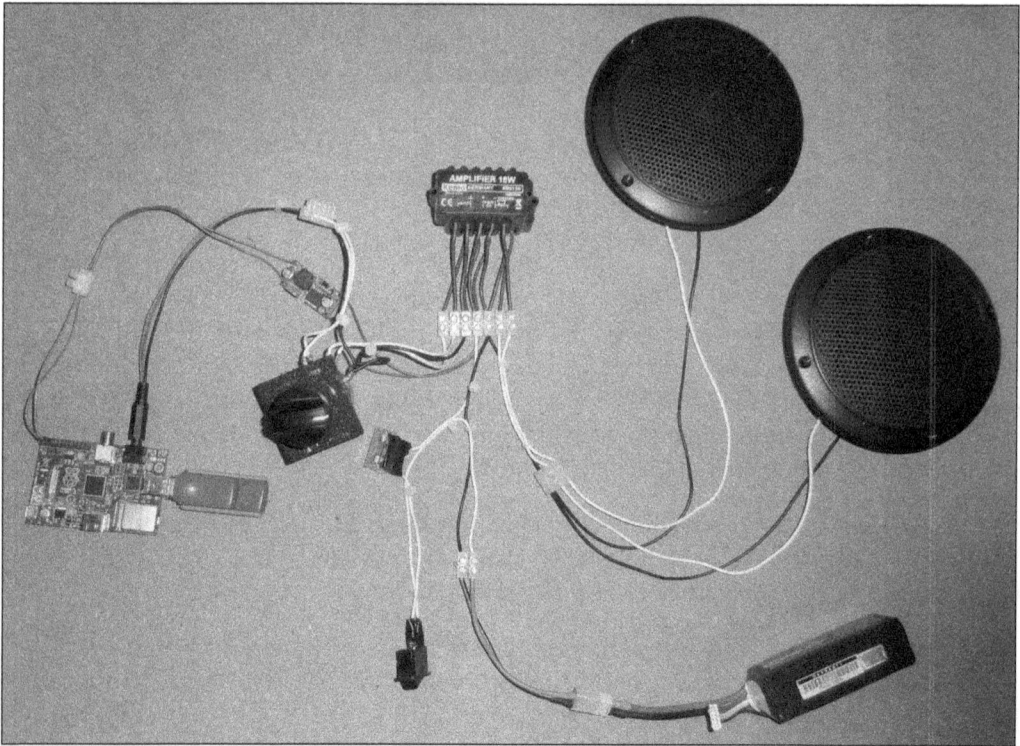

Once this is done, apply power once more and within a few seconds, the Pi should start booting up. If it does not, turn the power off immediately to prevent possible damage to the Pi and battery, and double-check all of the wiring against the block diagram shown earlier in the chapter.

Building the enclosure for the speaker system

Since we are using a premade flight case as the base for our speaker system's enclosure, all we have to do is cut a single panel that will hold the speakers, volume control, and power switch on a panel that is exposed. We can do this by opening the case, thus hiding the Pi, battery, and electronics behind it.

To make this panel, we will use a 3 mm **medium density fiberboard (MDF)**; this is a cheap material and is very easy to work with.

First, we will need to cut a square of MDF that is just smaller than the opening in the flight case. To do this, first measure the length and width of the inside of the flight case and mark this distance away from two edges of a sheet of MDF, as shown in the following image:

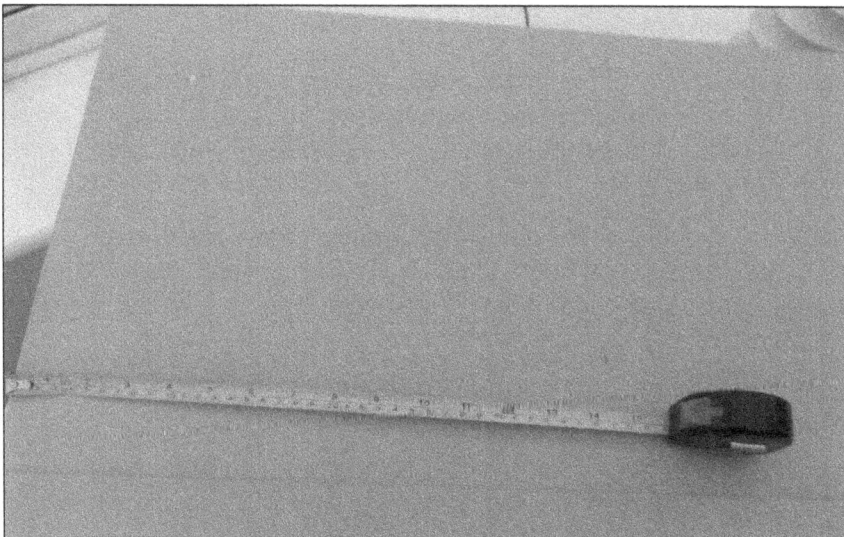

Next, take a try square and draw a line parallel to each edge in line with the markings in order to give an outline of where the square needs to be cut to get our panel as shown in the following figure.

> When using power tools, proper safety precautions should be undertaken. Eye protection should always be worn and mains-powered tools should be protected using a **residual current device (RCD)**.

Once this is done, we can take a jigsaw and cut along the lines to get the panel, which should be able to snugly fit in the opening of the flight case.

Now that we have the basic panel for the enclosure, we will cut the two speaker holes. Since different speakers are mounted in different ways, I assume that you are using the same speakers that are listed on the parts list here.

Mounting the speakers will first involve cutting a large hole into the sheet to set the speakers in and then drilling four smaller holes that are used to bolt the speaker to the panel. Fortunately, for the speakers, the large hole can be marked out easily by tracing around a CD.

Once you have the outline of the speaker positioned correctly, drill a 10 mm hole near the edge of each circle, as shown in the following image. This will allow us to get inside the circle with the jigsaw in order to cut a large hole in the panel.

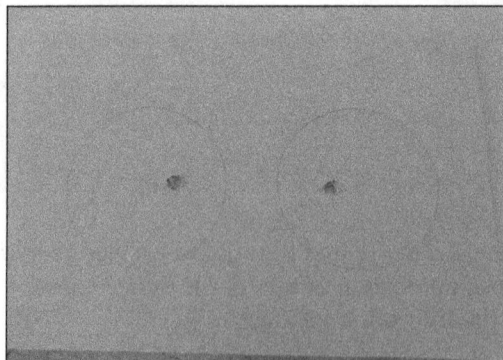

Once this is done, insert the blade of the jigsaw into the hole and cut around the outline of the circle for each speaker. It isn't vital that the holes are cut neatly or accurately, since the speaker will cover this edge when installed; however, it is important that the speaker sits flat when it is mounted on the cutout.

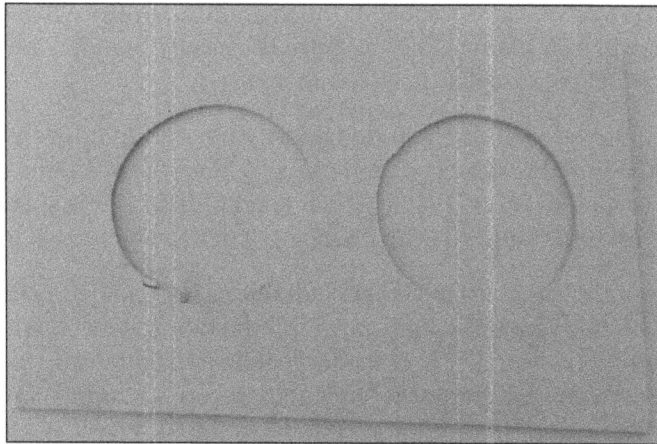

Next, we need to drill the mounting holes that will be used to bolt the speakers to the MDF panel; in this case, we will drill 4 mm holes and use M3 screws and nuts to mount the speakers.

First, mark the positions of each hole by placing the speaker into the hole and making a mark on the MDF through the hole in the speaker fascia (with a pencil, for example).

Next, drill a 4 mm hole in each marked position. It would be a good idea to check whether the holes line up with the speaker correctly by trial fitting it with just the screws; however, we will mount the speakers properly later.

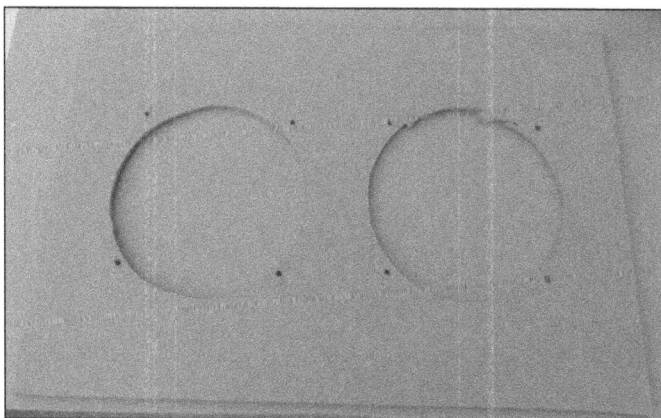

Next, we need to drill a single hole large enough for the shaft of the volume control. The best place to position this is in between the speakers, but far away enough to leave room for the front plate. Once the position is marked out, drill the hole and remove any loose pieces of material.

The hole for the power switch is probably the most difficult since it is a square hole. For this, we will drill two 10 mm holes and use the jigsaw to make the two ends square and remove the material in between them.

The two holes should be around 15-20 mm apart. This should allow a snug fit of the switch once the full hole has been cut out using the jigsaw. In this case, since the edge of the cut may be more visible, it is a good idea to take a small amount of material off in each pass and to keep checking whether the switch fits neatly.

Now that all the mounting holes have been cut out of the panel, it is time to mount each component on the panel. We will start with the two speakers, which can be mounted by inserting the speaker into the large hole and fastening it in place using an M3 machine screw in each mounting hole with a corresponding washer and nut. To make the wiring neater, it is a good idea to have the terminals of each speaker facing the same direction. I recommend having them face the back of the flight case.

Next, the power switch can be fitted; this requires you to disconnect the connections to the amplifier terminal blocks first. Once disconnected, this is simply a case of feeding the wiring and fuse holder through the mounting hole and pushing the switch into the hole. Once in place, it should be kept securely in place by friction alone.

Next, the volume control can be mounted by pushing the threaded shaft through the hole drilled for it from the back of the MDF panel. Place the plastic front plate over the shaft on the front of the MDF panel and fasten it in place using the included nuts. The knob should then be pushed on, ensuring that the indicator lines up with the minimum indicator on the plastic front panel.

By this time, the front of the MDF panel should look similar to the following image:

All that is left to do now is mount the DC-DC converter and amplifiers to the back of the panel, reconnect, and tidy up the wiring.

Since the amplifier modules have mounting holes, I used these to thread some large cable ties through and fastened them to the two speakers. This allows a secure mounting of the amplifiers that does not need additional holes to be drilled in the MDF panel.

The DC-DC converter can be mounted anywhere on the MDF panel using any suitable adhesive. I would recommend hot glue as it allows fairly easy removal without risking damage to the converter, but you can also use double-sided tape.

The next step is to reconnect all the wiring that is currently disconnected. While doing so, it is a good idea to trim any wires that are excessively long so that each wire is just long enough to reach where it should connect to. This is mainly done just to make the wiring tidier.

By now, the back should look as shown in the following image:

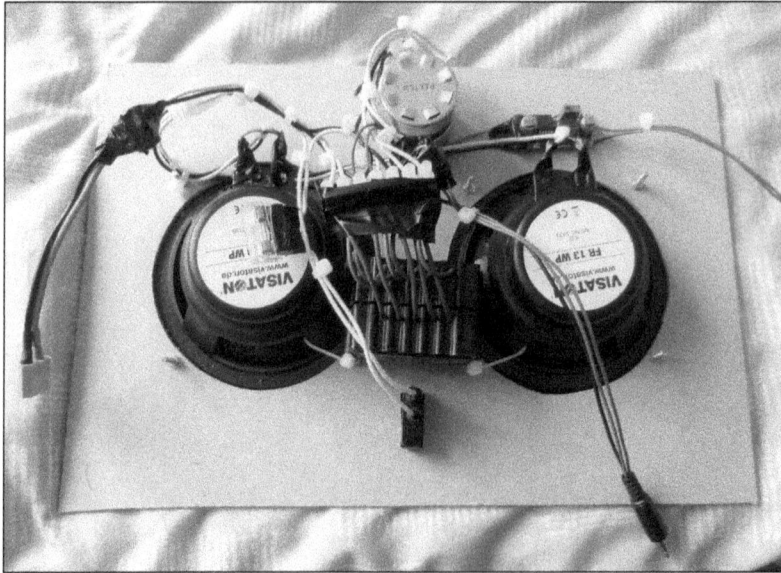

Assuming that you are using the same flight case that I used, there are two dividers included that make a perfect spacer to keep the MDF panel a good distance from the bottom of the flight case, the spacers should be placed around 40 mm from each side of the case.

All that is left to do now is reconnect the Pi and battery and give the system a test.

Running Logitech Media Server on the Pi

Our current solution is all well and good if you only want to use the system around the home and garden. However, to make the system truly portable, we need to move the media collection, Logitech Media Server, and wireless network to the Pi.

Creating a backup image of an SD card

Since we will now be making a few changes to the software running on the Pi, it may be worthwhile that you take an image of the SD card so that later, it is easy to restore the Pi to its working state.

Fortunately, this is a very simple thing to do, and since it is essentially just the reverse of writing the OS image to the card, it can be done with the dd utility:

```
sudo dd if=/dev/sdb of=working.img
```

This will create an image of the SD card at /dev/sdb and save it to the working.img file. This can later be rewritten to the SD card in the same way as a fresh OS image.

One thing worth noting about this method is that it will take an image of the entire SD card, including any free space. Hence, the size of the image is equal (or marginally smaller in the majority of cases) to the capacity of the SD card. This means that to restore the image, you need an SD card of at least the capacity of the card the image was taken from. For this reason, it is good to try and use an SD card that is just big enough for what you need, in order to both restore the image onto a larger range of SD cards and to reduce the amount of storage required to keep the images.

Automounting a USB storage device

Since its likely that your media collection may not entirely fit on a single SD card (as well as Raspbian), we will opt to store this on an external USB device, this could either be a USB memory stick or an external hard drive. The process of doing this is the same for all storage devices.

First, we need to know the path to the storage device and the filesystem it uses. Both can be obtained using the following command:

```
sudo blkid
```

This will give output similar to the following. Here, you can see the two partitions on the SD card (mmcblk0p1 and mmcblk0p2) as well as a USB memory stick (/dev/sda1). Ensuring that you assign a label to the partition while formatting it will help to make identification easier:

```
/dev/mmcblk0p1: SEC_TYPE="msdos" LABEL="boot" UUID="787C-2FD4"
TYPE="vfat"
/dev/mmcblk0p2: UUID="3d81d9e2-7d1b-4015-8c2c-29ec0875f762"
TYPE="ext4"
/dev/sda1: SEC_TYPE="msdos" LABEL="DANNIXON" UUID="321A-15D0"
TYPE="vfat"
```

Note the path to the device at the very start of the line and the partition type given by TYPE. We will need both of these pieces of information when we set up the partition to be mounted at the boot time.

Next, we will create a directory for the partition to be mounted on. This is the path that will be used to access the root of the partition when it is mounted. In this case, we will create a directory under /media. In Linux this is the directory used for mounting removable filesystems; the name of the directory is not critical, but something descriptive is recommended:

```
sudo mkdir /media/music
```

Now that the mount point has been created, we will modify the filesystem table (`fstab`) to automatically mount the drive when the Pi boots; this can be done using the `nano` text editor. The filesystem table needs to be modified as root:

```
sudo nano /etc/fstab
```

To add the partition of our USB device, the following line should be added to the end of the file, replacing `/dev/sda1` with the path to your partition and `vfat` with the partition type (which were discovered earlier):

```
/dev/sda1 /media/music vfat defaults 0 0
```

Once finished, press *Ctrl* + *X* to save and exit. Reboot the Pi using:

```
sudo reboot
```

Once the Pi has booted, check whether the partition has been mounted and is accessible using:

```
ls /media/music
```

This should show you the files and directories at the root of the partition on the USB storage device.

Installing Logitech Media Server

Now that we have the music collection stored locally with the Pi, we need to move our Logitech Media Server instance there. Officially, there is no support for LMS on the Pi, however, All Things Pi (`http://allthingspi.webspace.virginmedia.com/`) has already done the work of porting LMS to run on the Pi.

Firstly, there are a few more libraries that are required by Logitech Media Server that may need to be installed first. This can be done with the following command:

```
sudo apt-get install libjpeg8 libpng12-0 libgif4 libexif12 libswscale2
libavcodec53
```

Now, we can download and install the Debian version of Logitech Media Server from the Logitech website:

```
wget http://downloads.slimdevices.com/LogitechMediaServer_v7.7.2/
logitechmediaserver_7.7.2_all.deb
```

```
sudo dpkg -i logitechmediaserver_7.7.2_all.deb
```

As it is, the installation needs some modifications before it can be used on the Pi. Before we start with this, we need to ensure that LMS is not already running; this is done by attempting to stop the service:

```
sudo service logitechmediaserver stop
```

Next, we need to download and extract the required files that will be used to modify the LMS installation from All Things Pi:

```
wget http://allthingspi.webspace.virginmedia.com/files/lms-rpi-raspbian.tar.gz

tar -zxvf lms-rpi-raspbian.tar.gz
```

Now, we can perform the required modifications using the following commands:

```
sudo patch /usr/share/perl5/Slim/bootstrap.pm lms-rpi-bootstrap.patch
sudo mv arm-linux-gnueabihf-thread-multi-64int /usr/share/squeezeboxserver/CPAN/arch/5.14/
sudo mv libmediascan.so.0.0.0 libfaad.so.2.0.0 /usr/local/lib
sudo mv /usr/share/squeezeboxserver/Bin/arm-linux/faad /usr/share/squeezeboxserver/Bin/arm-linux/faad.old
sudo mv faad /usr/share/squeezeboxserver/Bin/arm-linux
sudo ln -s /usr/local/lib/libmediascan.so.0.0.0 /usr/local/lib/libmediascan.so
sudo ln -s /usr/local/lib/libmediascan.so.0.0.0 /usr/local/lib/libmediascan.so.0
sudo ln -s /usr/local/lib/libfaad.so.2.0.0 /usr/local/lib/libfaad.so
sudo ln -s /usr/local/lib/libfaad.so.2.0.0 /usr/local/lib/libfaad.so.2
sudo ldconfig
sudo chown -R squeezeboxserver:nogroup /usr/share/squeezeboxserver/
```

Once we are finished, Logitech Media Server should be ready to use. However, I had to reboot before I was able to navigate to the web interface:

```
sudo reboot
```

Once the Pi has booted, navigate to PI_IP:9000 (where PI_IP is the IP address of your Pi) to access the LMS web interface. Here, you can follow the same steps described earlier to set up your media library. Keep in mind that the web interface and media scanning may seem slightly slower than on a standard PC. This is mainly due to the lower system resources of the Pi.

Setting up the Pi as a Wi-Fi access point

Since we want to be able to use the speaker system wherever we go, we need a way to connect to the Pi without relying on the availability of a wireless network. The easiest way to do this is to turn the Pi into a Wi-Fi access point that we can connect to using a smartphone.

First, we will assign a static IP address to the Wi-Fi interface. Start by opening the interfaces file in nano:

```
sudo nano /etc/network/interfaces
```

Edit the file so that after the allow-hotplug wlan0 line, it looks like the following code. This code is telling the wlan0 interface to take a static IP address rather than using DHCP as was done previously:

```
allow-hotplug wlan0

iface wlan0 inet static
address 192.168.42.1
netmask 255.255.255.0

#iface wlan0 inet manual
#wpa-roam /etc/wpa_supplicant/wpa_supplicant.conf
#iface default inet dhcp
```

Next, we will set up the DHCP server, which will provide an IP address to any devices that connect to the Wi-Fi network:

```
sudo apt-get install isc-dhcp-server
sudo nano /etc/dhcp/dhcpd.conf
```

This will open nano to edit the DHCP server configuration. First, uncomment the authoritative line. This tells the server that it is the main DHCP server on the network. Next, comment out the following two lines:

```
option domain-name "example.org";
option domain-name-servers ns1.example.org, ns2.example.org;
```

Next, add the following lines to the end of the file:

```
subnet 192.168.42.0 netmask 255.255.255.0 {
  range 192.168.42.10 192.168.42.50;
  option broadcast-address 192.168.42.255;
  option routers 192.168.42.1;
  default-lease-time 600;
```

```
    max-lease-time 7200;
    option domain-name "local";
    option domain-name-servers 8.8.8.8, 8.8.4.4;
}
```

Then, we need to tell the DHCP server which interfaces to use. This is done by editing the following configuration file:

sudo nano /etc/default/isc-dhcp-server

Add wlan0 to the list of interfaces so that the line looks like this:

```
INTERFACES="wlan0"
```

Next, we will install and configure the access point daemon. This involves creating a configuration file for the access point:

sudo apt-get install hostapd

sudo nano /etc/hostapd/hostapd.conf

Add the following lines to the configuration file, replacing NETWORK and PASSWD with the SSID and key you wish to use for the wireless access point:

```
interface=wlan0
driver=nl80211
#driver=rtl871xdrv
ssid=NETWORK
hw_mode=g
channel=6
macaddr_acl=0
auth_algs=1
ignore_broadcast_ssid=0
wpa=2
wpa_passphrase=PASSWD
wpa_key_mgmt=WPA-PSK
wpa_pairwise=TKIP
rsn_pairwise=CCMP
```

Now, we need to tell the daemon to use this configuration file when it starts. This is done by editing the daemon startup options:

sudo nano /etc/default/hostapd

Replace the DAEMON_CONF line with the following:

```
DAEMON_CONF="/etc/hostapd/hostapd.conf"
```

Finally, reboot the Pi and you should be able to connect to the Wi-Fi network using the login used in the configuration file. You can then use either a web browser or smartphone application to connect to the Logitech Media Server instance at 192.168.42.1.

If the Wi-Fi network is not showing up in a search, you may need to use an alternative driver. To check whether this is the case, run the following commands:

```
sudo apt-get install iw
iw list
```

If you see a message similar to n180211 not found, then open /etc/hostapd/ hostapd.conf and swap the commented out driver lines so that rtl871xdrv is uncommented. Next, we need to download a modified version of hostapd using the following set of commands:

```
wget http://www.adafruit.com/downloads/adafruit_hostapd.zip
unzip adafruit_hostapd.zip
sudo mv /usr/sbin/hostapd /usr/sbin/hostapd.ORIG
sudo mv hostapd /usr/sbin
sudo chmod 755 /usr/sbin/hostapd
```

Once the commands have finished executing, reboot the Pi and you should be able to pick up the Wi-Fi network.

Summary

In this chapter, we took a look at some basic electronics that were to be used to power the Pi and external devices and to amplify the audio from the audio output on the Pi.

We also took the first steps to design and manufacture custom enclosures and fittings for hardware projects by adapting an existing case for the enclosure of the speaker system. In later projects in this book, we will use these skills to manufacture enclosures from scratch.

In the next chapter, we will look further into designing and manufacturing customized enclosures, as we build a mini tabletop arcade machine.

3
Mini Retro Arcade Cabinet

In this chapter, we will build a mini retro-style arcade cabinet, which runs a selection of emulators that can play games from a wide variety of game consoles and arcade machines. This will be done using an operating system called **PiPlay** (formally known as PiMAME).

An arcade cabinet is essentially a standard computer and monitor in a custom-built cabinet used to mimic the style and shape of retro arcade machines.

This project will also be the first that involves a significant amount of woodwork and carpentry in the making of the cabinet for the arcade system. Although it seems like a daunting task for anyone who has not undertaken a project like this in the past, the construction is relatively simple and can be done with common household tools.

To control the games, we will use a selection of arcade controls that are readily available online. We will interface them to the Pi using the GPIO port and some software written by Adafruit.

This project is based on a similar project built by Tony Dixon at Maker Space, Newcastle.

Requirements

For this project, you will need the hardware and tools. Here is the list of the hardware required:

- The Raspberry Pi
- A USB keyboard (for setup only)
- Arcade buttons and a joystick

- A monitor (and an HDMI adapter if needed)
- A sheet of 6 mm plywood (see the *Building the cabinet* section for the size required)
- A sheet of 12 mm plywood (see the *Building the cabinet* section for the size required)
- Female-to-female 0.1 inch pin jumpers

Tools required for this project are listed as follows:

- A soldering iron and solder
- Wire cutters
- A Pozidriv screwdriver
- A drill machine
- A 30 mm Forstner drill bit
- Sandpaper (80, 120, and 240 grit)
- A jigsaw

Setting up the input electronics

In this section, we will set up the input hardware to the arcade cabinet. The cabinet we will build comprises a joystick and seven push buttons. All of the devices used for this are simple digital logic devices that can be connected directly to the GPIO header on the Pi without external electronics.

Firstly, we will solder the connecting wires to each of our arcade buttons and joystick. The buttons used have three connections on them that are marked as **COM**, **NC**, and **NO**, which stand for **common**, **normally closed**, and **normally open**.

> The buttons and joystick that I have used are from a seller on eBay called **ultracabs** (http://www.ebay.co.uk/ usr/ultracabs) who sells a variety of hardware for arcade cabinets. While any buttons and joysticks should work, I will be using these in the instructions.

In our case, we want to create a circuit when the button is pressed, so we need to solder wires to COM and NO. In this case, we will use female-to-female 0.1 inch jumper wires with one end removed and stripped, as this will allow easier connection to the pins on the Pi GPIO port, as shown in the following image:

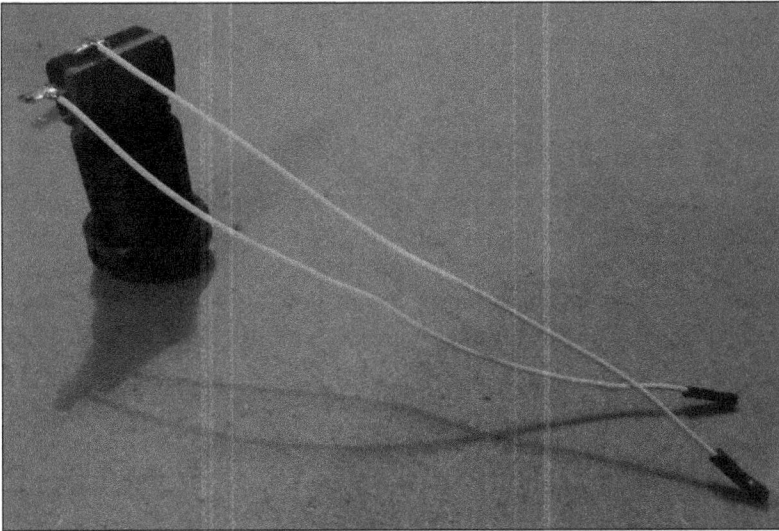

Next, we need to solder the same connecting wires onto the joystick. For this, there are four similar switches to what were used on the buttons around the underside of the joystick assembly that needs to be connected.

Note that the particular joystick I recommend only has COM and NO connections, so since there are only two connections on the switch, getting the wires connected in the correct way is less important here.

Here, it is worth connecting the COM connections of each switch together with short pieces of standard wire, so that we only need a single common wire running to the joystick.

Next, as with the buttons, solder a 0.1 inch jumper wire to each switch contact and a single jumper wire to one of the common connections:

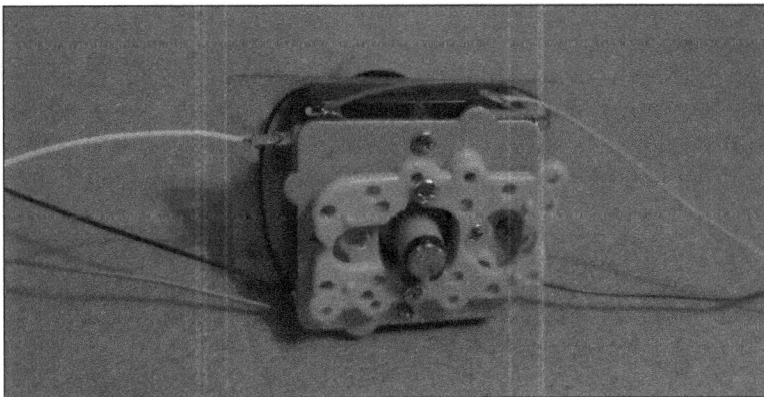

Once this is done, the electronics part of this project is pretty much complete. We will connect the buttons and joystick to the Pi later, once they are mounted on the cabinet.

Building the cabinet

Firstly, it is important to have a good idea of the dimension that we need for each part of the cabinet. The following diagram shows the dimension of the cabinet I made with the height and width of the monitor. While you are free to adapt the design to whatever style you like, be aware of the dimensions that are likely to change throughout the design. In the following diagram, note that all the sizes are in mm:

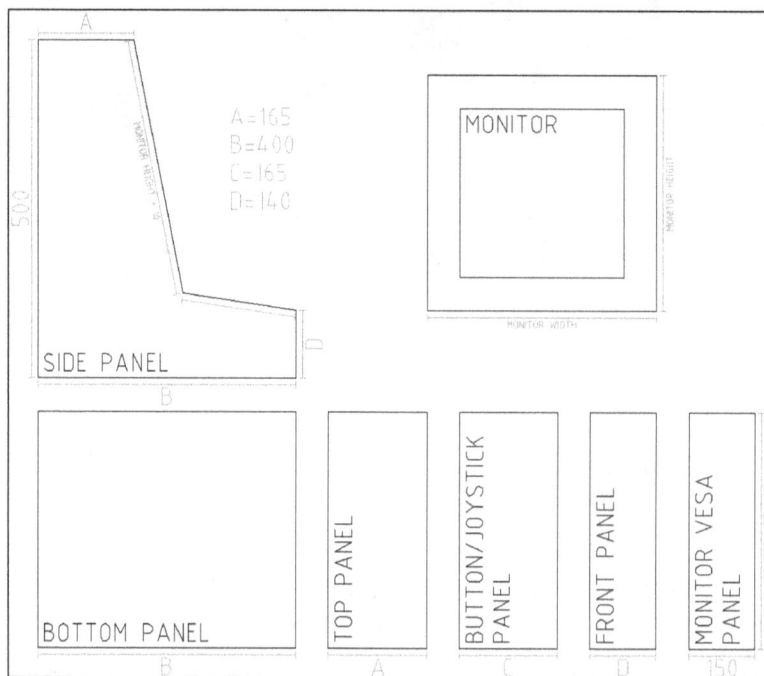

Note that the angle between the monitor and joystick panel is not fixed, as it will depend on the size of the monitor and joystick/button panel. The dimensions listed in the diagram are only a rough guide and you are encouraged to draw a side panel out in a scale of 1:1 to check the dimensions before deciding on them.

> When using power tools, proper safety precautions should be undertaken. Eye protection should always be worn and mains-powered tools should be protected using a **residual current device** (RCD).

The first parts we want to cut are the two side panels for the enclosure. These will both be cut from a 12 mm plywood. As we will be using a jigsaw to cut the panels, we will cut both the left-hand side and right-hand side panels at the same time, since it is very difficult to get exactly the same cut twice when you're guided by eye alone.

> For my cabinet, I opted to use Birch plywood, as it has a much nicer appearance and is stronger than standard plywood. However, it more expensive and can be harder to work with.

For this, we need to ensure that the two sheets of plywood do not move relative to each other during the cut. There are multiple ways to do this, but the way I chose was to screw the two sheets together at regular intervals just outside the cut line (refer to the following image). This is probably one of the best ways, as this method of fixing is very easy to remove and will withstand a lot of force (more than you will ever exert on it while sawing) before the sheets start to move.

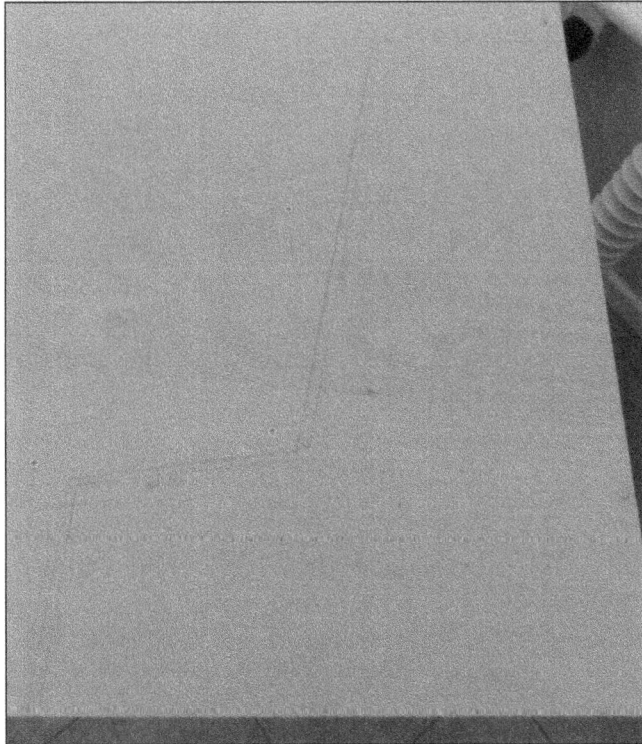

Once both the sheets of material are fixed together, you will need to mark out the cut path in faint pencil markings on one side of the material. Ensuring that this is as faint as possible will make it is easier to remove any leftover markings while sanding the panels down later.

Once the panels have been cut out as shown in the following image, they will have fairly untidy edges, especially when you cut against the grain of the top layer of material. As each panel is made, it is a good idea to take a piece of a low-grit sandpaper (around 40-60) and quickly remove any untidy edges. When it is time for the panel to be assembled in its final position, you should take time to sand the edges and surfaces with progressively higher grip sandpapers to achieve a smooth and tidy finish. A good progression would be 80, then 120, and then 240.

The grit classification of sandpaper is based on the number of abrasive particles per square inch of material. They can range from 24 (very coarse) to 1,000 (very fine).

Next, we will cut the bottom panel of the cabinet. Also, cut from the 12 mm plywood, as shown in the diagram at the start of this section. The width of this panel will be around the width of the monitor plus 10 mm, and the depth will be whatever the desired width of the cabinet is (in the case of the diagram, it is 400 mm).

As with the side panels, they should be sanded down to remove any rough edges. However, as only one edge will be exposed to the front of the cabinet, getting a perfect finish here is not essential.

Next, we will attach the bottom panel to the two side panels. To do this, we will use both screws through the side panels that go into the edge of the bottom panel and several plastic assembly fittings like the ones shown in the following image. This will help to ensure a good quality, durable joint.

> For a more permanent fitting, PVA wood glue can also be used on the joints between two plywood panels.

First, place the bottom panel on a flat surface and align the one side panel next to the matching edge of the bottom panel. Next, drill a series of pilot holes that are around 1-2 mm smaller than the screws that will fix the two panels together at regular intervals along the edge of the side panel. They will also screw the side panel to the bottom panel, as shown in the following image. The screws used here should be dome-headed, self-tapping wood screws around 1.5 inches long. Here, it is important to ensure that the pilot holes are deep enough to prevent the plywood from splitting as the screws are inserted.

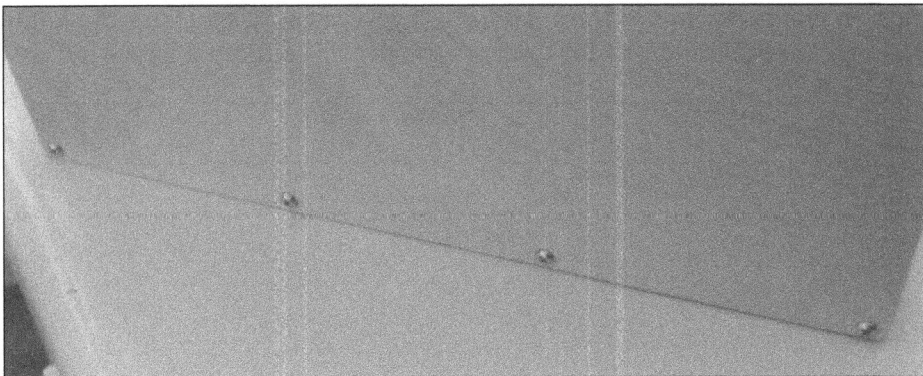

Next, on the inside of the cabinet, screw several of the plastic assembly joints at the corner between the two panels by using countersunk self-tapping wood screws around 3/4 inch long. Ensure that around 30 mm of space is left at each end to give enough clearance for other panels and their assembly joints, as shown in the following image. Repeat this process for the second side panel:

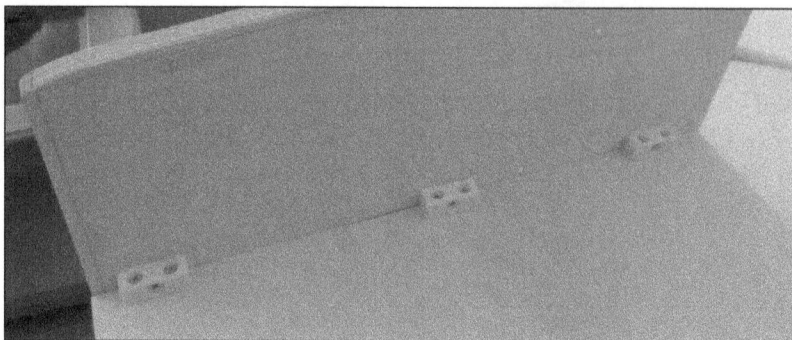

Next, we will cut the panel that will hold the monitor in place. This panel needs to be around 150 mm high, the same width as the bottom panel, and cut from 12 mm plywood. This can be marked out and cut in the same way as the other panels.

Once you've cut out the panel, follow the next diagram to mark out the four holes that will be needed to attach the monitor. Here, I am assuming that the monitor uses the VESA 100 standard, which is the most common size found on 15-22 inch computer monitors. It would be worth checking this standard when you're looking for a monitor for this project. VGA monitors with this type of mounting are very common on Internet auction sites and often sell very cheaply. Note that the following diagram is not to scale and that the center of the panel is indicated by the red cross:

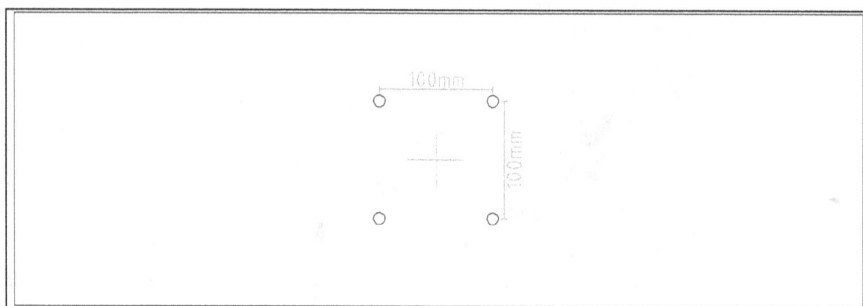

Once the VESA holes are drilled, you can prepare the monitor to be mounted on the panel by removing any desk stand it had (the procedure for doing so varies for each monitor; it is worth searching online if it is not obvious to you how it can be removed). Attach the monitor using four M4 machine screws in the holes you've just drilled, as shown in the following image. It is important to use a washer on both sides of the plywood panel to help spread the weight of the monitor and to prevent the screw heads from digging into the plywood.

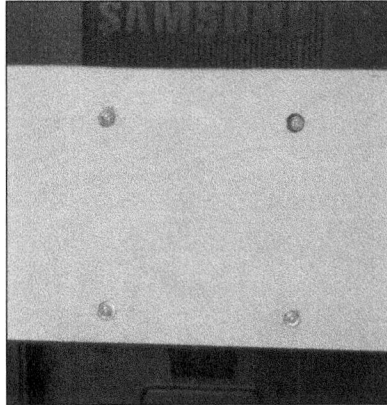

Next, we will attach the monitor mount to the two side panels. To make the positioning of the monitor easier, first, tip the cabinet to its side so that the monitor's weight is supported. Now, move the monitor panel until the monitor is in the desired position. This should leave at least 5 mm at the top for cooling and the bottom should be just above where the button panel will be.

Now, attach the monitor panel to the two side panels using two assembly joints on each side of the panel. This will keep the panel in place for now. However, as with the bottom panel, we need to add some longer screws that go through the side panel to provide enough support for the weight of the monitor.

To do this, unscrew the monitor and mark the outline of the monitor panel on the inside of each side panel and then remove the screws holding the assembly joints to the side panels. This will leave an indication that the panel was mounted.

Next, drill two holes in each side panel that will be used to guide the screws into the side of the monitor panel, as shown in the following image. It is important here to ensure that the position of the holes will not cause the screws to collide with the screws already in the panel from the assembly joints.

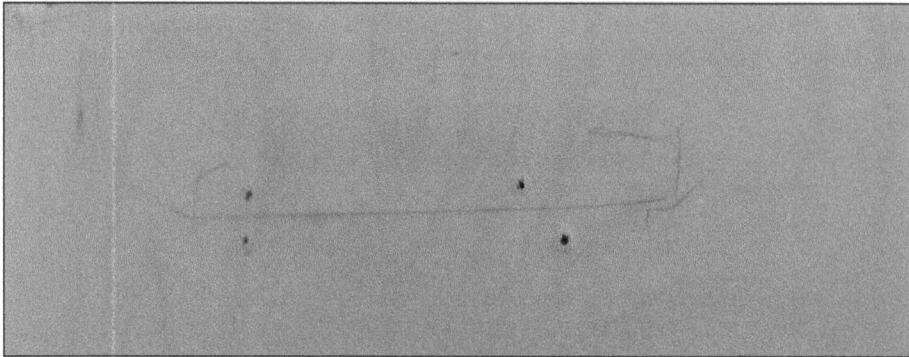

Once this is done, reattach the monitor panel with the assembly joints and use the holes drilled in the side panels to drill pilot holes in the edge of the monitor panel, similar to what was done in the bottom panel. To finish, screw two of the same screws used for the bottom panel into each side of the monitor panel and reattach the monitor. By now, the back of the cabinet should look similar to what is shown in the following image:

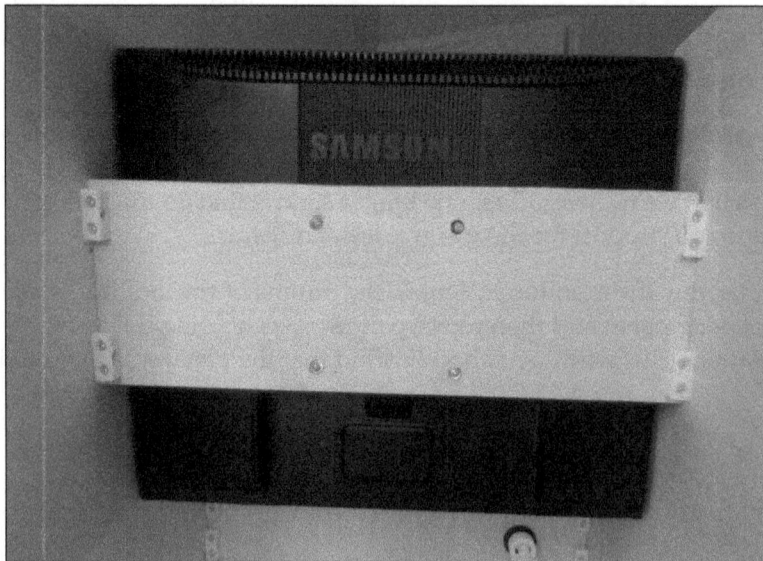

Next, we will cut the front, top, and button/joystick panels. All of these panels can be cut from 6 mm plywood and the width of these will be the same as the bottom and monitor panels. The exact width of these will depend on your design, based on the diagram earlier in this section. Once you have the dimensions of the panels, they can be cut in the same way as the other panels.

First, we will attach the top panel. This should be mounted on the top between the two side panels and can be held in place with two assembly joints on each side of the panel, as shown in the following image. Since this plywood is thinner, you will need to use half inch screws for this.

Next, we need to drill a hole in the front panel for the single-player arcade button. To do this, we will use a 30 mm Forstner drill bit. First, start by marking the center of the hole for the button. This will be used to align with the sharp point in the center of the drill bit.

Although holes like this are best drilled using a pillar drill or drill press, they can be drilled using a handheld electric drill (a battery-powered cordless drill is unlikely to have enough power to drive a Forstner bit of this size). It is important to hold the drill as vertical and steady as possible to ensure that the hole does not become out of shape by the drill as it moves relative to the panel.

When drilling by a handheld drill, it is best to start slow to ensure that the drill gets a good position in the center of the hole and gradually speed up to do the bulk of cutting. It may take several minutes to fully cut through the panel, and it is worth stopping occasionally to clean any material that has built up on the drill bit. Be careful when doing this, as friction can cause the drill bit to heat up enough to cause burns. The drilled hole is shown in the following image:

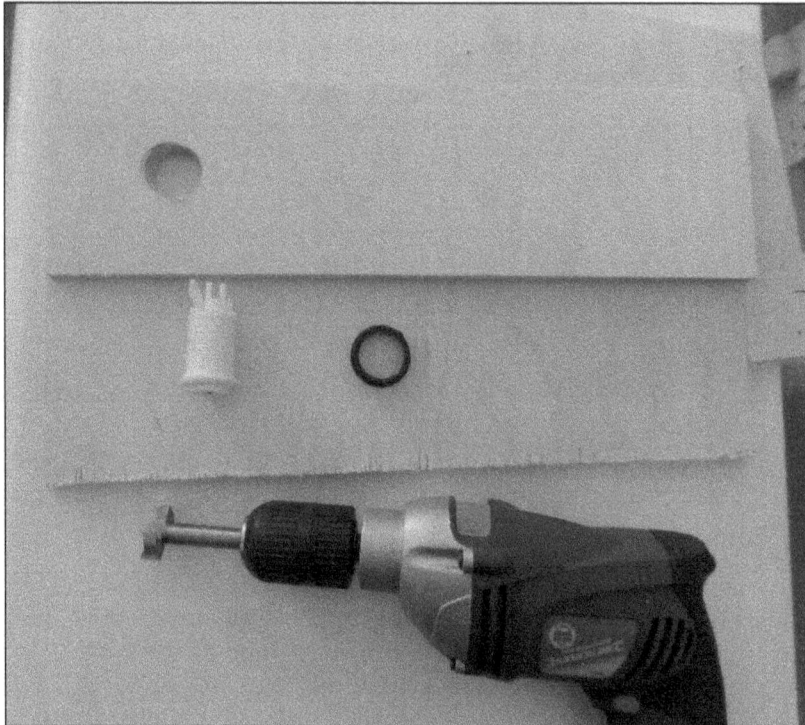

Once the hole is drilled, remove any loose material around the edges of the hole using medium-low grit sandpaper (either 80 or 120) and insert the button through the hole. To do this, you will have to remove the micro switch from the back side of the switch. In the switch that I used, this is done by lifting the clips on one side of the switch, which allows the micro switch to be levered out.

Once the switch is fitted and the edges of the panel are sanded down, the panel can be fitted using four assembly joints, as shown in the following image. Depending on the accuracy of the cut, you may find that the panel is a tight fit in between the two side panels. If this is the case, then loosen the screws that hold the side panels to the bottom panel so that the side panels can be moved outwards slightly. This allows the front panel to be inserted easily.

Note that in the preceding image, I used 12 mm plywood for the front panel. While it is possible to do this, it is not required. Drilling the 30 mm hole takes much longer.

Next, we want to mark the position of the buttons and joystick on the front panel. The best way to do this is to place the panel in position to see which position will feel most comfortable or intuitive to play. Once you have done this, mark the position of the center of each button and the joystick, as shown in the following image:

Now that we have the positions of each part to be mounted on this panel, we can start drilling the holes for them, starting with the joystick.

With the joystick, I recommend that you drill one 30 mm hole for the shaft of the joystick and four 4 mm holes for the mounting screws. Start by drilling the 30 mm hole centered on the mark you made for the center of the joystick. This hole will be cut using the 30 mm Forstner bit in the same way as the hole for the button on the front panel.

Once this is done, insert the joystick into the hole with the switch side on the back side of the panel (you will need to unscrew the red ball from the top of the joystick first) and mark the position of the four holes in the corner of the metal plate. This is where we will drill the holes that will be used to mount the joystick.

After the holes have been drilled, the panel should look something like what's shown in the following image:

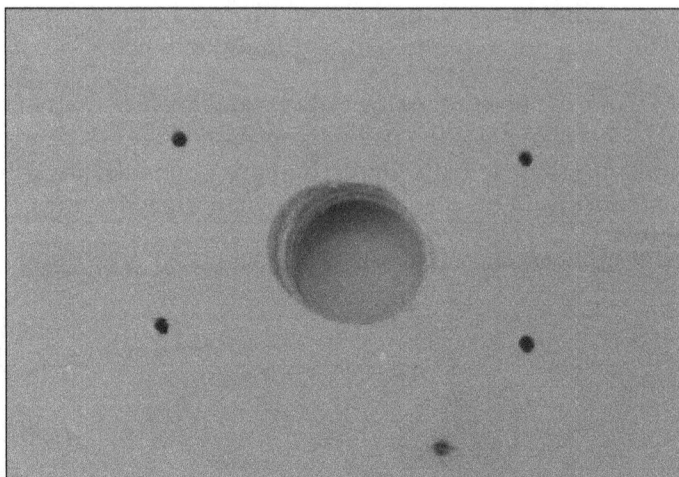

We will mount the joystick later on. Now, it is time to drill the holes for our arcade buttons. This is done in the same way as was done for the single-player button on the front panel.

Each of the buttons can now be mounted on the panel. While nonessential, mounting them so that all of the micro switches line up parallel to each other makes cable management easier, as shown in the upcoming image.

Next, we can fasten the joystick in position with four M3 machine screws by using a washer for both the sides of the metal plate on the joystick. Finally, place the round, black disc that came with the joystick over the joystick shaft and reattach the red ball.

By this point, the back of the front panel should look something like what's shown in the following image:

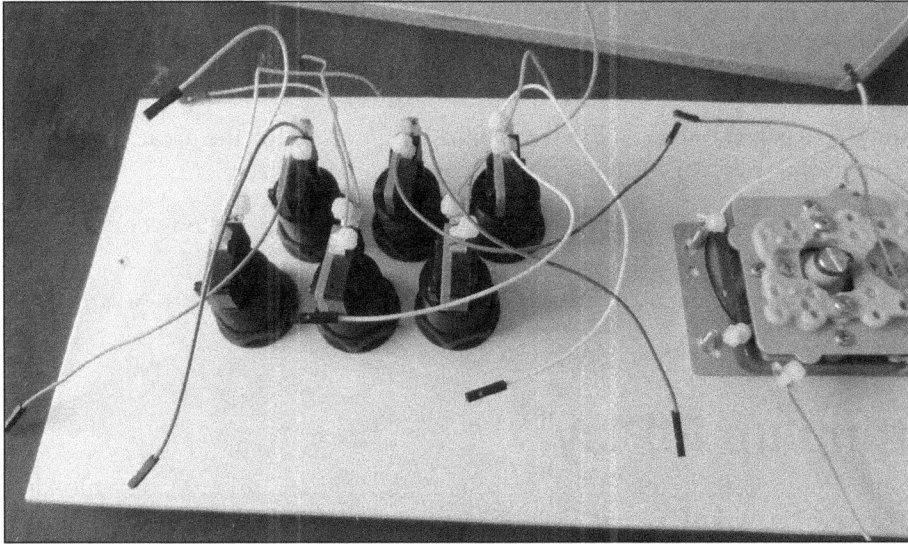

All that is left to do now is to attach the button/joystick panel to the rest of the cabinet. As with all the other panels, this can be easily done by using several assembly joints.

While it is possible to use four joints here to fix the panel in a single position, I found it useful to only attach the panel using two joints at the back of the panel (closest to the bottom of the monitor). This will allow the front panel to be lifted up for easy access to the Pi and wiring, as shown in the following image:

I also chose to use a set of male-to-female 0.1 inch jumper wires to extend the wires that had been soldered onto the button and joystick switches. Again, this is not essential, but may help to make wiring the switches to the Pi easier.

Of course, this is just one possible way to design the case for the arcade cabinet. Here are another two very unique designs of a similar project:

- `http://www.instructables.com/id/NaCade-The-Naked-Raspberry-Pi-Arcade-Machine/`
- `http://www.instructables.com/id/MAME-gaming-table-with-Raspberry-Pi/`

Setting up PiPlay

First, you should head to the PiPlay website (`http://pimame.org`), download the latest version of the OS, and write the image to an SD card. This is the same procedure that we followed with Raspbian in the two previous projects.

Once the image is written to the SD card, connect a network cable, USB keyboard, and monitor to the Pi and power it up. After a few minutes, you should see the PiPlay main screen, as shown in the following screenshot:

This shows a list of all the installed emulators and a count of how many games are installed for each one in the small red squares (obviously, for a clean install, there will not be any games installed).

PiPlay has a web interface that can be used to upload games to the arcade system. This is accessed using the IP address of the Pi, as shown in the following screenshot:

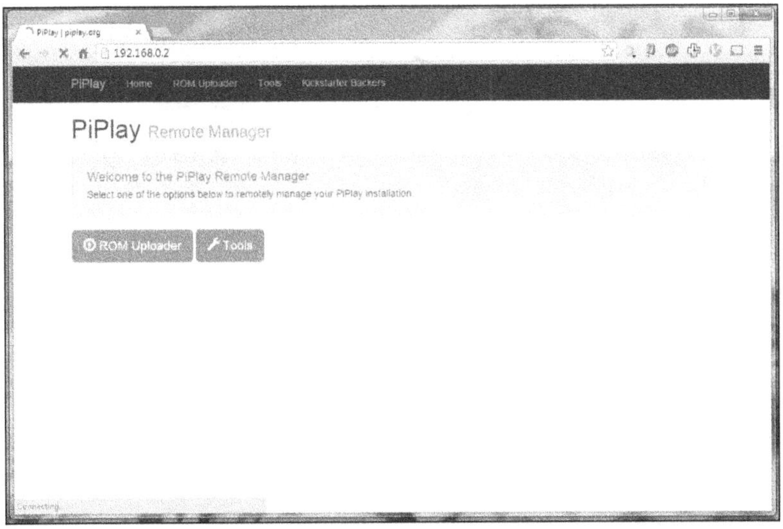

This interface can also be used to shutdown and reboot the Pi using the **Tools** menu. For now, we will use **ROM Uploader** to add a new game to the **Gameboy** emulator. The list of all the installed emulators is shown in the following screenshot:

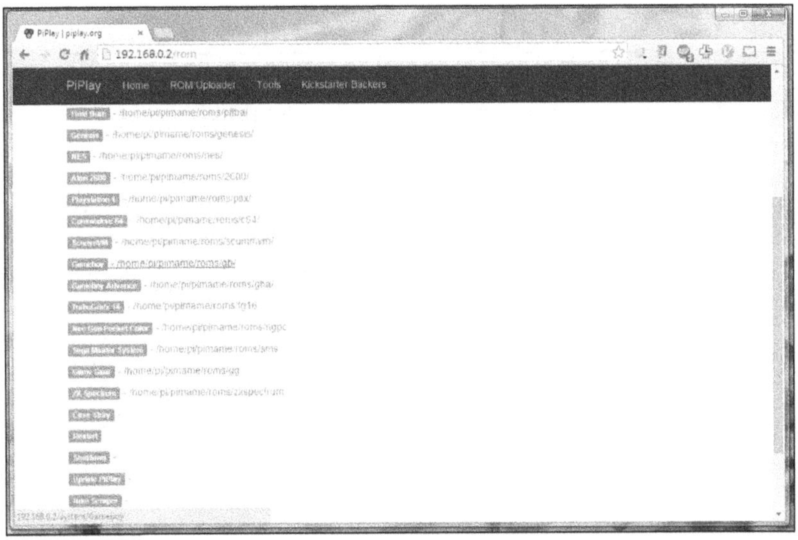

There are many websites where ROMs can be downloaded. If you're looking for a particular game, the best option is to use a search engine with a query containing the name of the game and the platform you want to emulate it on.

Here, we will select the **Gameboy** emulator. This shows a page where you can drag and drop any ROM files from your PC that are to be uploaded to the Pi:

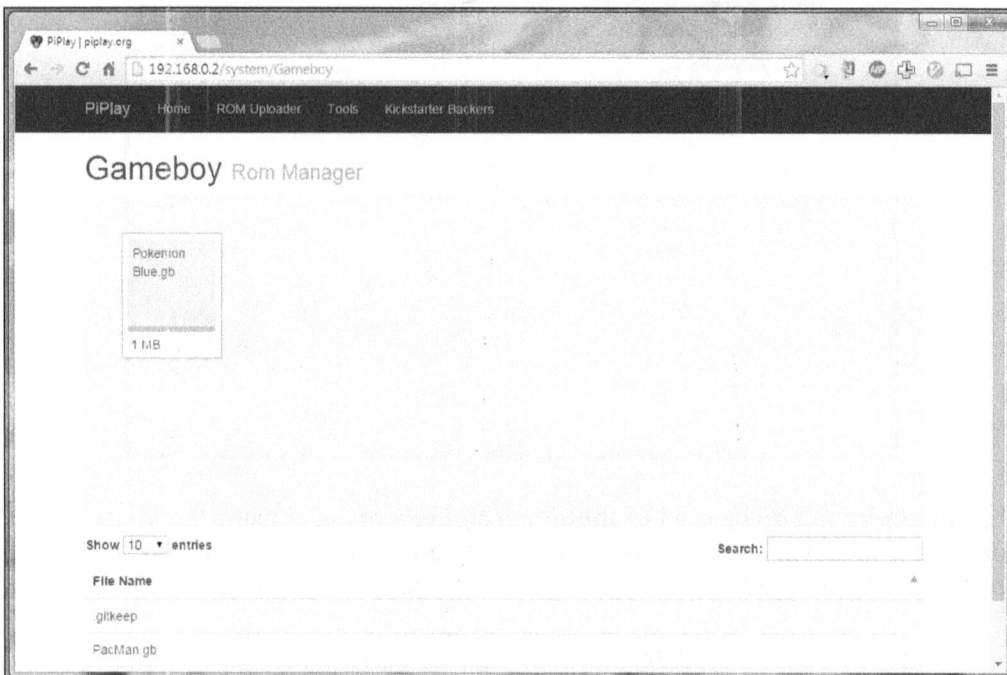

Once the upload is complete, the new game will be available in the menu for that emulator.

When a new game has been added for a certain emulator, PiPlay will ask whether you want to download its information from an online database, as shown in the following screenshot. This will automatically correct the name of the game and download a cover image if it is available; it is not required that you do this to play a game.

When an emulator is selected, a menu similar to the one shown in the following screenshot is shown, which lists all the games uploaded to the Pi for the current emulator. To start one, select it using the arrow keys and press *Enter*. To return to the main PiPlay menu, press *Esc*.

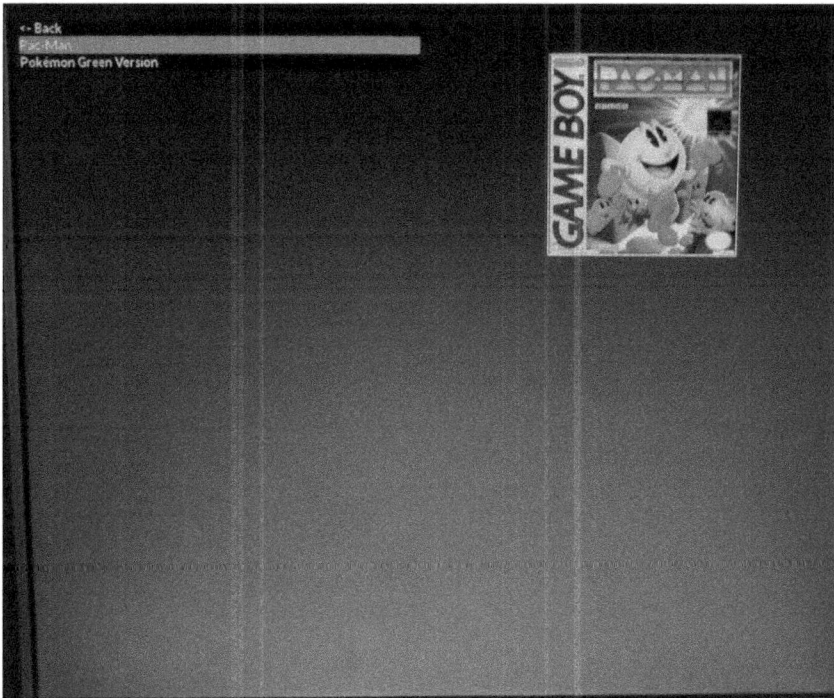

Using the buttons and joystick with PiPlay

While the ability to use GPIO inputs as input to emulators is planned for a future release of PiPlay, the current version does not support the use of switches connected via the GPIO port as input to game emulators. Hence, we need an additional piece of software to do this.

Fortunately, Adafruit has already written a driver that converts switch signals from the GPIO port to key presses (`https://github.com/adafruit/Adafruit-Retrogame`), which we will use for our arcade buttons and joystick.

First, we need to install some required programs and libraries that will allow us to recompile the retro game software when we make changes to it; these can be installed using:

```
sudo apt-get install git libexpat1 libexpat1-dev libncurses5 libncurses5-dev
```

Next, we will download the retro game software and move to the directory it was saved in by using the following two commands:

```
git clone https://github.com/adafruit/Adafruit-Retrogame.git
cd Adafruit-Retrogame
```

While there is already a precompiled version of the software available, it will not be suitable for the type of arcade system we have built. So, we need to make a few modifications to the code first. Use the following command to start editing the program:

```
nano retrogame.c
```

Next, look for the line that starts with ioStandard and replace the lines up to the END OF LIST marker with the following code. Note that if you are using a Pi B version 1, you need to replace 27 with 21 in this code:

```
ioStandard[] = {
    {   25,      KEY_LEFT      },
    {   11,      KEY_RIGHT     },
    {    8,      KEY_UP        },
    {    9,      KEY_DOWN      },
    {   24,      KEY_ENTER     },
    {   22,      KEY_S         },
    {   17,      KEY_D         },
    {   10,      KEY_Z         },
    {   23,      KEY_X         },
    {   27,      KEY_C         },
```

```
{    7,       KEY_ESC        },
{   -1,       -1             }
};
```

Once this is done, the code should look something like the following:

Once this is done, recompile the code using the following command:

`make`

This may take a couple of minutes and will output a message similar to the following:

```
pi@raspberrypi ~/Adafruit-Retrogame $ make
gcc  -Wall -O3 -fomit-frame-pointer -funroll-loops -s retrogame.c -o retrogame
strip retrogame
gcc  -Wall -O3 -fomit-frame-pointer -funroll-loops -s gamera.c -lncurses -lmenu
-lexpat -o gamera
strip gamera
pi@raspberrypi ~/Adafruit-Retrogame $
```

If this is the case, then all is good and you can move on to the next step. If you get a message with the word Error in it anywhere, then you will likely have errors in the syntax of the program code. In this case, check whether the code you have matches what's shown in the preceding screenshot. You can also get an error when one of the libraries used by the code is not installed correctly; in which case, try updating the installed packages using the following commands:

```
sudo apt-get update
sudo apt-get upgrade
sudo apt-get install git libexpat1 libexpat1-dev libncurses5 libncurses5-
dev
```

Once the retro game program is compiled successfully, we need to add a udev rule to ensure its compatibility with emulators using the latest SDL2 library. To do this, create a new rule file using the following command:

```
sudo nano /etc/udev/rules.d/10-retrogame.rules
```

On a single line, add the following code:

```
SUBSYSTEM=="input", ATTRS{name}=="retrogame",
ENV{ID_INPUT_KEYBOARD}="1"
```

Next, we want to ensure that the retro game program starts as soon as the OS boots in order to remove the need to attach a keyboard to the Pi. This can be done with an addition to the rc.local file:

```
sudo nano /etc/rc.local
```

Add the following line to the script just before the exit 0 line:

```
/home/pi/Adafruit-Retrogame/retrogame &
```

The script should now look similar to the following:

```
pi@raspberrypi: ~

  GNU nano 2.2.6                    File: /etc/rc.local

#!/bin/sh -e
#
# rc.local
#
# This script is executed at the end of each multiuser runlevel.
# Make sure that the script will "exit 0" on success or any other
# value on error.
#
# In order to enable or disable this script just change the execution
# bits.
#
# By default this script does nothing.

# Print the IP address
_IP=$(hostname -I) || true
if [ "$_IP" ]; then
  printf "My IP address is %s\n" "$_IP"
fi

/home/pi/Adafruit-Retrogame/retrogame &

exit 0




^G Get Help   ^O WriteOut   ^R Read File  ^Y Prev Page  ^K Cut Text    ^C Cur Pos
^X Exit       ^J Justify    ^W Where Is   ^V Next Page  ^U UnCut Text  ^T To Spell
```

This script is run at the end of the Linux boot sequence, so it is a good place to add code that should be executed after the operating system has finished booting.

Finally, reboot the Pi and move on to configure the buttons within PiPlay:

`sudo reboot`

The next step is to wire up the buttons and joystick to the GPIO port. This must be done, as shown in the following diagram, to ensure that the button mapping is as expected and based on the code changed in `retrogame.c`. It would be worth doing this wiring with the power to the Pi turned off to reduce the chances of mistakes and permanent damage to the Pi.

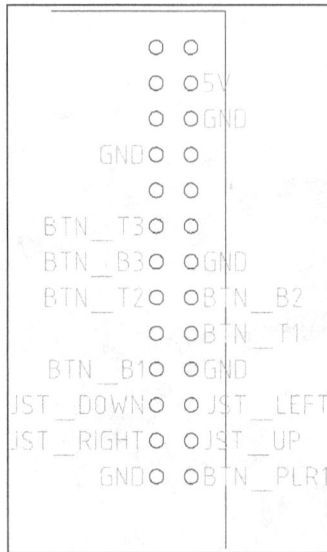

Note that **PLR1** is the button on the front panel, **B1-3** is the bottom row of buttons from left to right, and **T1-3** is the top row of buttons from left to right.

Once all the connections have been made, the inside of the front of the cabinet should look something like what's shown in the following image. Also note that the white HDMI to VGA converter allows you to use an old PC monitor for this project.

In the preceding image, you may notice that I am powering the Pi from a 5 V power supply, which is connected directly to the 5 V and ground pins on the GPIO port. This is not essential, but if you find that the Pi becomes unstable or has problems with USB devices or in maintaining a network connection, then this may be the case because the power supply cannot supply enough current. This can happen especially if you're using a HDMI to VGA converter, which requires a certain amount of power to operate.

Once this is done, repower the Pi. When the Pi boots back into PiPlay, you will notice that the joystick and button 1 will already be able to move the cursor and select emulators. However, you will need to configure the key mapping for the additional buttons used by each emulator.

To configure the joystick and buttons for a certain emulator, press the *Tab* key on the keyboard. This should bring up a menu similar to the one shown in the following image. Use the arrow keys to scroll down to **Controller Setup** and press *Enter*.

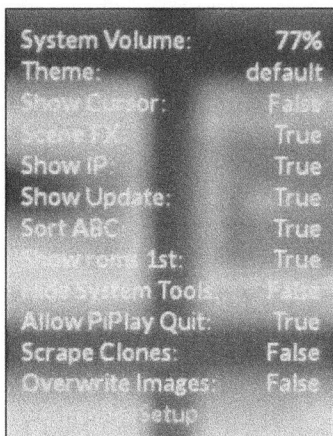

This will show another menu that shows all the emulators that PiPlay can control the key mapping of. Here, it is best to select a single emulator and assign its key mapping individually, for instance, select **arcade** from this menu.

This will then show a preview of the controller as shown in the following image and you will be prompted to press certain buttons to configure the key mapping. Certain emulators may have more buttons than what are available on the cabinet. In this case, they will have to be mapped to keys on the USB keyboard. (I have only found this to be the case with a couple of emulators, for example, the pause and credit buttons of MAME emulators have to be mapped to keys on the keyboard.)

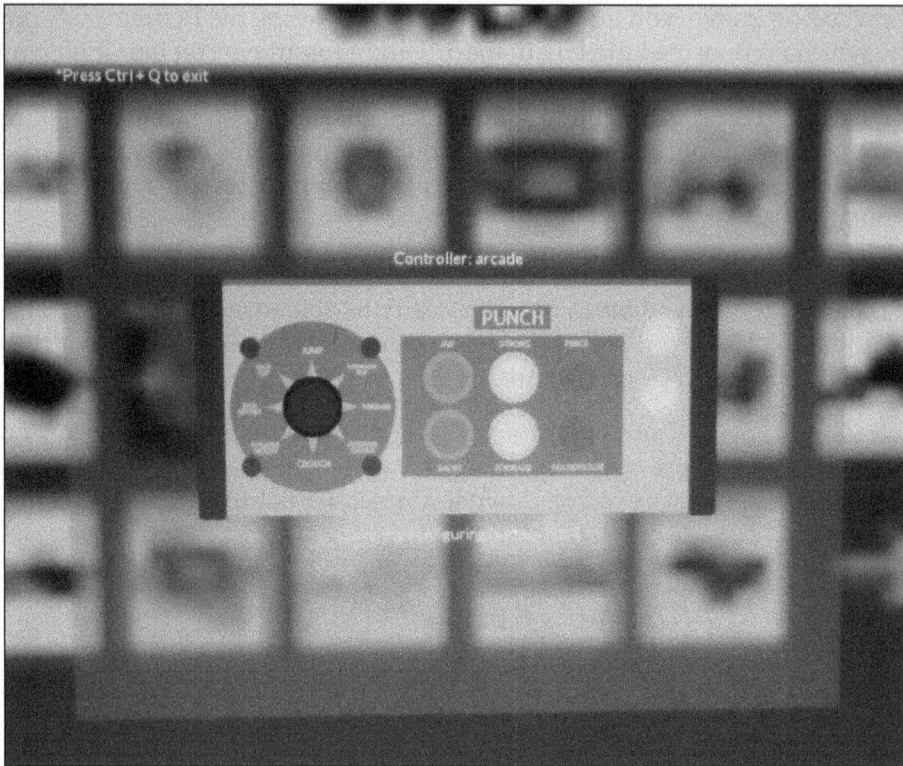

Once this is done, you will be taken back to the main menu and can then select any of the emulators using the joystick and arcade buttons. Note that the top-left arcade button is used to select a menu option and the front, single-player button is used to return to the PiPlay main menu.

Summary

In this chapter, we had a good look at the process of designing and building a custom enclosure for a project based on the requirements of specific parts that are to be used in the project.

We also made more use of the GPIO port on the Pi by using it as an additional input device to control a variety of games made available on the PiPlay operating system.

In the next chapter, we will use the Raspberry Pi camera module to create a location-aware time-lapse recorder that can be used to record a series of still images over a long period of time.

4
GPS-enabled
Time-lapse Recorder

One of the possible uses of the Raspberry Pi camera module is the recording of time-lapse captures, which takes a still image at a set interval over a long period of time. This can then be used to create an accelerated video of a long-term event that takes place (for example, a building being constructed).

One alteration to this is to have the camera mounted on a moving vehicle. Use the time lapse to record a journey; with the addition of GPS data, this can provide an interesting record of a reasonably long journey.

In this chapter, we will use the Raspberry Pi camera module board to create a location-aware time-lapse recorder that will store the GPS position with each image in the EXIF metadata.

To do this, we will use a GPS module that connects to the Pi over the serial connection on the GPIO port and a custom Python program that listens for new GPS data during the time lapse.

For this project, we will use the Raspbian distribution. Instructions on how this is installed can be found in *Chapter 1, Raspberry Pi Pirate Radio*.

What you will need

This is a list of things that you will need to complete this project. All of these are available at most electronic components stores and online retailers:

- The Raspberry Pi
- A relatively large SD card (at least 8 GB is recommended)

- The Pi camera board
- A GPS module (http://www.adafruit.com/product/746)
- 0.1 inch female to female pin jumper wires
- A USB power bank (this is optional and is used to power the Pi when no other power is available)

Setting up the hardware

The first thing we will do is set up the two pieces of hardware and verify that they are working correctly before moving on to the software.

The camera board

The first (and the most important) piece of hardware we need is the camera board. Firstly, start by connecting the camera board to the Pi.

Connecting the camera module to the Pi

The camera is connected to the Pi via a 15-pin flat, flex ribbon cable, which can be physically connected to two connectors on the Pi. However, the connector it should be connected to is the one nearest to the Ethernet jack; the other connector is for display.

1. To connect the cable first, lift the top retention clip on the connector, as shown in the following image:

2. Insert the flat, flex cable with the silver contacts facing the HDMI port and the rigid, blue plastic part of the ribbon connector facing the Ethernet port on the Pi:

3. Finally, press down the cable retention clip to secure the cable into the connector. If this is done correctly, the cable should be perpendicular to the **printed circuit board** (**PCB**) and should remain seated in the connector if you try to use a little force to pull it out:

4. Next, we will move on to set up the camera driver, libraries, and software within Raspbian.

Setting up the Raspberry Pi camera

Firstly, we need to enable support for the camera in the operating system itself by performing the following steps:

1. This is done by the `raspi-config` utility from a terminal (either locally or over SSH). Enter the following command:

   ```
   sudo raspi-config
   ```

   This command will open the following configuration page:

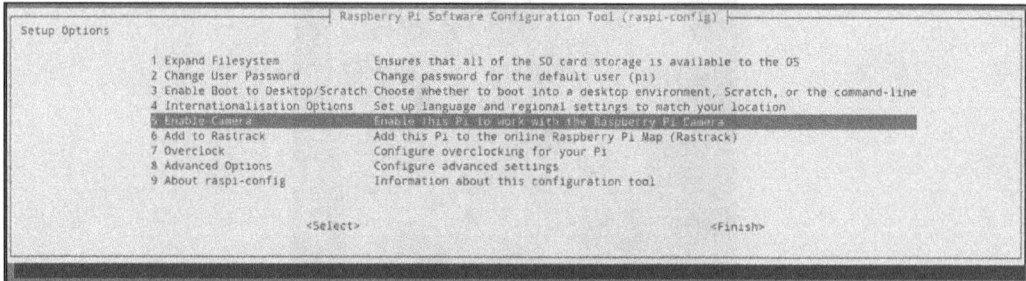

   This will load the configuration utility. Scroll down to the **Enable Camera** option using the arrow keys and select it using *Enter*.

2. Next, highlight **Enable** and select it using *Enter*:

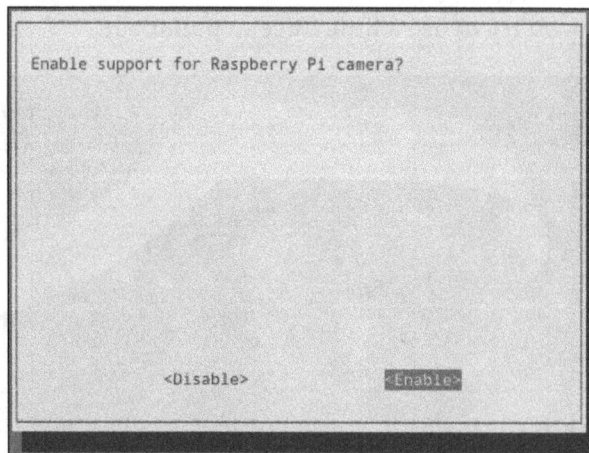

   Once this is done, you will be taken back to the main `raspi-config` menu. Exit `raspi-config`, and reboot the Pi to continue.

3. Next, we will look for any updates to the Pi kernel, as using an out-of-date kernel can sometimes cause issues with the low-level hardware, such as the camera module and GPIO. We also need to get a library that allows control of the camera from Python.

   Both of these installations can be done with the following two commands:

   ```
   sudo rpi-update
   sudo apt-get install python-picamera
   ```

4. Once this is complete, reboot the Pi using the following command:

   ```
   sudo reboot
   ```

5. Next, we will test out the camera using the `python-picamera` library we just installed.

   To do this, create a simple test script using `nano`:

   ```
   nano canera_test.py
   ```

6. The following code will capture a still image after opening the preview for 5 seconds. Having the preview open before a capture is a good idea as this gives the camera time to adjust capture parameters of the environment:

   ```python
   import sys
   import time
   import picamera

   with picamera.PiCamera() as cam:
       cam.resolution = (1280, 1024)
       cam.start_preview()
       time.sleep(5)
       cam.capture(sys.argv[1])
       cam.stop_preview()
   ```

7. Save the script using *Ctrl* + *X* and enter *Y* to confirm. Now, test it by using the following command:

   ```
   python camera_test.py image.jpg
   ```

8. This will capture a single, still image and save it to `image.jpg`. It is worth downloading the image using SFTP to verify that the camera is working properly.

The GPS module

Before connecting the GPS module to the Pi, there are a couple of important modifications that need to be made to the way the Pi boots up.

By default, Raspbian uses the on-board serial port on the GPIO header as a serial terminal for the Pi (this allows you to connect to the Pi and run commands in a similar way to SSH). However, this is of little use to us here and can interfere with the communication between the GPS module and the Pi if the serial terminal is left enabled. This can be disabled by modifying a couple of configuration files:

1. First, start with:

   `sudo nano /boot/cmdline.txt`

2. Here, you will need to remove any references to ttyAMA0 (the name for the on-board serial port). In my case, there was a single entry of `console=ttyAMA0,115200`, which had to be removed. Once this is done, the file should look something like what is shown in the following screenshot:

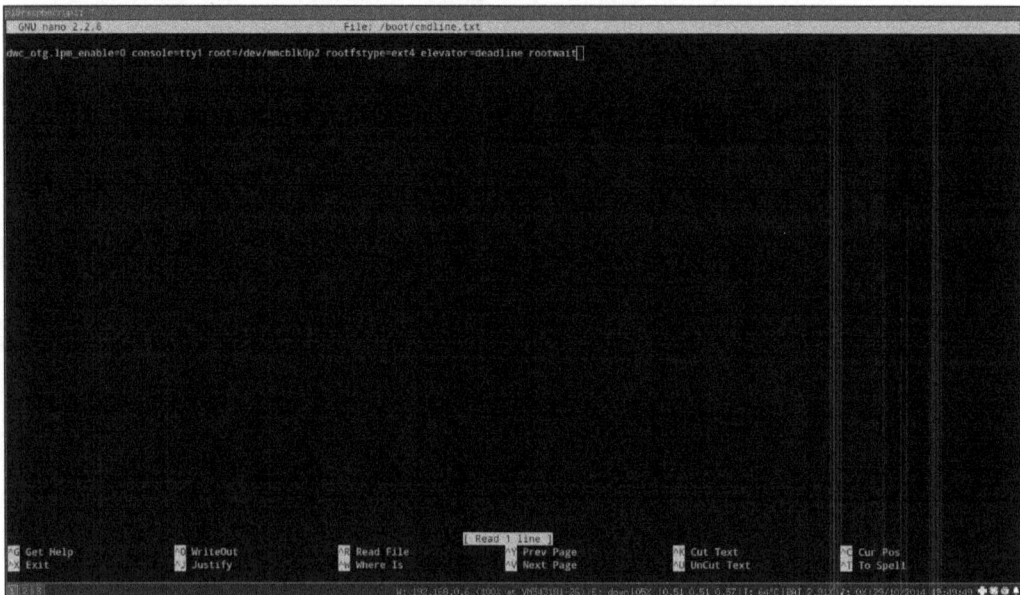

3. Next, we need to stop the Pi by using the serial port for the TTY session. To do this, edit this file:

   `sudo nano /etc/inittab`

4. Here, look for the following line and comment it out:

    ```
    T0:23:respawn:/sbin/getty -L ttyAMA0 115200 vt100
    ```

    Once this is done, the file should look like what is shown in the following screenshot:

```
pi@raspberrypi: ~
  GNU nano 2.2.6                                            File: /etc/inittab

pf::powerwait:/etc/init.d/powerfail start
pn::powerfailnow:/etc/init.d/powerfail now
po::powerokwait:/etc/init.d/powerfail stop

# /sbin/getty invocations for the runlevels.
#
# The "id" field MUST be the same as the last
# characters of the device (after "tty").
#
# Format:
#  <id>:<runlevels>:<action>:<process>
#
# Note that on most Debian systems tty7 is used by the X Window System,
# so if you want to add more getty's go ahead but skip tty7 if you run X.
#
1:2345:respawn:/sbin/getty --noclear 38400 tty1
2:23:respawn:/sbin/getty 38400 tty2
3:23:respawn:/sbin/getty 38400 tty3
4:23:respawn:/sbin/getty 38400 tty4
5:23:respawn:/sbin/getty 38400 tty5
6:23:respawn:/sbin/getty 38400 tty6

# Example how to put a getty on a serial line (for a terminal)
#
#T0:23:respawn:/sbin/getty -L ttyS0 9600 vt100
#T1:23:respawn:/sbin/getty -L ttyS1 9600 vt100

# Example how to put a getty on a modem line.
#
#T3:23:respawn:/sbin/mgetty -x0 -s 57600 ttyS3


#Spawn a getty on Raspberry Pi serial line
#T0:23:respawn:/sbin/getty -L ttyAMA0 115200 vt100

^G Get Help          ^O WriteOut          ^R Read File
^X Exit              ^J Justify           ^W Where Is
```

5. After both the files are changed, power down the Pi using the following command:

    ```
    sudo shutdown -h now
    ```

Next, we need to connect the GPS module to the Pi GPIO port. One important thing to note when you do this is that the GPS module must be able to run on 3.3 V or at least be able to use a 3.3 V logic level (such as the Adafruit module I am using here).

[📝 As with any device that connects to the Pi GPIO header, using a 5 V logic device can cause irreparable damage to the Pi.]

Next, connect the GPS module to the Pi, as shown in the following diagram. If you are using the Adafruit module, then all the pins are labeled on the PCB itself. For other modules, you may need to check the data sheet to find which pins to connect:

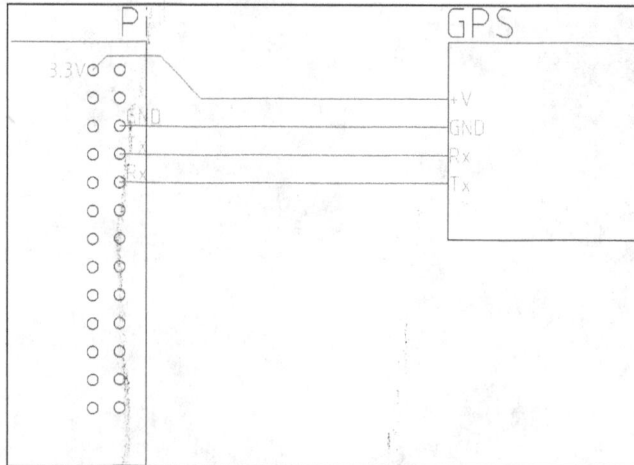

Once this is completed, the wiring to the GPS module should look similar to what is shown in the following image:

After the GPS module is connected and the Pi is powered up, we will install, configure, and test the driver and libraries that are needed to access the data that is sent to the Pi from the GPS module:

1. Start by installing some required packages. Here, gpsd is the daemon that managed data from GPS devices connected to a system, gpsd-clients contains a client that we will use to test the GPS module, and python-gps contains the Python client for gpsd, which is used in the time-lapse capture application:

   ```
   sudo apt-get install gpsd gpsd-clients python-gps
   ```

2. Once they are installed, we need to configure gpsd to work in the way we want. To do this, use the following command:

   ```
   sudo dpkg-reconfigure gpsd
   ```

3. This will open a configuration page similar to raspi-config. First, you will be asked whether you want gpsd to start on boot. Select **Yes** here:

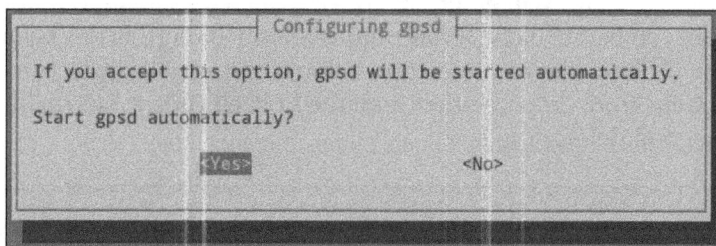

4. Next, it will ask whether we are using USB GPS receivers. Since we are not using one, select **No** here:

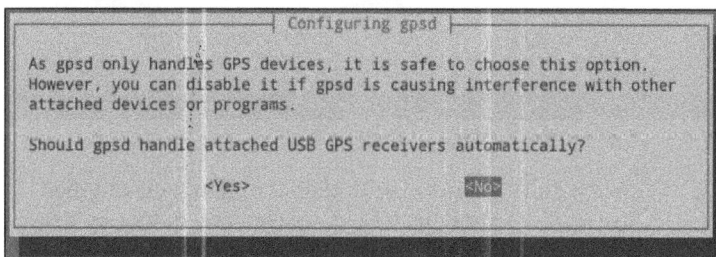

5. Next, it will ask for the device (that is, serial port) the GPS receiver is connected to. Since we are using the on-board serial port on the Pi GPIO header, enter /dev/ttyAMA0 here:

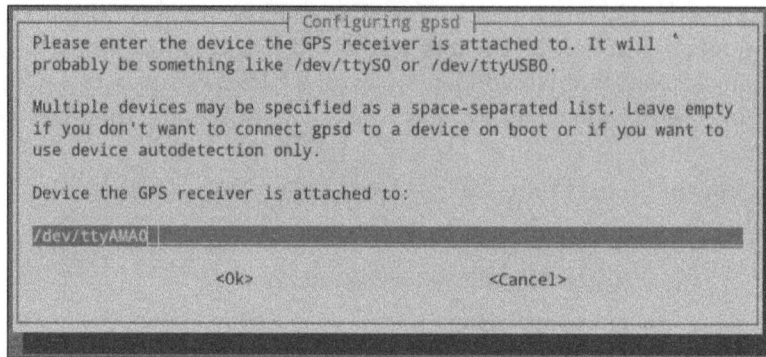

```
┤ Configuring gpsd ├
Please enter the device the GPS receiver is attached to. It will
probably be something like /dev/ttyS0 or /dev/ttyUSB0.

Multiple devices may be specified as a space-separated list. Leave empty
if you don't want to connect gpsd to a device on boot or if you want to
use device autodetection only.

Device the GPS receiver is attached to:

/dev/ttyAMA0

            <Ok>                        <Cancel>
```

6. Next, it will ask for any custom parameters to pass to gpsd, when it is executed. Here, we will enter -n -G. -n, which tells gpsd to poll the GPS module even before a client has requested any data (this has been known to cause problems with some applications) and -G tells gpsd to accept connections from devices other then the Pi itself (this is not really required, but is a good debugging tool):

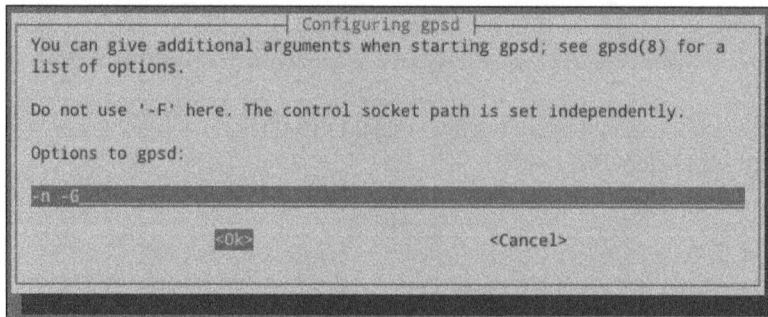

```
┤ Configuring gpsd ├
You can give additional arguments when starting gpsd; see gpsd(8) for a
list of options.

Do not use '-F' here. The control socket path is set independently.

Options to gpsd:

-n -G

            <Ok>                        <Cancel>
```

> When you start gpsd with the -G option, you can then use cgps to view the GPS data from any device by using the command where [IP] is the IP address of the Pi:
>
> cgps [IP]

7. Finally, you will be asked for the location of the control socket. The default value should be kept here so just select **Ok**:

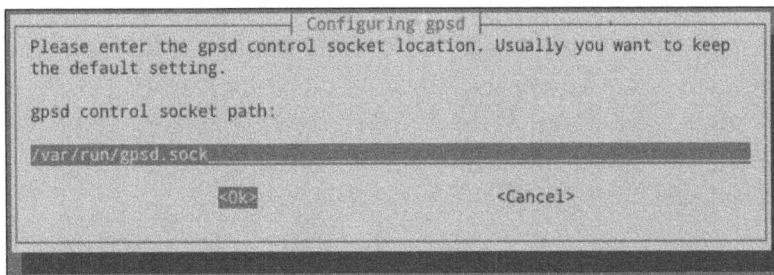

```
┌─────────────────── Configuring gpsd ──────────────────────┐
│ Please enter the gpsd control socket location. Usually you want to keep │
│ the default setting.                                        │
│                                                             │
│ gpsd control socket path:                                   │
│                                                             │
│ /var/run/gpsd.sock                                          │
│                                                             │
│          <Ok>                          <Cancel>             │
└─────────────────────────────────────────────────────────────┘
```

8. After the configuration is done, reboot the Pi and use the following command to test the configuration:

`cgps -s`

This should give output similar to what is shown in the following screenshot, if everything works:

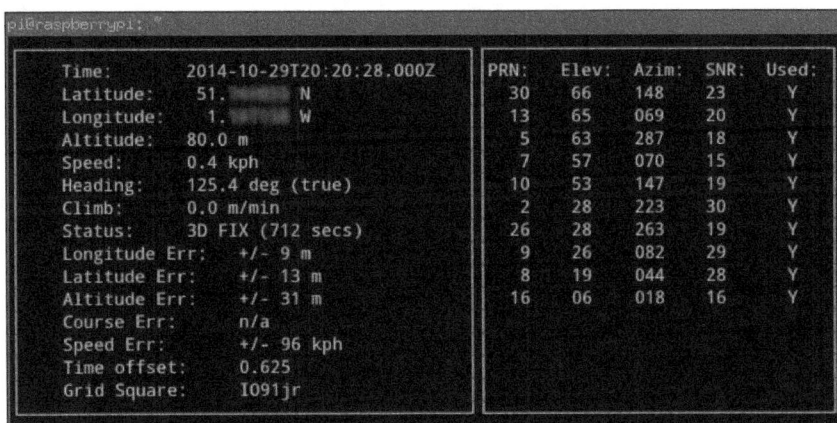

```
pi@raspberrypi: ~

┌──────────────────────────────────────┐┌───────────────────────────────────┐
│ Time:        2014-10-29T20:20:28.000Z ││ PRN:  Elev:  Azim:  SNR:  Used:   │
│ Latitude:      51.      N             ││  30    66    148    23     Y      │
│ Longitude:      1.      W             ││  13    65    069    20     Y      │
│ Altitude:    80.0 m                   ││   5    63    287    18     Y      │
│ Speed:       0.4 kph                  ││   7    57    070    15     Y      │
│ Heading:     125.4 deg (true)         ││  10    53    147    19     Y      │
│ Climb:       0.0 m/min                ││   2    28    223    30     Y      │
│ Status:      3D FIX (712 secs)        ││  26    28    263    19     Y      │
│ Longitude Err:   +/- 9 m              ││   9    26    082    29     Y      │
│ Latitude Err:    +/- 13 m             ││   8    19    044    28     Y      │
│ Altitude Err:    +/- 31 m             ││  16    06    018    16     Y      │
│ Course Err:      n/a                  ││                                   │
│ Speed Err:       +/- 96 kph           ││                                   │
│ Time offset:     0.625                ││                                   │
│ Grid Square:     IO91jr               ││                                   │
└──────────────────────────────────────┘└───────────────────────────────────┘
```

If the status indication reads **NO FIX**, then you may need to move the GPS module into an area with a clear view of the sky for testing. If cgps times out and exits, then gpsd has failed to communicate with your GPS module. Go back and double-check the configuration and wiring.

Setting up the capture software

Now, we need to get the capture software installed on the Pi.

1. First, copy the `recorder` folder onto the Pi using FileZilla and SFTP.

2. We need to install some packages and Python libraries that are used by the capture application. To do this, first install the Python setup tools that I have used to package the capture application:

```
sudo apt-get install python-setuptools git
```

3. Next, run the following commands to download and install the `pexif` library, which is used to save the GPS position from which each image was taken into the image EXIF data:

```
git clone https://github.com/bennoleslie/pexif.git pexif
cd pexif
sudo python setup.py install
```

4. Once this is done, SSH into the Pi can change directory to the `recorder` folder and run the following command:

```
sudo python setup.py install
```

5. Now that the application is installed, we can take a look at the list of commands it accepts using:

```
gpstimelapse -h
```

This shows the list of commands, as shown in the following screenshot:

```
pi@raspberrypi ~ $ gpstimelapse -h
usage: gpstimelapse [-h] [-v] [--gps GPS] [-f FOLDER] [-n FILENAME]
                    [-d DISTANCE] [-i INTERVAL] [--width WIDTH]
                    [--height HEIGHT] [--log-file LOG_FILE]
                    [--log-level LOG_LEVEL]

GPS enabled timelapse recorder

optional arguments:
  -h, --help            show this help message and exit
  -v, --verbose         Increases console verbosity
  --gps GPS             Specifies address to connect to cgps daemon (default
                        localhost::2947)
  -f FOLDER, --folder FOLDER
                        Specifies folder to save timelapse recordings in
  -n FILENAME, --filename FILENAME
                        Filename pattern for image files
  -d DISTANCE, --distance DISTANCE
                        Distance in meters to have moved between captures
  -i INTERVAL, --interval INTERVAL
                        Time in seconds between captures
  --width WIDTH         Height of captured images
  --height HEIGHT       Width of captured images
  --log-file LOG_FILE   File to save log to
  --log-level LOG_LEVEL
                        Logging level [DEBUG,INFO,WARNING,ERROR,CRITICAL]
pi@raspberrypi ~ $
```

A few of the options here can be ignored; `--log-file`, `--log-level`, and `--verbose` were mainly added for debugging while I was writing the application. The `--gps` option will not need to be set, as it defaults to connect to the local `gpsd` instance, which if the application is running on the Pi, will always be correct.

The `--width` and `--height` options are simply used to set the resolution of the captured image. Without them, the capture software will default to capture 1248 x 1024 images.

The `--interval` option is used to specify how long, in seconds, to wait before it captures another time-lapse frame. It is recommended that you set this value at least 10 seconds in order to avoid filling the SD card too quickly (especially if the time lapse will run over a long period of time) and to ensure that any video created with the frames is of a reasonably length (that is, not too long).

The `--distance` option allows you to specify a minimum distance, in kilometers, that must be travelled since the last image was captured and before another image is captured. This can be useful to record a time lapse where, whatever holds the Pi, may stop in the same position for periods of time (for example, if the camera is in a car dashboard, this would prevent it from capturing several identical frames if the car is waiting in traffic).

This option can also be used to capture a set of images based alone on the distance travelled, disregarding the amount of time that has passed. This can be done by setting the `--interval` option to 1 (a value of 1 is used as data is only taken from the GPS module every second, so checking the distance travelled faster than this would be a waste of time).

The folder structure is used to store the frames. While being slightly complex at first sight, this is a good method that allows you to take multiple captures without ever having to SSH into the Pi.

Using the `--folder` option, you can set the folder under which all captures are saved. In this folder, the application looks for folders with a numerical name and creates a new folder that is one higher than the highest number it finds. This is where it will save the images for the current capture.

The filename for each image is given by the `--filename` option. This option specifies the filename of each image that will be captured. It must contain `%d`, which is used to indicate the frame number (for example, `image_%d.jpg`).

For example, if I pass `--folder captures --filename image_%d.jpg` to the program, the first frame will be saved as `./captures/0/image_0/jpg`, and the second as `./captures/0/image_1.jpg`.

Here are some examples of how the application can be used:

- `gpstimelapse --folder captures --filename i_%d.jpg --interval 30`: This will capture a frame in every 30 seconds

- `gpstimelapse --folder captures --filename i_%d.jpg --interval 30 --distance 0.05`: This will capture a frame in every 30 seconds, provided that 50 meters have been travelled

- `gpstimelapse --folder captures --filename i_%d.jpg --interval 1 --distance 0.05`: This will capture a frame in every 50 meters that have been travelled

Now that you are able to run the time-lapse recorder application, you are ready to configure it to start as soon as the Pi boots. Removing the need for an active network connection and the ability to interface with the Pi to start the capture.

1. To do this, we will add a command to the `/etc/rc.local` file. This can be edited using the following command:

   `sudo nano /etc/rc.local`

2. The line you will add will depend on how exactly you want the recorder to behave. In this case, I have set it to record an image at the default resolution every minute. As before, ensure that the command is placed just before the line containing `exit 0`:

```
  GNU nano 2.2.6                                            File: /etc/rc

#!/bin/sh -e
#
# rc.local
#
# This script is executed at the end of each multiuser runlevel.
# Make sure that the script will "exit 0" on success or any other
# value on error.
#
# In order to enable or disable this script just change the execution
# bits.
#
# By default this script does nothing.

# Print the IP address
_IP=$(hostname -I) || true
if [ "$_IP" ]; then
   printf "My IP address is %s\n" "$_IP"
fi

/usr/local/bin/gpstimelapse -i 60 -f /home/pi/captures -n frame_%d.jpg

exit 0
```

Now, you can reboot the Pi and test out the recorder. A good indication that the capture is working is the red LED on the camera board that lights up constantly. This shows that the camera preview is open, which should always be the case with this application.

Also note that, the capture will not begin until the GPS module has a fix. On the Adafruit module, this is indicated by a quick blink every 15 seconds on the fix LED (no fix is indicated by a steady blink once per second).

One issue you may have with this project is the amount of power required to power the camera and GPS module on top of the Pi. To power this while on the move, I recommend that you use one of the USB power banks that have a 2 A output (such power banks are readily available on Amazon).

Using the captures

Now that we have a set of recorded time-lapse frames, where each has a GPS position attached, there are a number of things that can be done with this data. Here, we will have a quick look at a couple of instances for which we can use the captured frames.

Creating a time-lapse video

The first and probably the most obvious thing that can be done with the images is you can create a time-lapse video in which, each time-lapse image is shown as a single frame of the video, and the length (or speed) of the video is controlled by changing the number of frames per second.

One of the simplest ways to do this is by using either the ffmpeg or avconv utility (depending on your version of Linux; the parameters to each are identical in our case). This utility is available on most Linux distributions, including Raspbian. There are also precompiled executables available for Mac and Windows. However, here I will only discuss using it on Linux, but rest assured, any instructions given here will also work on the Pi itself.

To create a time lapse, form a set of images. You can use the following command:

```
avconv -framerate FPS -i FILENAME -c:v libx264 -r 30 -pix_fmt yuv420p
OUTPUT
```

Here, FPS is the number of the time-lapse frames you want to display every second, FILENAME is the filename format with %d that marks the frame number, and OUTPUT is the output's filename. This will give output similar to the following:

```
dan@dan-desktop ~/8> avconv -framerate 10 -i frame_%d.jpg -c:v libx264 -r 30 -pix_fmt yuv420p out.mp4
avconv version 9.16-6:9.16-0ubuntu0.14.04.1, Copyright (c) 2000-2014 the Libav developers
  built on Aug 10 2014 18:16:02 with gcc 4.8 (Ubuntu 4.8.2-19ubuntu1)
Input #0, image2, from 'frame_%d.jpg':
  Duration: 00:00:19.50, start: 0.000000, bitrate: N/A
    Stream #0.0: Video: mjpeg, yuvj420p, 1248x1024, 10 fps, 10 tbr, 10 tbn
[libx264 @ 0x1418920] using cpu capabilities: MMX2 SSE2Fast SSSE3 SSE4.2 AVX
[libx264 @ 0x1418920] profile High, level 3.2
[libx264 @ 0x1418920] 264 - core 142 r2389 956c8d8 - H.264/MPEG-4 AVC codec - Copyleft 2003-2014 - http://www.v
ideolan.org/x264.html - options: cabac=1 ref=3 deblock=1:0:0 analyse=0x3:0x113 me=hex subme=7 psy=1 psy_rd=1.00
:0.00 mixed_ref=1 me_range=16 chroma_me=1 trellis=1 8x8dct=1 cqm=0 deadzone=21,11 fast_pskip=1 chroma_qp_offset
=-2 threads=6 lookahead_threads=1 sliced_threads=0 nr=0 decimate=1 interlaced=0 bluray_compat=0 constrained_int
ra=0 bframes=3 b_pyramid=2 b_adapt=1 b_bias=0 direct=1 weightb=1 open_gop=0 weightp=2 keyint=250 keyint_min=25
scenecut=40 intra_refresh=0 rc_lookahead=40 rc=crf mbtree=1 crf=23.0 qcomp=0.60 qpmin=0 qpmax=69 qpstep=4 ip_ra
tio=1.25 aq=1:1.00
Output #0, mp4, to 'out.mp4':
  Metadata:
    encoder         : Lavf54.20.4
    Stream #0.0: Video: libx264, yuv420p, 1248x1024, q=-1--1, 30 tbn, 30 tbc
Stream mapping:
  Stream #0:0 -> #0:0 (mjpeg -> libx264)
Press ctrl-c to stop encoding
frame=  583 fps= 36 q=32766.0 Lsize=    3151kB time=19.37 bitrate=1332.7kbits/s
video:2936kB audio:0kB global headers:0kB muxing overhead 7.298904%
[libx264 @ 0x1418920] frame I:4     Avg QP:19.83  size: 57603
[libx264 @ 0x1418920] frame P:304   Avg QP:22.15  size:  9391
[libx264 @ 0x1418920] frame B:275   Avg QP:23.90  size:   475
[libx264 @ 0x1418920] consecutive B-frames: 33.3% 11.3%  0.5% 54.9%
[libx264 @ 0x1418920] mb I  I16..4:  8.7% 78.5% 12.8%
[libx264 @ 0x1418920] mb P  I16..4:  0.5%  1.6%  0.1%  P16..4: 46.7%  4.4%  4.8%  0.0%  0.0%    skip:41.9%
[libx264 @ 0x1418920] mb B  I16..4:  0.0%  0.0%  0.0%  B16..8:  9.4%  0.0%  0.0%  direct: 0.0%  skip:90.5%  L0:
46.1% L1:53.5% BI: 0.4%
[libx264 @ 0x1418920] 8x8 transform intra:74.1% inter:81.3%
[libx264 @ 0x1418920] coded y,uvDC,uvAC intra: 53.9% 48.1% 14.9% inter: 10.1% 24.0% 0.3%
[libx264 @ 0x1418920] i16 v,h,dc,p: 20% 48%  7% 25%
[libx264 @ 0x1418920] i8 v,h,dc,ddl,ddr,vr,hd,vl,hu: 12% 13% 31%  7%  7% 11%  6%  5%  9%
[libx264 @ 0x1418920] i4 v,h,dc,ddl,ddr,vr,hd,vl,hu: 19% 16% 19% 10%  9% 11%  6%  5%  7%
[libx264 @ 0x1418920] i8c dc,h,v,p: 61% 22% 13%  4%
[libx264 @ 0x1418920] Weighted P-Frames: Y:33.2% UV:32.9%
[libx264 @ 0x1418920] ref P L0: 62.6%  8.1% 11.9% 10.5%  6.9%
[libx264 @ 0x1418920] ref B L0: 96.1%  2.1%  1.8%
[libx264 @ 0x1418920] ref B L1: 98.3%  1.7%
[libx264 @ 0x1418920] kb/s:1323.95
dan@dan-desktop ~/8>
```

Exporting GPS data as CSV

We can also extract GPS data from each of the captured time-lapse images and save it as a **comma-separated value** (CSV) file. This will allow us to import the data into third-party applications, such as Google Maps and Google Earth.

To do this, we can use the frames_to_gps_path.py Python script included in the code for this chapter. This takes the file format for the time-lapse frames and a name for the output file.

For example, to create a CSV file called `gps_data.csv` for images in the `frame_%d.jpg` format, you can use the following command:

```
python frames_to_gps_points.py -f frame_%d.jpg -o gps_points.csv
```

```
dan@dan-HP-G62 ~/c/8> python ~/RaspberryPi-Blueprints/04-GPSTimelapseRecorder/frames_to_gps_path.py -f frame_%d.jpg -o gps_data.csv
Getting points from images with format: frame_%d.jpg
       (first index = 0, last index = 9223372036854775807)
Reducing point count (max 500)
Saving CSV file: gps_data.csv
dan@dan-HP-G62 ~/c/8>
```

The output is a CSV file in the following format:

```
[frame number],[latitude],[longitude],[image filename]
```

The script also has the option to restrict the maximum number of output points. Passing the `--max-points N` parameter will ensure that no more than `N` points are in the CSV file. This can be useful for importing data into applications that limit the number of points that can be imported.

Summary

In this chapter, we had a look at how to use the serial interface on the GPIO port in order to interface with some external hardware. The knowledge of how to do this will allow you to interface the Pi with a much wider range of hardware in future projects.

We also took a look at the camera board and how it can be used from within Python. This camera is a very versatile device and has a very wide range of uses in portable projects and ubiquitous computing.

You are encouraged to take a deeper look at the source code for the time-lapse recorder application. This will get you on your way to understand the structure of moderately complex Python programs and the way they can be packaged and distributed.

In the following chapter, we will take a more intricate look at how to interface with external hardware as we build a home theater PC.

Home Theater PC 5

In this chapter, we will create a low-power home theater PC capable of playing a variety of local media files from a USB memory stick or hard drive as well as the content stored on your local network and cloud services, such as YouTube.

To do this, we will use the OpenELEC (`http://openelec.tv`) operating system, which is an operating system designed specifically for home theater PCs running on the Pi.

We will also create a custom enclosure for the media PC that will house a 20 column by 4 row (20 x 4) LCD, which can be used by XBMC to display information of the currently playing media or information related to the cursor position in the onscreen menu. We will also include a set of buttons that can be used to control XBMC without a USB keyboard or any other remote; both these and the LCD will be interfaced directly to the GPIO port on the Pi.

What you will need

This is the list of parts and materials you will need for this project. They can be purchased at any electronic components stores and online retailers.

- The Raspberry Pi
- A USB keyboard (for setup only)
- A 600 x 600 mm sheet of a 3 mm MDF
- A 20 x 4 LCD (`www.amazon.co.uk/2004-Characters-Display-Module-Blacklight/dp/B009GXWFSM`)
- 0.1 inch female-to-female jumper wires
- A small section of stripboard/prototyping board (`www.maplin.co.uk/p/veroboard-copper-stripboard-100x160mm-a62rl`)

- Two 10 K multiple turn potentiometers (`http://cpc.farnell.com/1/1/24068-trimmer-24-turn-10k-m64z103kb40-vishay-spectrol.html`)

- A row of 0.1 inch pin headers (`http://cpc.farnell.com/starconn-connectors/phw-40-rv/0-1-pm-header-single-row-40-pms/dp/CN00870`)

- A row of 0.1 inch right-angled pin headers (`http://cpc.farnell.com/starconn-connectors/phw-40-rd/0-1-pin-header-right-angle-40-pms/dp/CN00871`)

- A DC barrel jack (`http://cpc.farnell.com/1/1/1498-2-1mm-dc-socket-psg01769-pro-signal.html`)

- Six push-to-make (PTM) buttons (`www.rapidonline.com/electronic-components/miniature-red-push-to-make-switch-78-0100`)

In this project, we will also use a new manufacturing technique: laser cutting. While I don't expect a laser cutter to be a tool that many people actually own, access to it is more readily available than you think. It is worth checking whether there is a hackspace in your local area. If so, they may either have a machine that you would be able to use (or at least have someone who can help you machine your design) or may be able to point you in the right direction for where you can have it done locally. Alternatively, there are many services that allow you to upload a design online and pay to have it cut from the material of your choice.

> Hackspaces are community-organized (and usually community funded) workspaces that provide a variety of tools and equipments that may not usually be available to you. They also provide a good place where you can collaborate on projects and seek advice from the experts for a problem you are facing in your own projects.

Setting up OpenELEC

OpenELEC is a very minimal operating system that is preconfigured with the XBMC media center software (`http://kodi.tv`) and a range of utilities specifically set up for home media sharing, such as the Samba file server.

First, head to `http://openelec.tv/get-openelec` and (under **RaspberryPi Builds**) download the latest stable SD image (the title will be something like what is indicated in the following screenshot). Once you have the file downloaded, decompress it and write it to your SD card.

Under Windows, you need to use software such as 7-Zip (www.7-zip.org) to decompress this type of file.

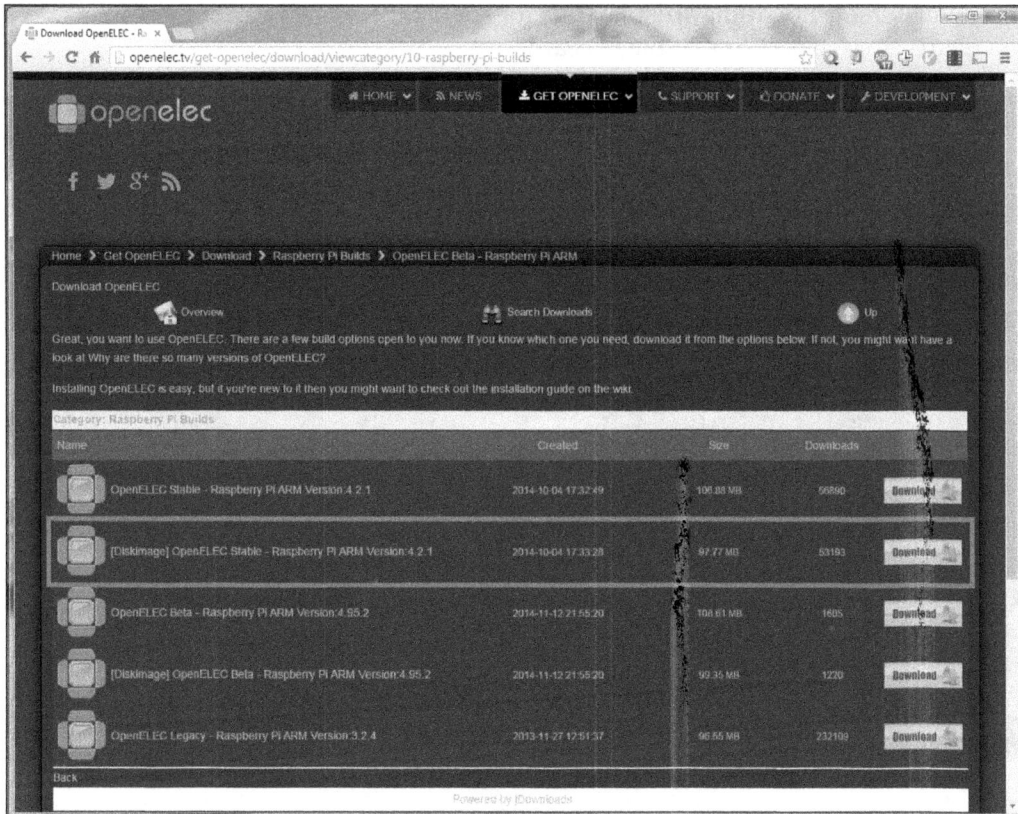

On Linux and Mac, the following command can be used, where FILENAME is the name of the file that you downloaded from the OpenELEC website:

```
gzip -d FILENAME.gz
```

Once you have the SD image written to the card, it is time to boot the Pi for the first time. Here, you need the Pi connected to a TV or monitor (here, I will be using HDMI) and a USB keyboard connected to it. I will also connect a USB Wi-Fi adapter, but you can easily just use an Ethernet connection instead of Wi-Fi.

For now, we can power the Pi from a USB connection, as we are yet to connect any additional peripherals to it. However, later on, we need to power the Pi using a more substantial 5 V power supply to provide enough power for the Pi and the LCD.

The first boot and initial setup

When you first boot OpenELEC, it will show a screen something similar to the following screenshot. It may display this for some time, as it is currently resizing the media storage partition of the SD card.

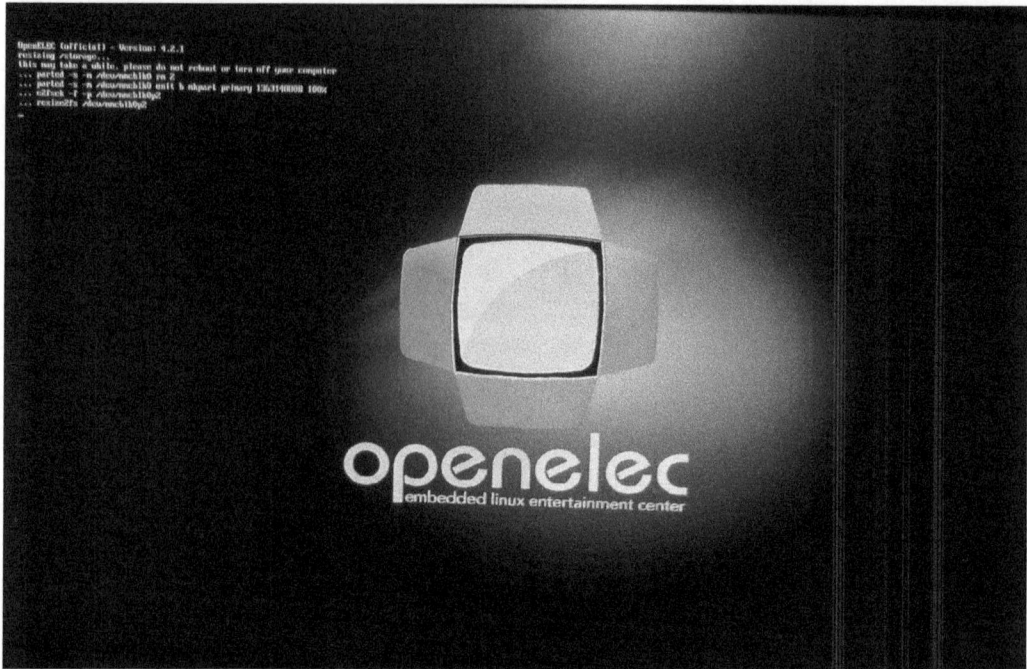

When OpenELEC boots, it will boot straight into XBMC. Since this is the first time it has been booted, you will also be greeted with the OpenELEC first-time setup wizard. This often takes a while to be displayed after XBMC has started.

To navigate the menus, simply use the arrow keys to move the cursor and *Enter* to select a menu option; perform the following steps:

1. First, you are asked by OpenELEC to select the appropriate regional settings. Select the button that defaults to **English** to change the settings and select **Next** to continue.

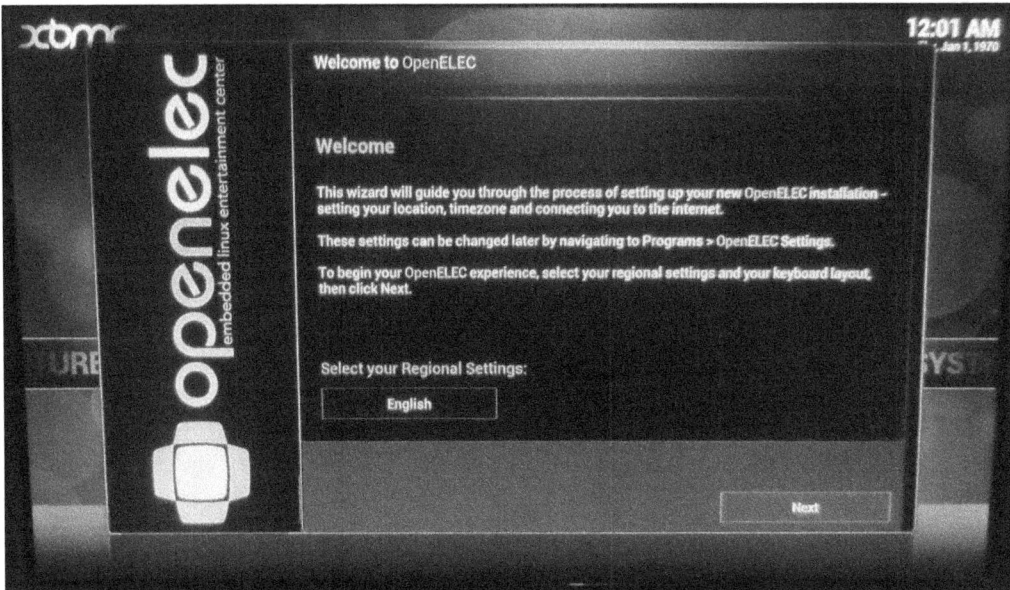

2. Next, you are asked to enter a new hostname for the media center. It is not required that you change it. However, if you intend to have multiple media centers, then it would be essential as no two devices should share a hostname. This will make identification of the Pi on the network easier.

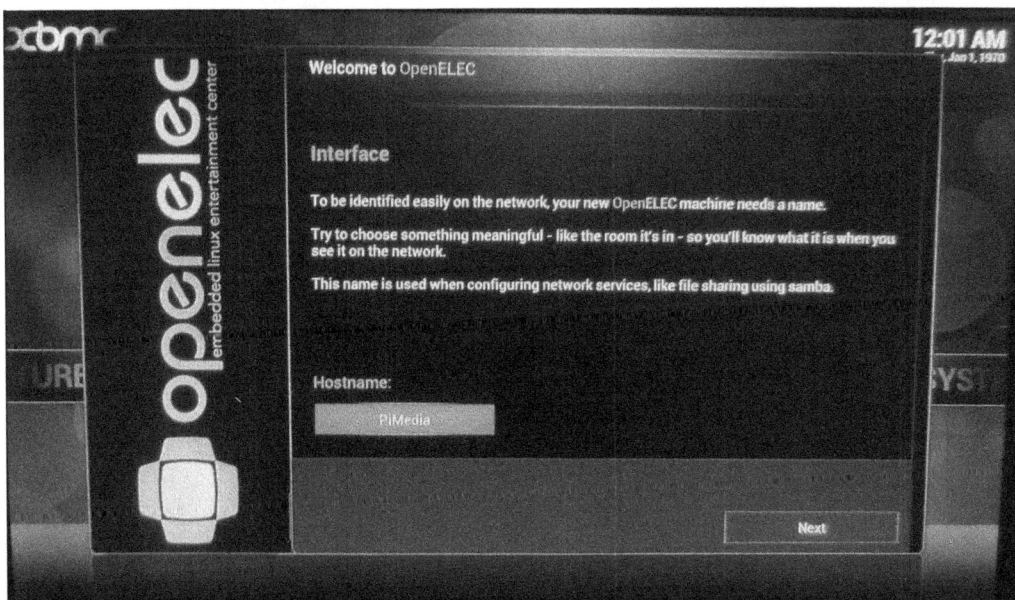

3. The next option asks you to configure network interfaces. As we are using Wi-Fi, we cannot do anything here yet, as wireless adapters are disabled by default and wired connections do not require configuration. Just select **Next** to continue.

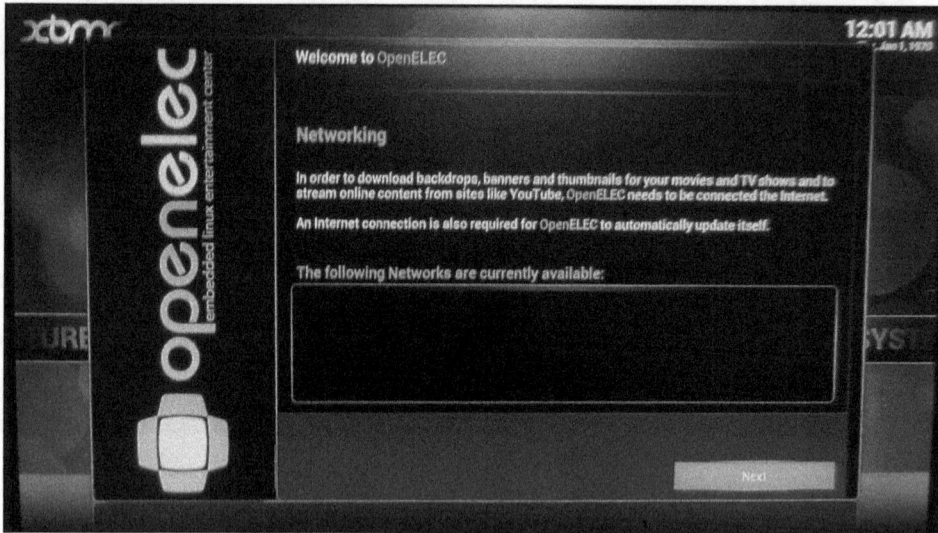

4. Next, you will be asked what servers you want to enable on the Pi. By default, SSH is disabled and Samba is enabled. I would recommend you to enable both, as you will need SSH to configure the LCD and buttons and Samba to upload media to the Pi.

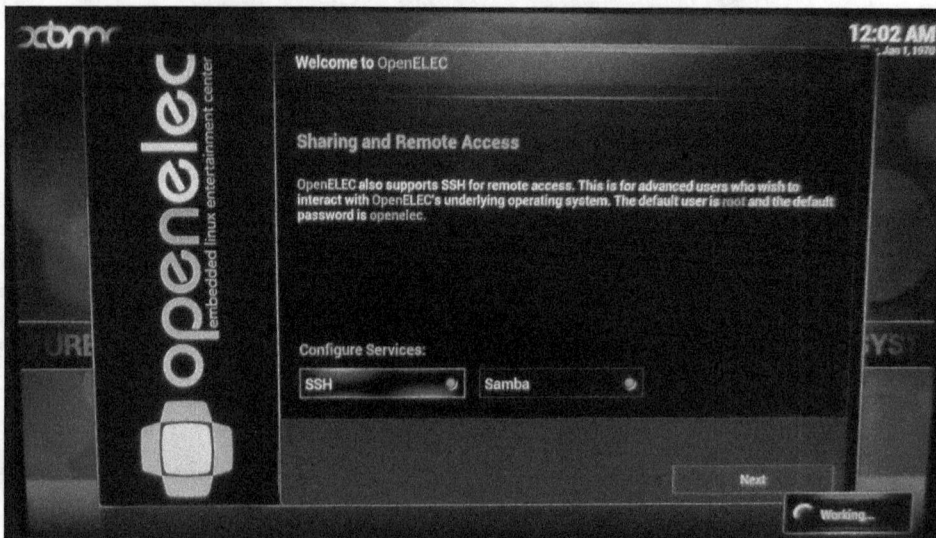

5. After this step, the initial configuration is complete. Select **Next** to return to the XBMC home screen.

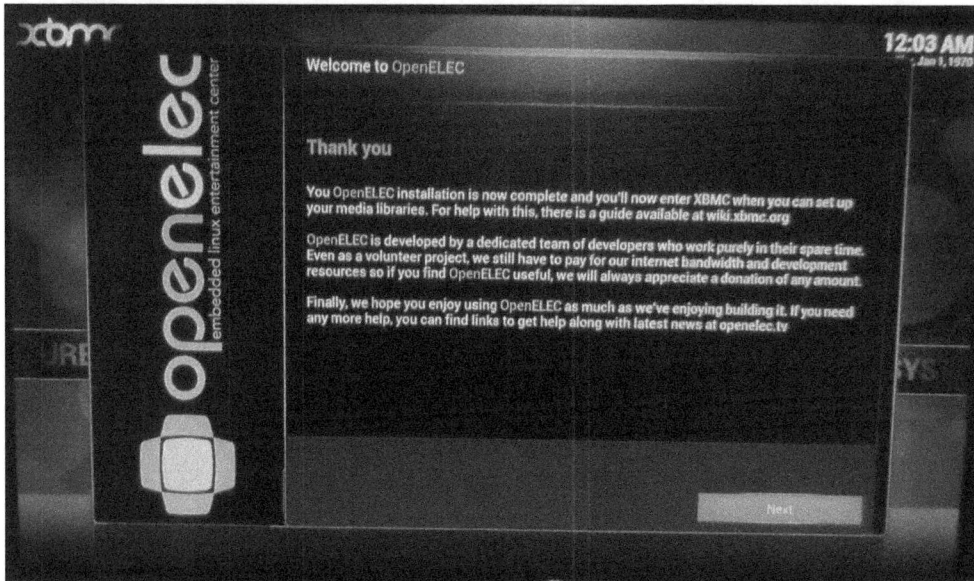

6. For now, there is one additional setting that we need to change. To do this, navigate to the **Settings** option under the **SYSTEM** menu using the arrow keys and the *Enter* key.

7. Next, navigate to the **System** menu and select it using *Enter*.

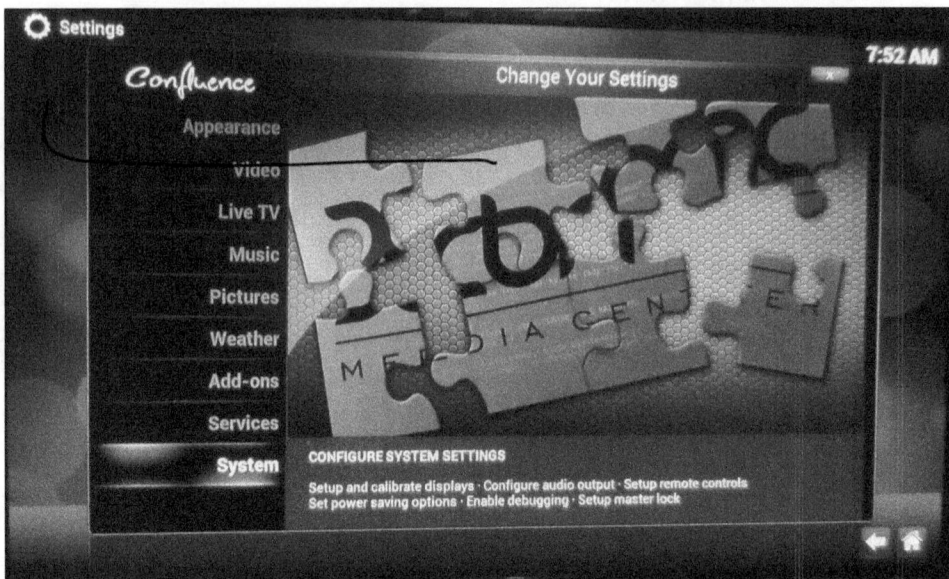

8. Next, navigate to **Input devices** and disable the **Enable mouse and touch screen support** option, as neither of these devices will be used with XBMC the way we will be using them.

9. On this menu, settings are automatically saved when they are changed, so you can now use *Esc* to go back until you return to the main menu.

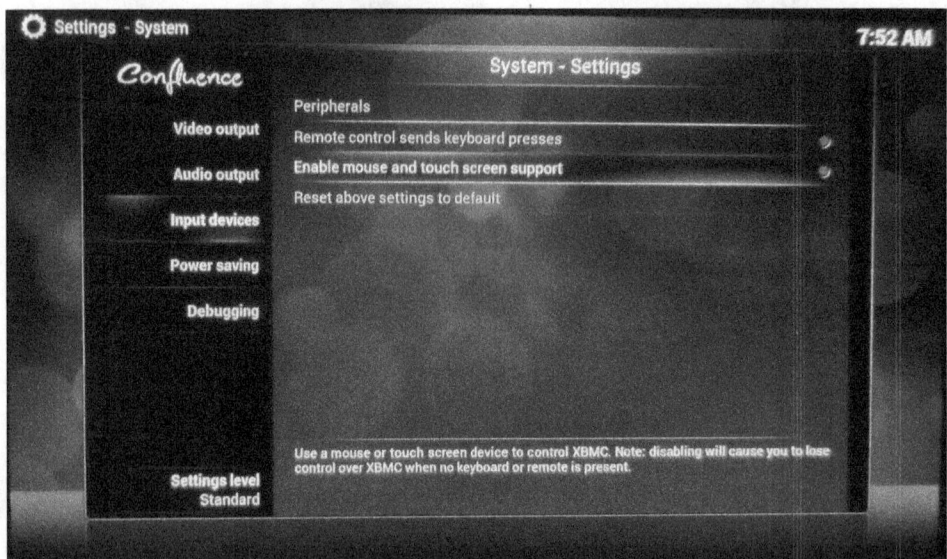

Connecting the Pi to a wireless network

If you plan to use Wi-Fi to connect to your network, then you will need to first enable it in order to join your wireless network. Using Wi-Fi as opposed to Ethernet allows you to install the media PC without having to worry about running an Ethernet cable to it. However, your network performance will be lower, so it is only recommended if it is essential. To connect to the wireless network, perform the following steps:

1. Select the **OpenELEC** option under the **SYSTEM** menu:

2. From here, navigate to **Network** and select the **Active** option under **Wireless Networks**. This will enable the Wi-Fi adapter and start searching for wireless networks in range.

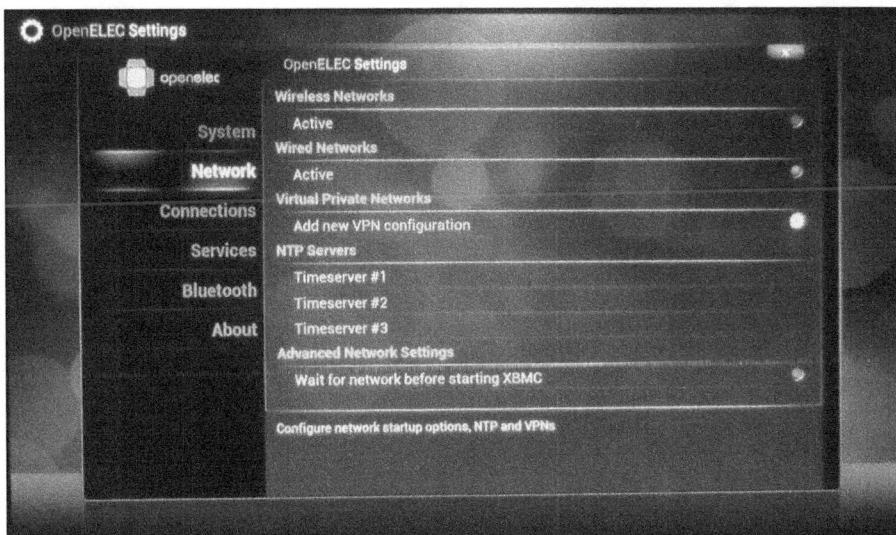

3. To connect to a network, navigate to the **Connections** menu. Here, you should see a list of the Wi-Fi networks that have been found in your range. To connect to one of them, navigate to it, press *Enter*, and select the option **Join**.

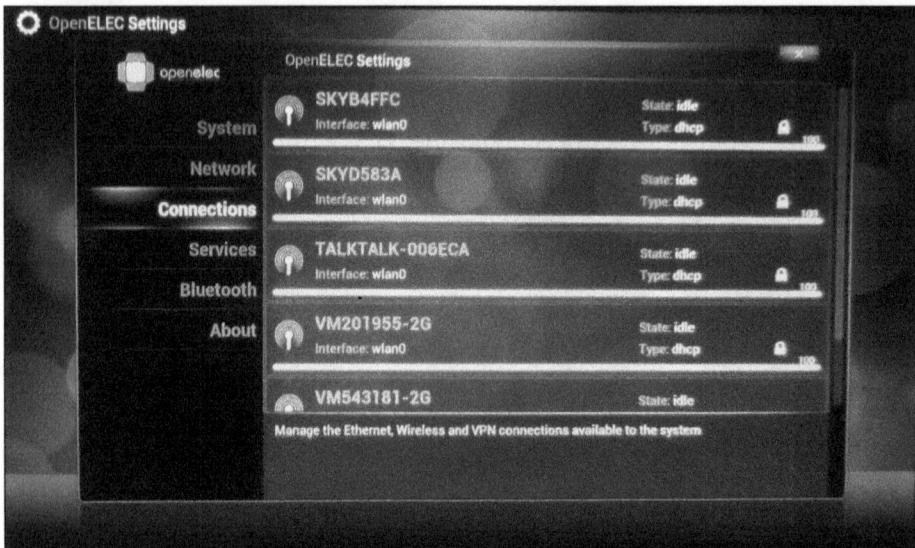

4. You will then be asked for the password for the network. Type it in and press *Enter*. Once done, this will return to the **Connections** menu; you should now see that the network you selected has an IP address listed alongside it. This shows that the connection was successful.

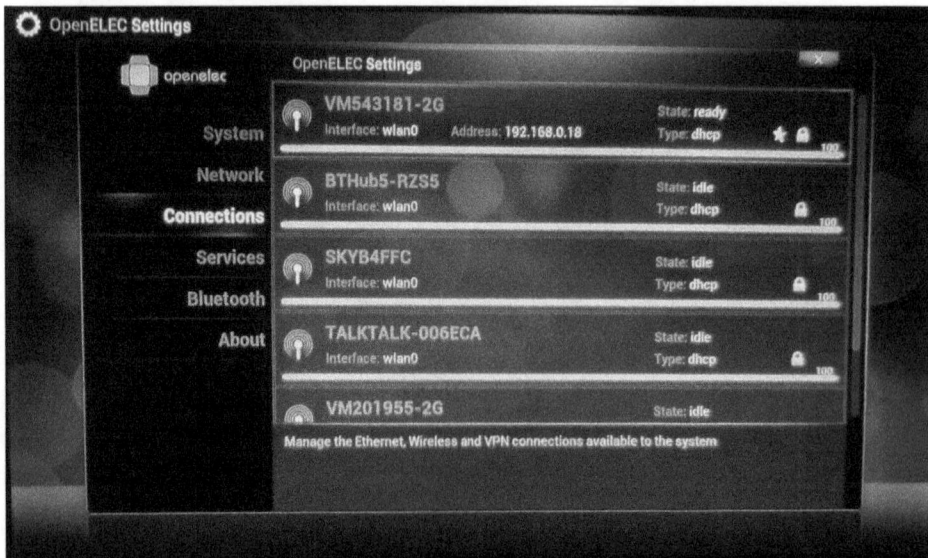

Uploading media files to the Pi

The easiest way to upload media to the Pi is by accessing the Samba file shares that are provided by the Pi.

The shares are split by the type of content that should be stored on them. A few of the most common ones are:

- `Music`: This is used to store music files, for example, `.mp3`
- `Pictures`: This is used to store image files, for example, `.jpeg`, `.png`
- `Videos`: This is used to store video files, for example, `.mkv`, `.mp4`
- `Userdata`: This is where the XBMC configuration files are stored

Windows

On Windows, you can use Windows Explorer to browse all shares on a server at once. To do this, press *WinKey* + *R* to open the run prompt and enter `\\IP\`, where `IP` is the IP address of the Pi, and click on **OK**.

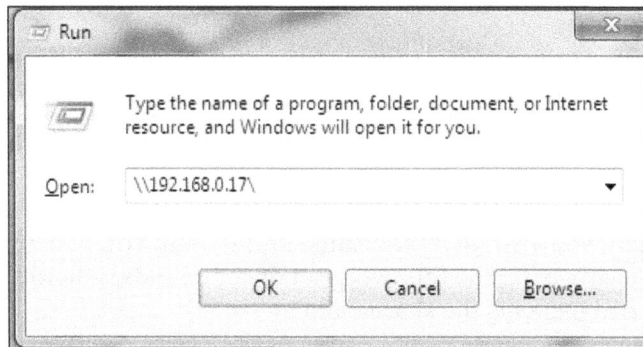

This will open a Windows Explorer window, which will allow you to browse the shares on the Pi and copy files to and from it, as if it were a local folder.

When you've moved the files, simply close the Explorer window.

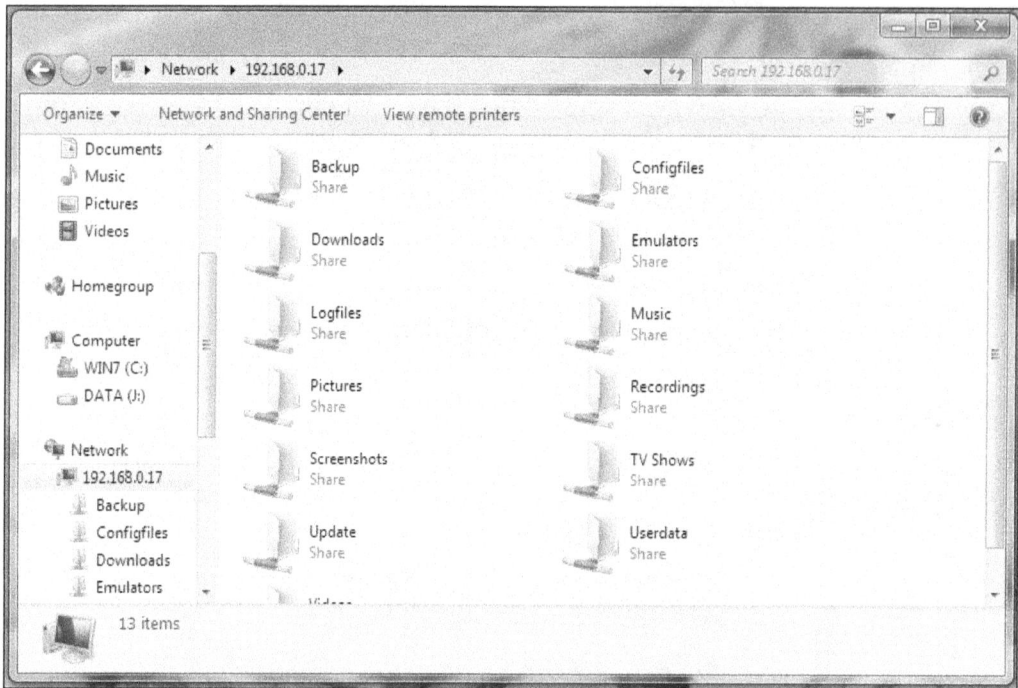

Linux

On Linux, assuming you also know the name of the share you want to add files to, you can mount a share using the following set of commands, where IP is the IP address of the Pi and SHARE is the share name:

1. First, we need to create a directory where the Samba share will be mounted (known as the **mount point**). This only has to be done once.

   ```
   sudo mkdir /media/openelec
   ```

2. Next, use the following command to mount the Samba share to the just-created mount point:

   ```
   sudo mount -t cifs //IP/SHARE /media/openelec
   ```

3. You will be asked for a password, but since OpenELEC does not put a password on Samba shared by default, just press *Enter*.

4. If the command exits without an error, you can go ahead and copy files to `/media/openelec` to upload them to the Pi. If you do get an error, then you may be missing a package needed to mount Samba shares. This can be fixed using the following command, which is used to install any missing packages:

   ```
   sudo apt-get install samba4 cifs-utils
   ```

5. When you've moved the files, you should unmount the Samba share using the following command:

   ```
   sudo umount /media/openelec
   ```

Shutting down the Pi

To shut down the Pi, you can use the power menu in XBMC, which can be found in the bottom-left corner of the home screen in the form of a power symbol.

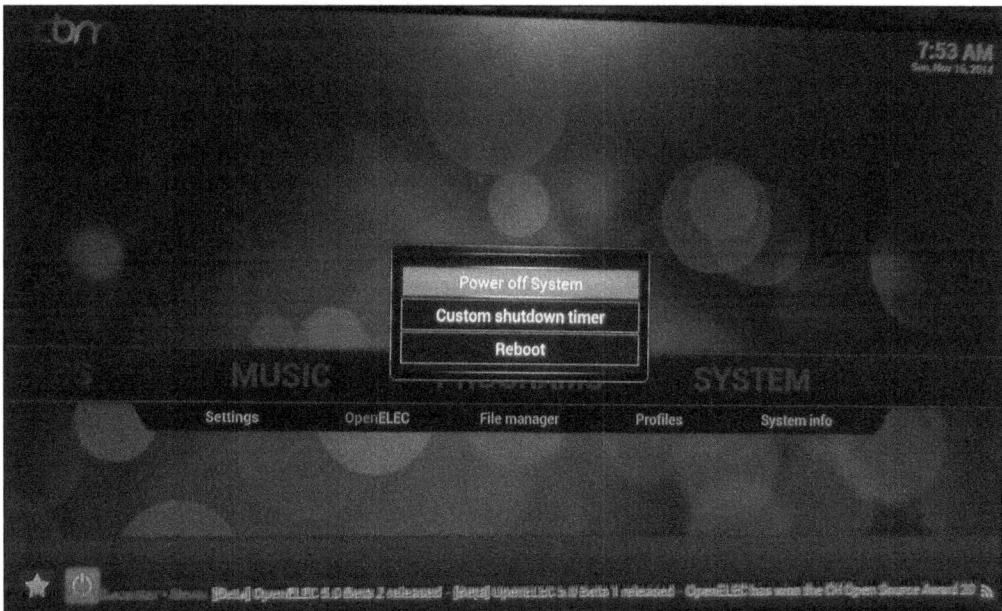

This will give you the option to shut down and reboot the Pi as well as the ability to set a shutdown timer, which will shut down the Pi after a given amount of time has elapsed.

Setting up the LCD

Now that we have configured OpenELEC, we can start adding our own hardware to the media center, starting with the LCD:

1. First, we will start by making a small board that will be used to mount two potentiometers (or variable resistors), which will allow the adjustment of the backlight brightness and contrast for the LCD. This board will also have a few 0.1 inch pin headers that will be used to connect the switches and various power supplies.

   ° To construct this board, first take a piece of strip board (also known as **prototyping board**) and cut a 1" x 2" section using a pair of side cutters. Then, cut a strip of 0.1" of a right-angled pin header to the length indicated in the following diagram. Arrange them on the component-side of the strip board (that is, the side with no copper strips) and solder them to the board.

   Take extra care here not to bridge the gap between the copper strips, and ensure that the copper surface is clean before you start soldering. The surface can be cleaned by rubbing it with some high-grit sandpaper, or preferably, wet and dry paper. In the following figure, note that the yellow strips represent the copper strips on the board. This is viewed from the component side of the board:

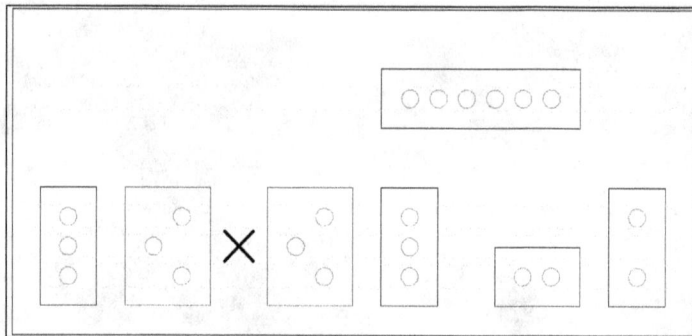

○ Once the pin headers are in place, note that there is a cross on the diagram. This mark is used to indicate that the copper strip must be cut in this position. The easiest way to do this is to take a 4 mm drill bit and rotate it by hand in the hole already drilled in the solder side until the copper connection is removed by the drill bit. If need be, this can be verified by checking the resistance across either side of the cut using a multimeter.

2. Next, insert the two potentiometers, as shown in the preceding diagram, and solder them to the board. When you're done, you will need to trim the excess material from the pins with the help of adjacent pins or tracks to prevent this from shorting.

3. We can connect the LCD to the Pi using several 0.1 inch female-to-female jumper wires by following the wiring information shown in the following image. Note that since the LCD and backlight may draw a significant amount of power, an external 5 V supply is needed here that is connected to the +5 V and GND connections to the far right of the board we have just soldered.

This connector should be soldered, as shown in the preceding photograph, where the red wire is +5 V and the white wire is ground. If in doubt about the pinout of the connector, you can verify it by testing the pairs of the pins using a multimeter, when there is a power adapter connected.

The following two diagrams provide details for the wiring of the home theater PC. Note that all connections should be made directly to the other pin with the same label, with the exception of those that are used for buttons (that is, all starting with **B_**), in which the push-to-make button should be wired in series with this connection.

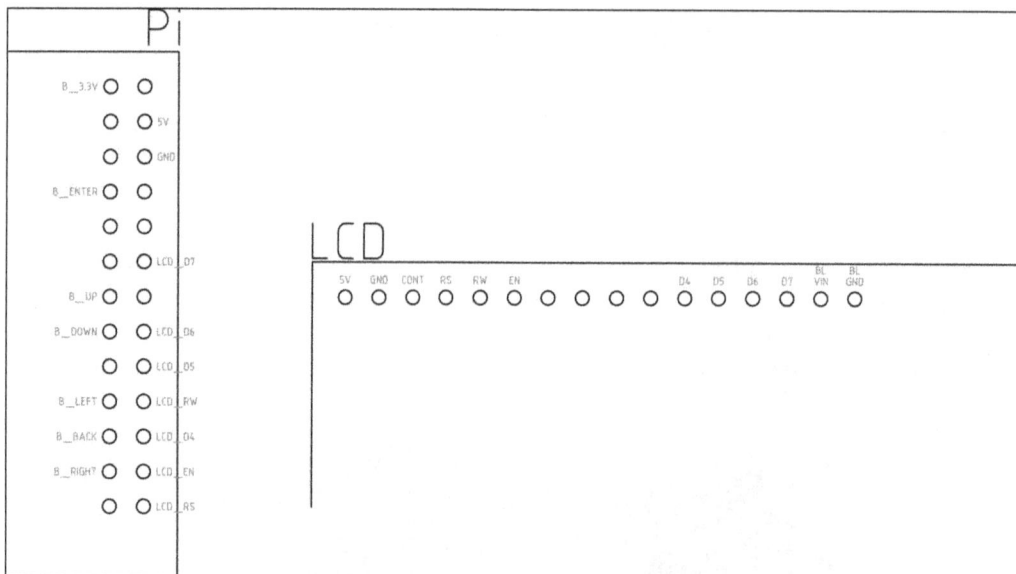

Pi

B_3.3V

5V

GND

B_ENTER

LCD_D7

B_UP

B_DOWN LCD_D6

LCD_D5

B_LEFT LCD_RW

B_BACK LCD_D4

B_RIGHT LCD_EN

LCD_RS

LCD

5V GND CONT RS RW EN   D4 D5 D6 D7 BL VIN BL GND

The following diagram details the connections to the power distribution board. Note that the +5 V and GND pins on the far right of the board are to be connected to the input power from the power supply.

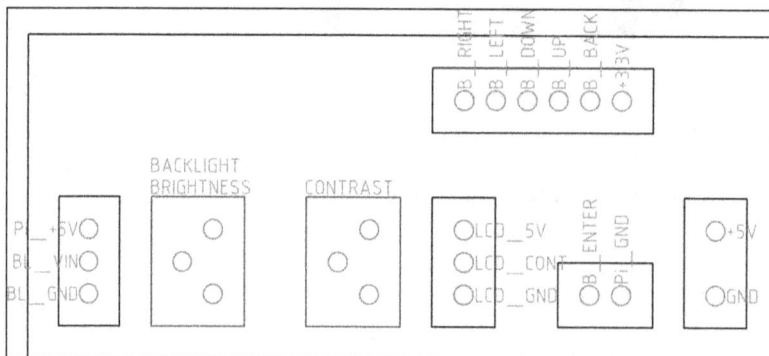

OB_RIGHT OB_LEFT OB_DOWN OB_UP OB_BACK O+3.3V

BACKLIGHT BRIGHTNESS   CONTRAST

P_+5V   OLCD_5V   OB_ENTER   O+5V
BL_VIN   OLCD_CONT   OPi_GND
BL_GND   OLCD_GND   OGND

Once this is complete, it is time to configure the software that will communicate with the LCD and allow XBMC to update the display. The software that will actually interface with the LCD is called **LCDproc**. This is preinstalled on OpenELEC, so it only requires configuration.

All that is required now is to move the `LCDd.conf` file included with this project to the `/storage/.config` directory on the SD card. This can be easily done over SFTP, as we have done in the previous projects.

After opening the file, you will see the following important lines:

- Line 53 tells LCDproc that we want to use the HD44780 driver for the display we are connecting to.

- Lines 76-82 are used to specify the test that is to be shown on the LCD as the operating system boots up and shuts down.

- Line 539 tells the HD44780 driver that our display is connected to the GPIO port on the Pi. This configuration option is a device-specific option that was added due to its popularity that it uses the Pi for this purpose.

- Line 581 tells the HD44780 driver how big our display is in number of columns by number of rows.

> HD44780 is a very common LCD controller chip made by Hitachi. You will find either this specific chip or one that is command identical to it is pretty much every character LCD module. The 16-pin interface is usually a good sign as it can be used with drivers that support HD44780.

Once the `LCDd.conf` file has been moved:

1. Reboot the Pi using the following command. You should be able to see the hello message displayed shortly after the Pi starts to boot:

   ```
   reboot
   ```

   You may need to adjust the backlight and contrast controls to get the clearest text on the display. This can be done using a small, flat screwdriver with the small brass screws on the two potentiometers. As they are multiple turn potentiometers, it may take a while before you see a noticeable difference in the display.

   If the hello message is not displayed, then you may have made a mistake when wiring the LCD. Double-check the wiring and reboot again.

2. Next, we need to install the LCDproc add-on to XBMC in order to enable it to communicate with LCDproc and show information on the display. This is done from the **Add-ons** menu, which can be found under the main settings menu of XBMC:

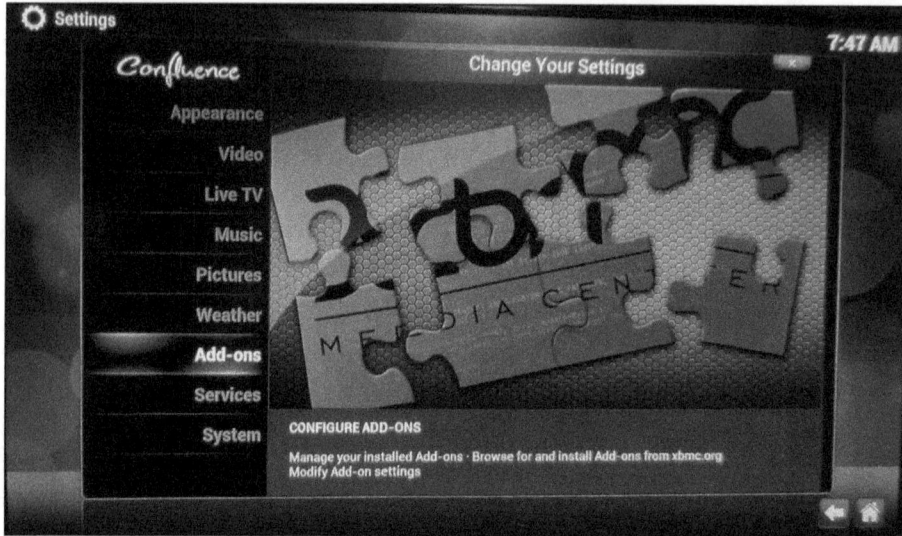

3. From here, select **Search**, enter `lcd`, and press *Enter*.

This search should find the **XBMC LCDproc** add-on. If no results were found, try rebooting the Pi, as I found problems with the list of add-ons not being updated if the network connection was just set up.

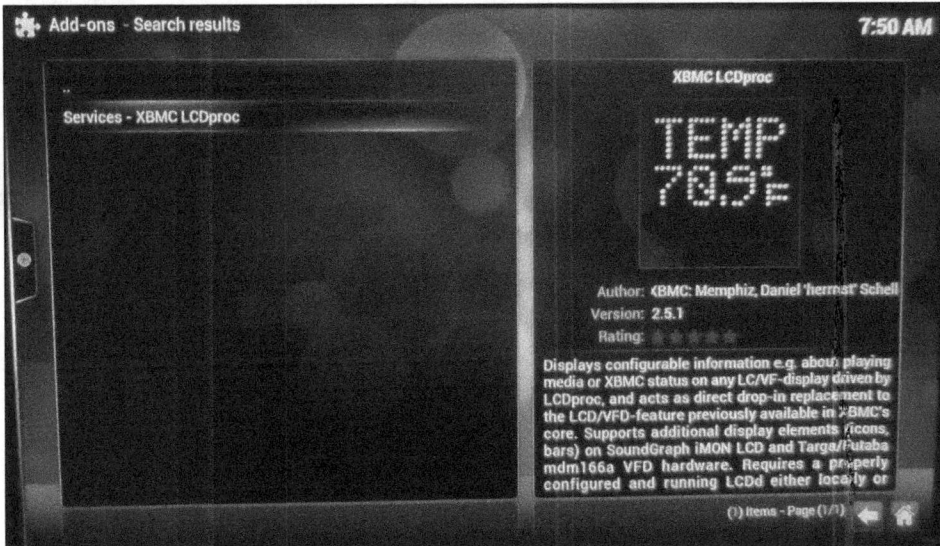

4. Select the LCDproc add-on using *Enter* and select the **Install** option. This will now download and install the add-on. When the process is complete, you will see a notification in the bottom right of the screen, and the entry in the search results will have an **Enabled** indicator next to it.

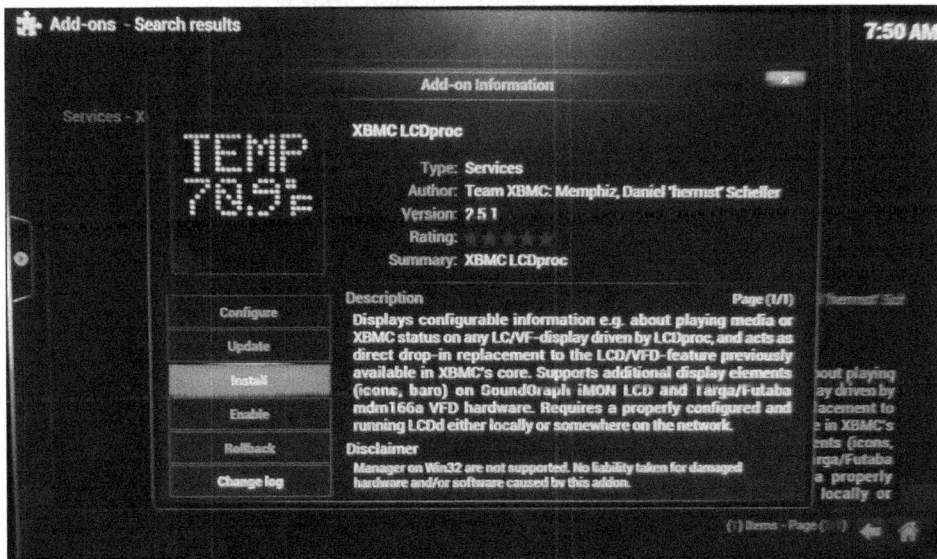

5. When this is done, select the add-on from the search results again, and select the **Configure** option.

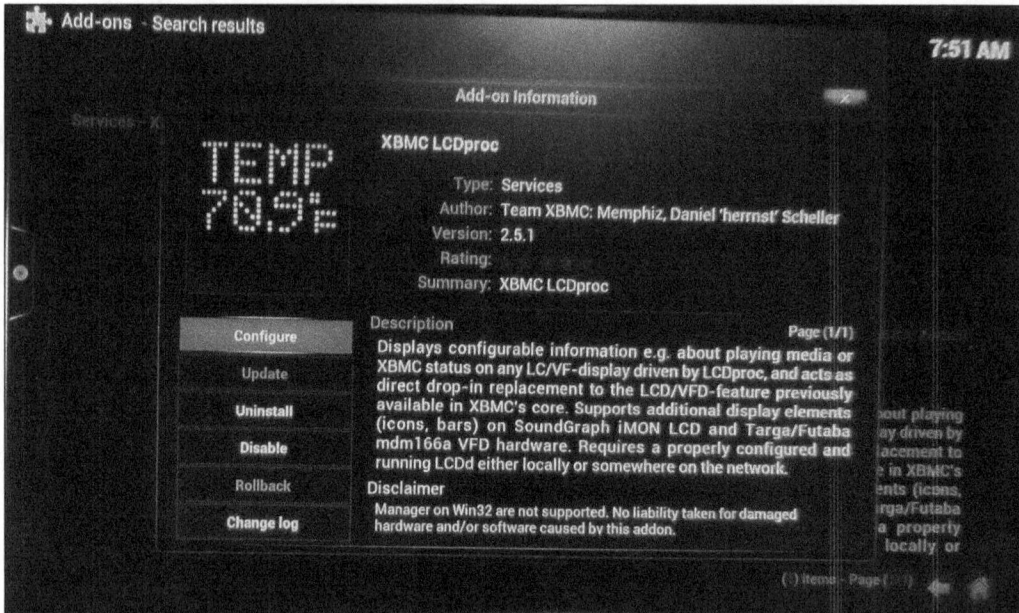

This has some options that control how certain text is displayed. Some options you may wish to change here are:

- ° **Navigation display duration**: This is the duration of how long the display will show the menu position after it is changed.

- ° **Scroll mode**: This changes the way text wraps around the display, when it is scrolling. It is best to try both and see which you prefer.

- ° **Delay for scrolling text**: This controls the speed of the text scrolling. If it is set to 0, text scrolling will be disabled.

Other options under **Backlight** and **Connection** are not as important, as we do not have a backlight that LCDproc can control and we don't want to change the default connection information.

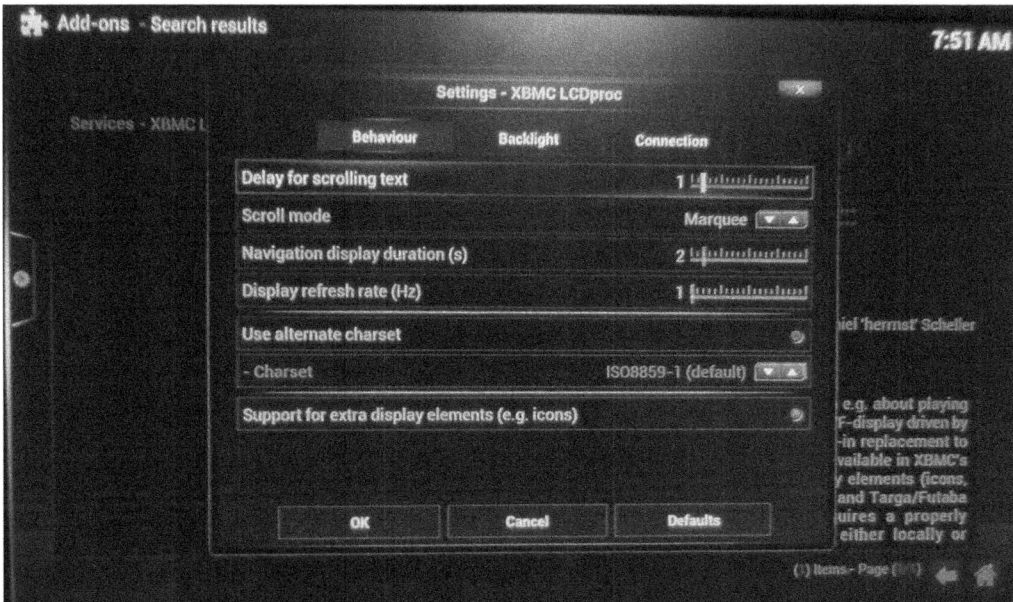

6. When finished, save any changes you've made to the settings by selecting **OK**.

7. Finally, you can customize the way information is displayed on the LCD by uploading an LCD.xml file to the Pi. This is then read by XBMC; it dictates what should be shown on each line of the LCD in a range of different situations.

I have included a sample LCD.xml file in the files for this project. This should be uploaded to the user data folder within XBMC, which can be accessed either through SFTP via /storage/xbmc/userdata or through Samba via the Userdata share.

There is documentation and some further sample LCD configuration files available on the XBMC wiki at http://kodi.wiki/view/LCD.xml.

Setting up the switches

The next piece of hardware we will set up is the six switches that will be used for the four direction keys, back, and enter. Although they can be easily remapped to whatever set of controls you like.

1. The first step here is to solder wires with a 0.1 inch female pin socket at one end to each switch terminal. This process is very similar to what we did for the arcade buttons in *Chapter 3, Mini Retro Arcade Cabinet*.

2. Once this is done, it would be worth wrapping the connections in some insulation tape to give the cables extra relief from the strain, as shown in the following image:

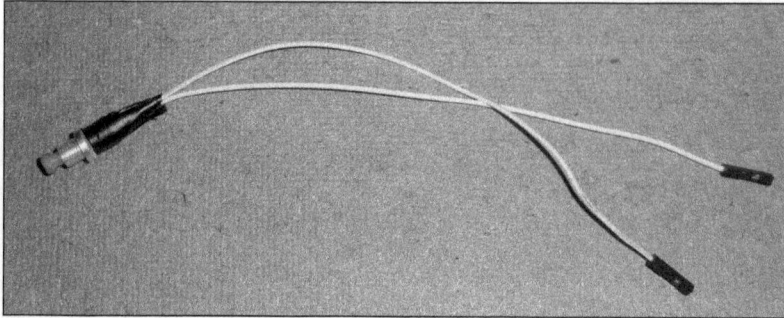

3. Next, it is time to wire the switches to the Pi. To do this, we will follow the same wiring diagrams used in the previous section to connect the LCD.

   Once this is done, we can move on to the software setup for the buttons. To interface with the GPIO hardware, we will use the sysfs bindings that are available by reading and writing to files under the /sys/class/gpio/ directory. This method is used because OpenELEC does not include the library to access GPIO through Python, and because the operating system runs mostly from a read-only filesystem, it is difficult to install this library.

4. If you wish to use a different button mapping, then you can change it in the lines 131-136 of button_watcher.py:

```
BUTTONS['enter']   = (4,  'Input.Select')
BUTTONS['back']    = (9,  'Input.Back')
BUTTONS['up']      = (27, 'Input.Up')
BUTTONS['down']    = (22, 'Input.Down')
BUTTONS['left']    = (10, 'Input.Left')
BUTTONS['right']   = (11, 'Input.Right')
```

> Note that for the revision 1 board, the up button must be swapped from GPIO 27 to GPIO 21.

Here, the first entry in the tuple for each button is the GPIO number (not the pin number) the button is connected to and the second entry is the command that is sent to the XBMC API when the button is pressed.

Changing the values for these entries allows you to remap the buttons to any functions supported by the API. Full documentation of the API is available on the XBMC wiki (`http://kodi.wiki/view/JSON-RPC_API/v4`). Here is a list of some common remote control functions that can be used:

- ○ `Input.Up`: This navigates up in the GUI
- ○ `Input.Down`: This navigates down in the GUI
- ○ `Input.Left`: This navigates left in the GUI
- ○ `Input.Right`: This navigates right in the GUI
- ○ `Input.Select`: This selects the current item in the GUI
- ○ `Input.Back`: This navigates back one level in the GUI
- ○ `Input.Home`: This returns to the home menu in the GUI
- ○ `Player.PlayPause`: This pauses or resumes playback
- ○ `Player.Stop`: This stops playback
- ○ `Player.GoPrevious`: This takes you to the previous item in the playlist
- ○ `Player.GoNext`: This takes you to the next item in the playlist

5. Once you have the buttons mapped according to your liking, go ahead and copy the `button_watcher.py` script to the `/storage/.config/` directory on the SD card. This is easily done by using SFTP.

6. When this is done, use the following command to run the script and test each of the buttons:

```
python /storage/.config/button_watcher.py
```

If all is well, you should see an output similar to the following on the console and XBMC should react according to what the button has been configured to do in `button_watcher.py`. To exit the script, press *Ctrl + C*.

If you see an error stating that the device is busy or unavailable, check the mapping in `button_watcher.py` and ensure that all of the GPIO port numbers are correct and that you have not mapped a button over another button or the LCD.

1. When the script is working as intended, it is time to configure it in order to start it when OpenELEC boots up. This is done in a slightly different manner in OpenELEC, as opposed to Raspbian. First, we must create a script that OpenELEC looks for to run on startup:

    ```
    touch /storage/.config/autostart.sh
    chmod +x /storage/.config/autostart.sh
    nano /storage/.config/autostart.sh
    ```

2. Here, the first command creates the file, the second command makes the file executable, and the third opens it in nano for us to edit. Here, we will add the following line to the end of the file:

    ```
    #!/bin/sh
    python /storage/.config/button_watcher.py &
    ```

3. This tells the shell to run the Python script in the background (noted by the `&` trailing). Now, simply exit nano using *Ctrl* + *X* and reboot the Pi using the following command:

    ```
    reboot
    ```

When the Pi has booted back into OpenELEC and XBMC is running, you should now be able to use the buttons right away.

Final assembly

The first thing you must do before getting the parts for the case machined is decide which video connector you will use. You can use either HDMI or composite video and 3.5 mm audio jacks. This will determine which side of the Pi is next to the side of the enclosure, since the two video outputs are on the opposite sides of the board and as such, there are differences between the designs of each enclosure.

For both types of enclosure, the files in the enclosure folder in the files for this project must be machined. There are two folders, `hdmi` and `composite_video`, that contain the parts specific to each video output type.

The parts needed for each type are shown in the following figure:

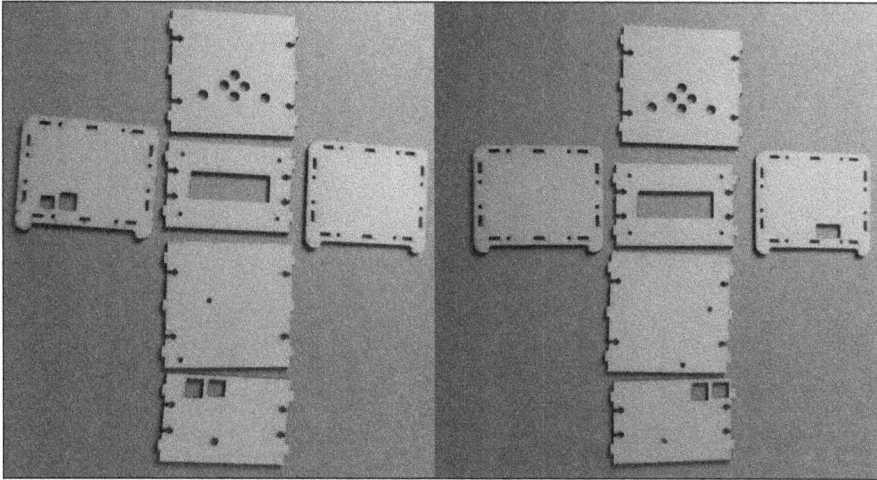

The two enclosure variants: composite video on the left and HDMI on the right

Once you have the parts you need for the enclosure type you have decided to build, it would be a good idea to remove any wiring already done so far to make the assembly process easier.

Once this is done, perform the following steps:

1. Start by mounting the LCD into the front panel. This should be done with four M4 machine screws and nuts. Ensure that you do not over tighten the nuts and put excess strain on the PCB.

   The front panel is symmetrical with the horizontal center of the LCD module, so it does not matter which side or which orientation the front panel is in when you mount the LCD. Do try to pick the side that is better looking.

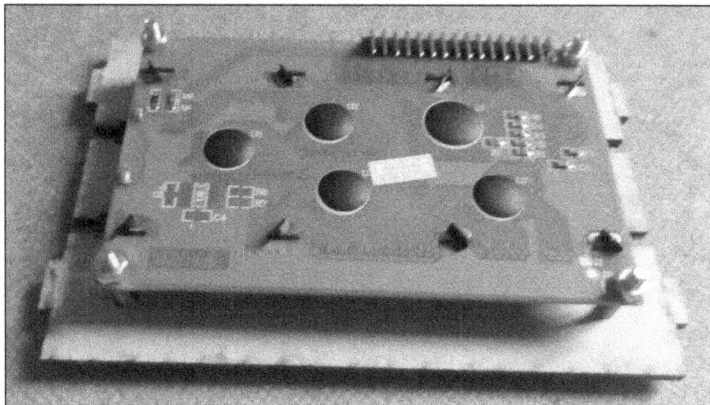

2. Next, mount each of the push buttons in the top panel using the washers and nuts that came with the buttons, as shown in the following image:

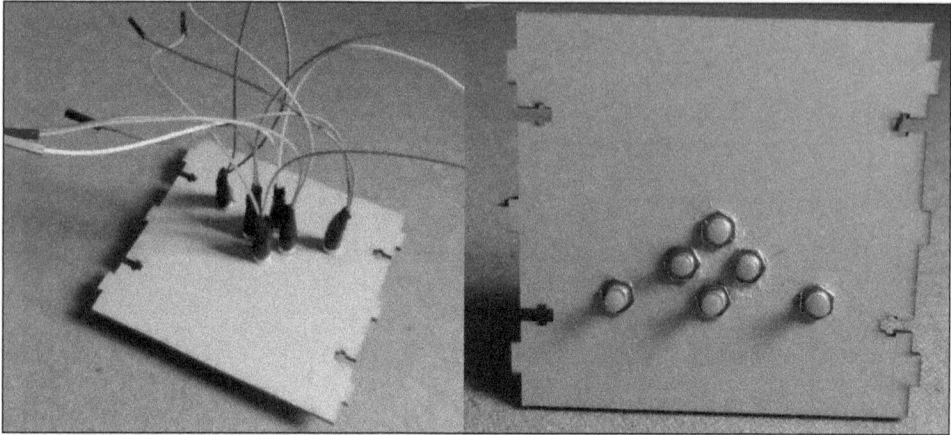

3. Next, we can assemble the top, bottom, back, and side panels that will include the cutout for the video connector, that is, if you are building the composite video version of the enclosure, you will have the opposite side attached to what is shown in the following image:

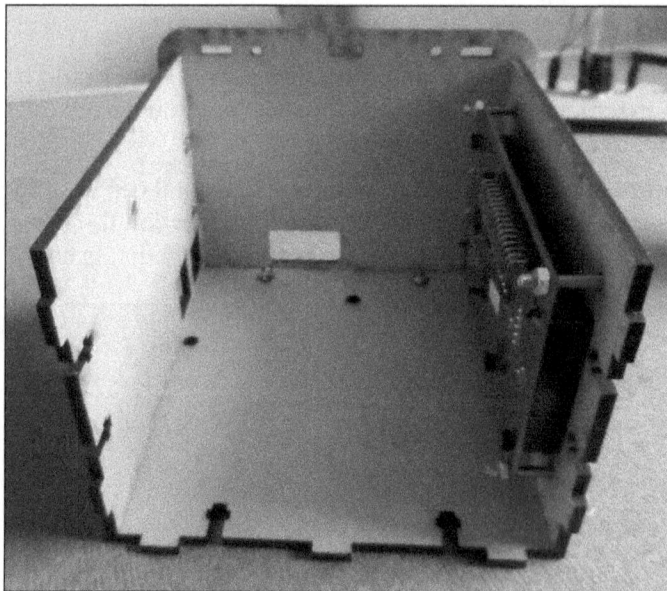

4. Around the edge, the middle panels connect to the side panels. Here, you will see a series of fittings similar to those shown in the following image. These require an M4 nut to be inserted into the slot and an M4 machine screw to be inserted through the hole in the side panel, as shown in the following image:

The screw fitting—before being tightened (left) and after being tightened (right)

> It is important not to over tighten these screw fittings, as the load is taken entirely by the approximately 2 mm of MDF that is in contact with each nut.

5. Next, mount the Pi into the enclosure using two M4 machine screws through the bottom panel. Here, it is useful to use a stack of watchers to space the PCB apart from the bottom panel to help remove strain in the PCB. Before doing this, it is important to verify that the washers you intend to use are small enough to prevent causing a short with any exposed components at the bottom of the Pi.

This is also a good point to start rewiring the Pi, LCD, and the small board we made to control the LCD brightness and contrast.

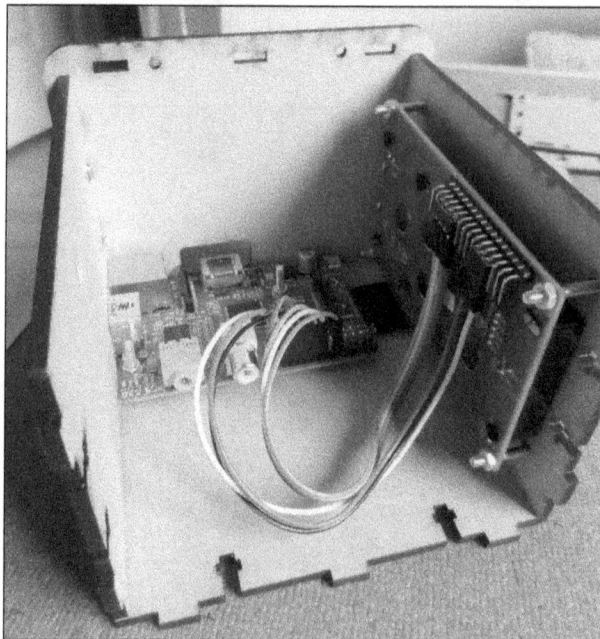

6. Next, we will rewire the buttons to the Pi as before and attach the top panel in the same way as the other three.

   By this point, the media center wiring should be complete. Now, you can mount the DC barrel jack that will be used to power the Pi externally to the back panel using the nut and washer that was supplied with it.

7. At this point, you are ready to attach the remaining side panel and give the media center a test before fastening the remaining screw fixings.

8. If all seems to be good and both the LCD and buttons work as intended, you can go ahead and fasten the remaining side panel using the same screw fixings that were used for the other side.

    Here, it is important to keep the enclosure tilted so that if one of the nuts falls out of the slot, it will fall outside of the enclosure rather than inside it.

Summary

In this chapter, we looked at yet more hardware that can be used with the GPIO port on the Pi and additional ways in which it can be controlled by software.

We also took a look at another application-specific operating system available for the Pi, how they can be very different to the general Raspbian OS, and how the approach to solve a problem (such as the buttons in this project) has to be changed based on the environment in which it will be implemented.

We also took a quick look at how to use laser cutting to manufacture professional quality enclosures quickly and easily. This is a very versatile manufacturing process and can be used to create some very impressive products. I would highly recommend you to consider it in any projects you may undertake in the future.

In the next chapter, we will look at how to interface the Raspberry Pi with a variety of sensors using the Arduino prototyping platform to create an outdoor weather station.

6
Outdoor Weather Station

In this chapter, we will make an outdoor weather station that is accessible over the Internet, which will allow remote monitoring and recording of the weather conditions.

To do this, we will have a look at a new skill that will allow us to take some existing sensors and adapt them for use in our project—reverse engineering. This is essentially the process of taking a part of an existing product and deriving the communication method between it and the rest of the product, so that you can replace either a specific part or a whole product.

We will also take a quick look at how to use the Pi as a web server and the method used to develop and deploy a Python web application.

What you will need

This is a list of all the parts you will need in order to complete this project. Most of these are available at high-street electronic components stores and online distributors:

- A Raspberry Pi
- A Wi-Fi dongle
- A long micro USB cable
- A clear/translucent Tupperware box
- A DHT11 (`www.adafruit.com/product/386`) or DHT22 (`www.adafruit.com/products/385`) sensor
- BMP180 (`www.adafruit.com/product/1603`)
- A Maplin anemometer (wind speed sensor) (`www.maplin.co.uk/p/maplin-replacement-wind-speed-sensor-for-n96fy-n82nf`)
- A Maplin wind direction sensor (`www.maplin.co.uk/p/maplin-replacement-wind-direction-sensor-for-n96fyn96gy-n81nf`)

- A Maplin rain gauge (www.maplin.co.uk/p/maplin-replacement-rain-gauge-for-n25frn96fyn96gy-n77nf)

- An Arduino Uno (www.adafruit.com/product/50)

- A selection of resistors (www.maplin.co.uk/p/e12-025w-resistor-610-piece-pack-fa08j)

- A 1 inch square section of a stripboard (www.maplin.co.uk/p/veroboard-copper-stripboard-100x160mm-a62rl)

- A row of four 0.1 inch pin headers

- A strip of terminal blocks

- Male-to-male pin jumper wires

- Female-to-female pin jumper wires

Note that even though I have specifically listed an Arduino Uno, any standard 8-bit AVR-based Arduino should work fine for this project, for example, the Uno, Mega, Nano, and Duemilanove.

I have also specified two different DHT sensors that can be used. The only real difference between them is that DHT22 has a wider operating range than DHT11; DHT11 can read temperatures between 0 and 50 degrees Celsius and humidity between 20 and 80 percent **RH (relative humidity)**, whereas the DHT22 can read temperatures between -40 to 80 degrees Celsius and humidity between 0 to 100 percent RH.

We will make use of different valued resistors a couple of times. These are small devices that are used to limit the flow of current through a circuit. Their resistance is measured in Ohms and is denoted by Ω. Since these devices do not have their resistance value printed on them, a color code must be used. To find the color code used to denote a particular resistance, a good reference chart can be found at www.digikey.co.uk/en/resources/conversion-calculators/conversion-calculator-resistor-color-code-4-band. Throughout this chapter, resistors are referred to by both value and color code.

Note that we will not use the full pack of resistors I provided a link to. However, they are very handy to have as having to order parts like resistors as and when they are needed slows down this type of electronics project.

Reverse engineering the Maplin sensors

Before we start creating our own electronics to take readings from these sensors, we need to start with a little theory and testing to get a good understanding of how these sensors work and how we will be able to interact with them.

Understanding the sensors

To start with, let's take a look at the mechanics and electronics used in the devices to know how the official device would have taken measurements from them (note that you do not have to disassemble your sensors here).

We will start with probably the simplest of all three—the rain gauge. If we unclip the top section, we will be able to notice a seesaw-like mechanism that carries water from the spout of the funnel in the top covered section to either the left-hand side or right-hand side of the sensor, depending on the position of the seesaw.

With each movement, the seesaw triggers a reed switch, a small switch that is activated using a magnet in the center of the seesaw that completes a circuit, which can be monitored by the measurement device.

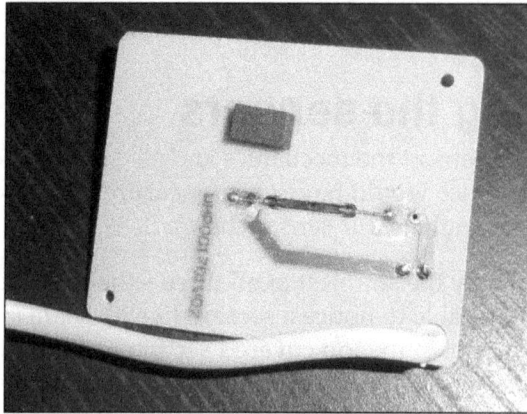

While this method is quite effective at measuring when there is rainfall, it cannot accurately determine how much rainfall there has been, as this will partially depend on the rate of rainfall. Since this relationship is not linear, it would take more effort than what it is worth to derive. Simply representing the number of times the switch is triggered over a given sample time will be sufficient for our weather station.

Let's move on to the anemometer now. This is the device that will be used to determine how fast the wind is blowing. If you remove the three screws at the bottom of the sensor, we can notice that it has a similar reed switch. By attaching a multimeter in resistance mode, we can tell that the switch pulses closed circuit and then open circuit twice per revolution of the sensor.

Given that we are able to measure time relatively accurately (up to millisecond precision) using Arduino, we can use the signal from this reed switch to measure the **revolutions per minute (RPM)** travelled by the anemometer. Then, we can multiply this by the circumference of the anemometer measured from the center of the cups to find the distance travelled by a single cup in one minute. Finally, convert this result to a standard unit (in our weather station this will be in **miles per hour (MPH)**) to get the wind speed.

The final (and most interesting) sensor is the wind direction sensor. This is essentially a vane that points in a given direction if force is exerted on the side of the vane by the wind. If we open the bottom of this sensor, we can see a **printed circuit board (PCB)** that contains eight reed switches and a socket, which is used to connect the anemometer.

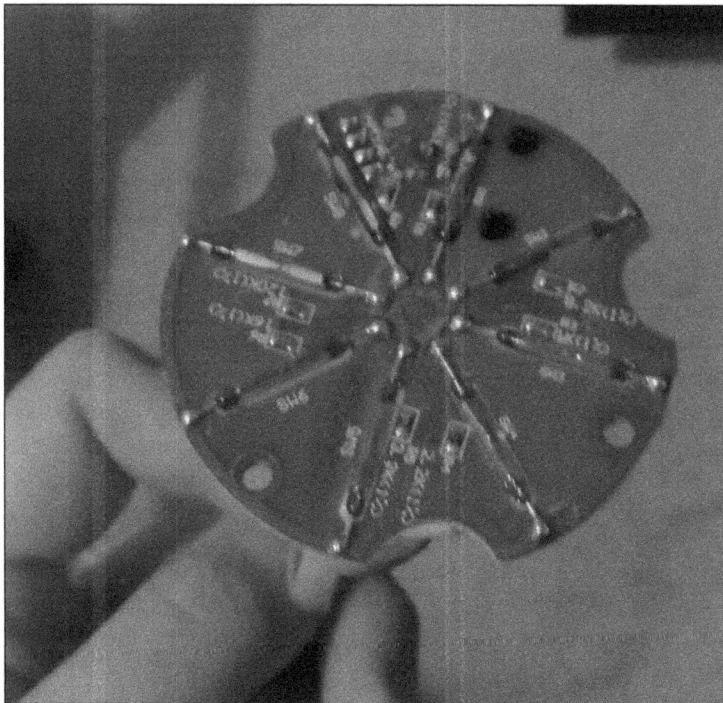

If you remove this PCB, you can see that the two middle connections of the socket are connected directly to the middle two connections of the cable running from the wind direction sensor, leaving just the outer two wires of the cable for the direction sensor.

On the reverse side of the PCB, you will also notice eight resistors marked with a given unique resistance on the PCB. Here, every reed switch has its own resistance (as shown in the following circuit diagram), and because of the spacing of the switches, only one can be activated at once. Therefore, by measuring the resistance across the circuit, you can set the position of the direction sensor accurate to 45 degrees.

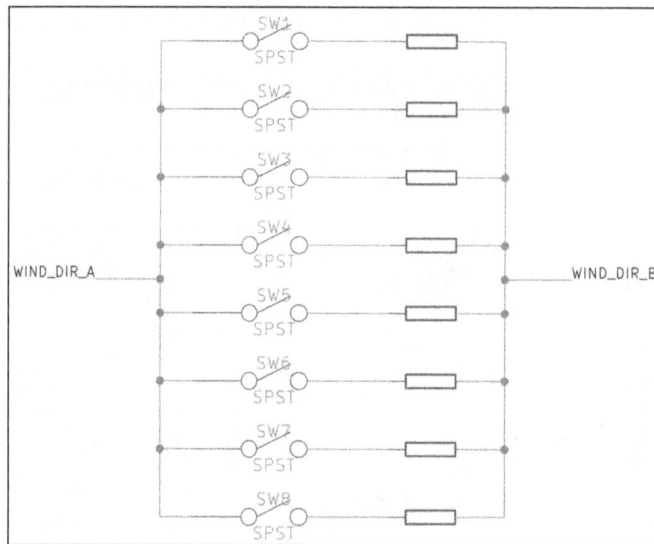

Now that we know exactly how each of the sensors work, we can start interfacing them with our own electronics. Since this involves the need for accurate timing to measure the wind speed, we cannot use the Raspberry Pi to directly take readings from the sensors, as the Pi runs a **scheduled** operating system. This means that a given task can be stopped and restarted at random times without notice, which causes problems when you have code that must keep an accurate track of time.

Arduino, however, is a real-time system. This means that the code you write will never be stopped or paused (with the exception of interrupts). This allows you to ensure that certain parts of it will be executed in a given amount of time. Arduino also supports hardware interrupts on its GPIOs, which allow a function to be called whenever the state of a given pin changes. This will be used with both the rain sensor and anemometer to keep a precise track of the readings taken from these sensors.

Although it is not originally sold as a weather sensor, we will also be including a **light-dependent resistor (LDR)**, which will be used to measure ambient light levels. As the name suggests, this is essentially a resistor that has a resistance that varies depending on the intensity of the light hitting its surface.

Since this is an analogue output (as with the wind direction sensor), we cannot use the Pi to take readings from it, as the GPIO pins on the Pi are only digital, whereas Arduino has several analogue inputs that can be used with sensors such as this.

Now is a good time to go over some of the theory of how the inputs to microcontrollers such as Arduino work. With both of our digital inputs here, we will essentially connect a switch between the input pin and ground pin. The chip used on Arduino has a **pull-up** resistor on each pin, which can be toggled in the software. This can be used to essentially make the reading from the pin read high unless there is a path to the ground with a lower resistance than the pull-up resistor, which in our case will be the reed switches that have negligible resistance.

With the analogue inputs, we will use an additional resistor to create what is called a **potential divider**. This is a circuit that, as the name suggests, outputs a voltage that is somewhere in between two input voltages, in our case, 5 V and ground (0 V). The potential divider makes it possible for a microcontroller to measure resistance by first converting it to voltage.

Wiring

Now that we have an idea of how our sensors work, we can start to create the circuit that will allow us to interface with the sensors. Since a lot of the sensors are quite simple, this is a relatively easy task.

Firstly, we need to prepare the Maplin weather sensors to be connected to Arduino. While this can be done by purchasing the correct type of socket for the connectors they come fitted with, it will be easier in this case to simply cut them off and connect them using strips of terminal blocks. To do so, perform the following steps:

1. Cut the two connectors off the ends of the long cables that are connected to the rain gauge and wind direction sensor. Do not remove the connection from the anemometer as this connects it to the socket on the wind direction sensor.

2. Remove around 1-2 inches of the grey insulation to expose the colored wires.

3. Strip around 10 mm of insulation from each of the colored wires.

4. Connect the two wires from the rain gauge to one side of a strip of two terminal blocks.

5. Connect the four wires from the wind direction sensor to one side of a strip of four terminal blocks in the order black, red, yellow, and green. This should be the same order for the wires arranged inside the cable.

6. Insert a 1 kΩ resistor (color-coded as brown, black, and red) between the black and red wires coming from the wind direction sensor on the same side as them on the terminal block.

7. On the other side of each of the terminal blocks, attach a male-to-male pin jumper wire. Note that the color does not have to match with that of the wire from the sensors. Whenever we refer to these wires, we will refer to them by the color of the wire from the sensor.

By now, the wiring from the sensors should look something like what is shown in the following image:

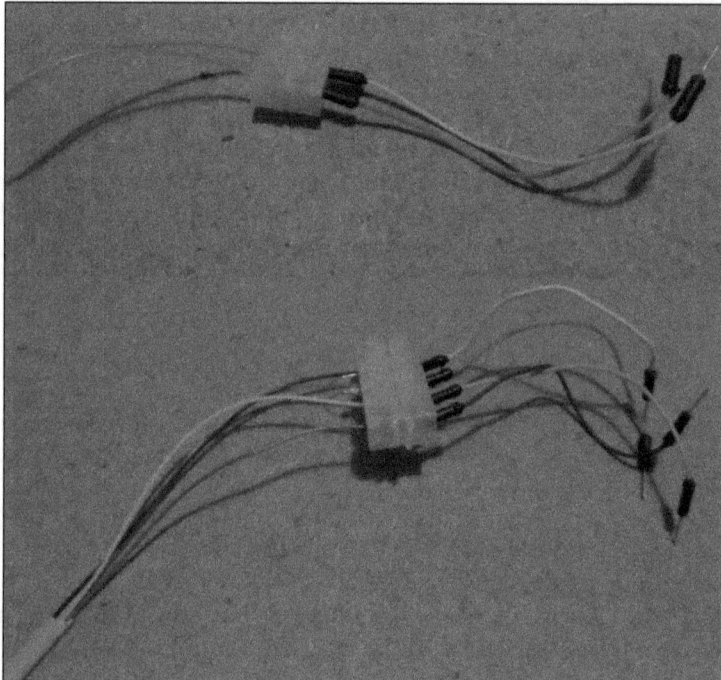

Next, we will prepare the LDR:

1. Take a strip of three terminal blocks and connect the LDR to the center and the leftmost terminal.

2. On the same side, connect a 4.7 kΩ resistor to the rightmost terminal and the center terminal.

3. On the other side of the terminal block, connect a male-to-male pin jumper wire to each terminal.

Now, the terminal block with the LDR should look similar to the following image:

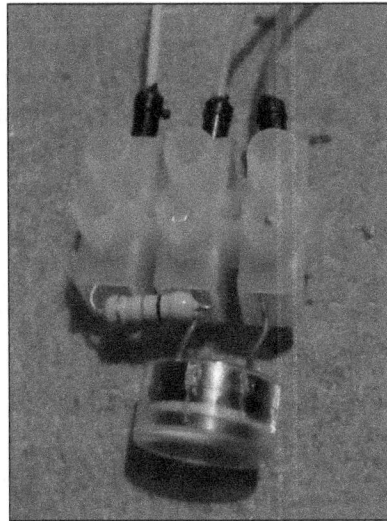

Now that we have the circuits required for our sensors built, we can connect them to the Arduino, as shown in the following diagram. This same wiring diagram will work for the majority of Arduino boards, including the Uno, Mega, Leonardo, and Duemilanove:

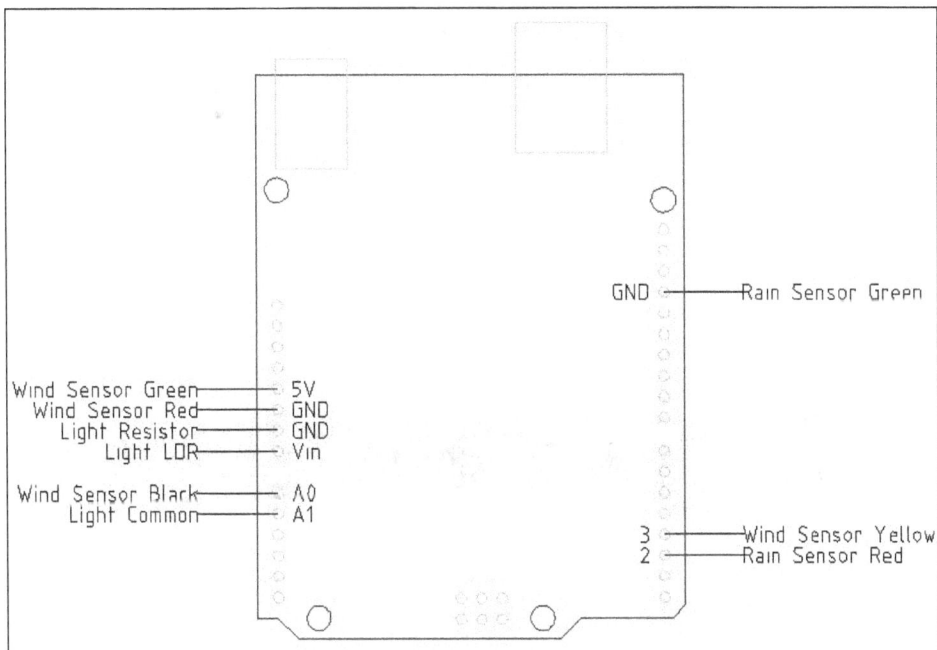

Setting up your Arduino

The final step to be taken for the sensors to work is uploading the software that will monitor the sensors and report information back to the Pi via your Arduino. To do this, we need to first download and install version 1.0.6 of the Arduino IDE from http://arduino.cc/en/main/software. When it is installed, follow these instructions to compile and upload the code to your Arduino and perform the following steps:

1. Connect your Arduino to your computer and open the Arduino IDE.

2. Select **File** and **Open** and browse to the MaplinWeatherInstrumentDriver folder in the project files. Open the Arduino sketch inside that folder. When loaded, it should look something like the following screenshot:

3. Select the type of Arduino on which you will be uploading the program by navigating to **Tools | Board**.

4. Select the serial port your Arduino is attached to by navigating to **Tools | Serial Port**.

5. Now, click on the upload button in the top-left corner of the Arduino IDE. This is the round button with an arrow pointing to the right. The Arduino IDE will then give a message that it is uploading the sketch to the board, as in the following screenshot:

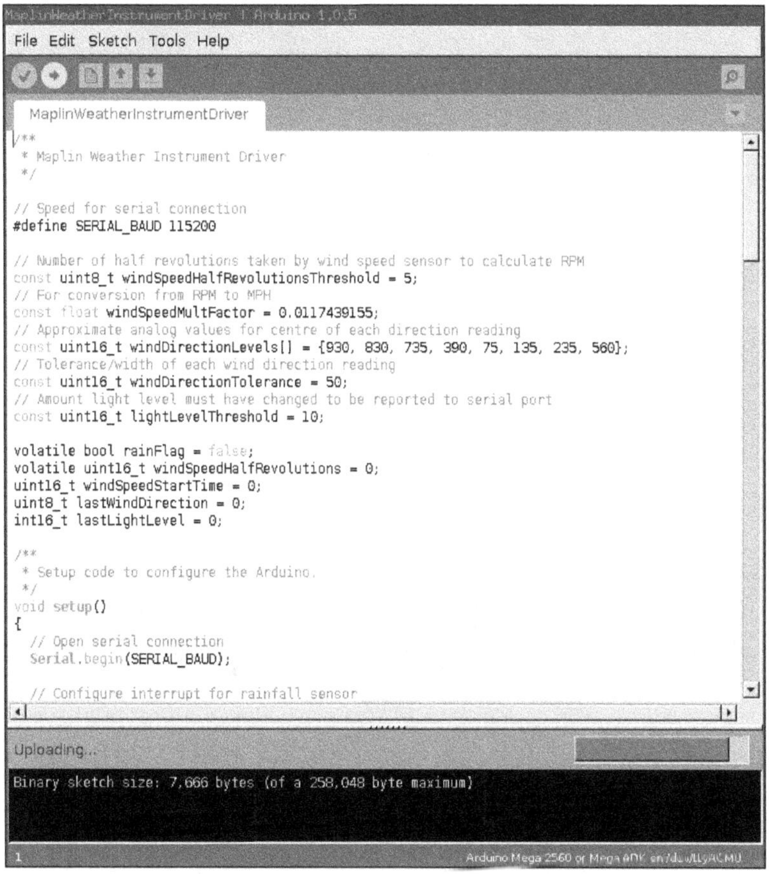

Assuming that the upload is completed successfully, you should see the message **Done uploading** in the IDE, as shown in the following screenshot:

If you get an error here, then check whether your board and serial port options are correct. If the error still persists, then disconnect your Arduino and restart the Arduino IDE and try again. This usually fixes any problems that occur here.

Once the upload is complete, you can open the serial monitor using the button in the top-right corner of the Arduino IDE that has the magnifying glass symbol to check whether the sensors are working correctly. Here, you should be able to manually move the sensors and see the output printed to the serial console.

> In regards to wind direction, the direction is represented by a value of 0 to 7, where 0 is north. The value increases in 45 degree increments, so 1 is north east, 2 is east, and so on. This goes on up to 7, which is north west.

The following screenshot displays the output printed in the serial console:

Setting up the remaining sensors

Now that we have the Maplin sensors and the LDR working properly, using the Arduino board, we can turn our focus to the remaining sensors that will measure temperature, humidity, and the barometric pressure.

For this, we will use DHT11 or DHT22 to measure the temperature and humidity and BMP180 to measure the barometric pressure. These devices can be interfaced directly to and powered from the GPIO port on the Pi.

DHT11/22

DHT11 and DHT22 use a one-wire communication protocol to send data back to the Pi, which requires an additional 10 K (brown, black, and orange) resistor to be added between the data and 3.3 V pins on the sensor. The easiest way to do this is by mounting the DHT sensor, resistor, and a row of male pin headers on a small section of a stripboard, as shown in the following diagram:

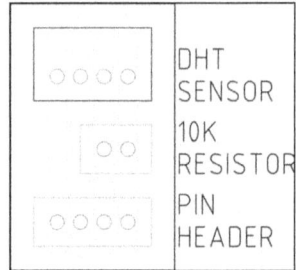

Once this is complete, the board should look similar to the following image:

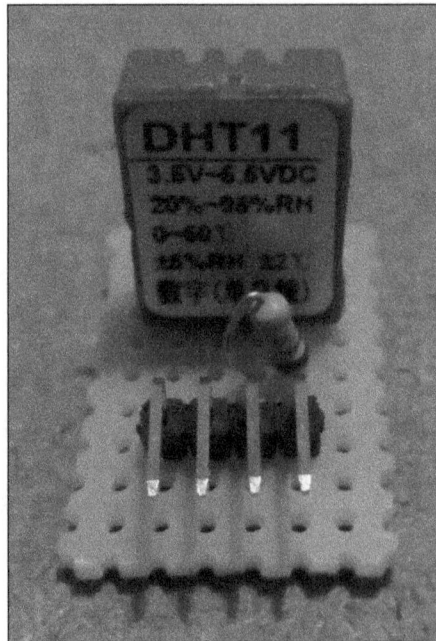

The copper tracks run vertically from the top of the preceding image to the bottom. As this is simply a task of adding a resistor across two tracks, there is no need to create any breaks in the copper tracks.

Now that we have a board for the DHT11/22 sensor, we can make the following connections to the Pi GPIO port by using female-to-female pin jumper wires:

- Pin 1 (the leftmost pin in the preceding image) to the Pi pin 6 (GND)
- Pin 2 should not be connected
- Pin 3 to the Pi pin 7 (GPIO 4)
- Pin 4 (the rightmost pin in the preceding image) to the Pi pin 1 (3.3 V)

Once the wiring is complete, we can now configure the software for the DHT11/22 sensor with the following steps:

1. First, install some packages that will be needed to set up the drivers:

   ```
   sudo apt-get install build-essential git
   ```

2. Next, clone the repository for the Adafruit driver and the BMP180 sensor:

   ```
   git clone https://github.com/adafruit/Adafruit_Python_DHT.git
   ```

3. Change the directory to the repository we just cloned and run the setup script:

   ```
   cd Adafruit_Python_DHT
   sudo python setup.py install
   ```

4. To ensure that the sensor is working correctly, change the directory to the `examples` directory and run the sample script. Note that if you're using the DHT22 sensor, you will need to change 11 to 22 in the following command:

   ```
   cd examples
   sudo ./AdafruitDHT.py 11/22 4
   ```

Assuming that everything went as it should, you should see an output similar to the following screenshot, with the readings taken from the sensor:

If this output is not produced, go back to the wiring and setup steps and ensure that the sensor is wired and configured correctly. It is worth double-checking the soldering on the stripboard to ensure that the sensor is wired with the correct pin and that there are no solder bridges between the tracks on the stripboard.

BMP180

The BMP180 sensor comes almost ready to use and requires no external circuitry to connect it to the Pi, as it uses the very common and standardized **I2C** bus. The only assembly step to perform here is to solder the row of 0.1 inch pin headers on to the PCB. Be careful when you do this and do not get the iron too close to any of the components already mounted on the PCB.

Once the pins are in place, we can then wire the sensor to the Pi. This is done by making the following connections between the sensor PCB and the Pi GPIO header by using female-to-female pin jumper wires:

- VIN to the Pi pin 17 (3.3 V)
- GND to the Pi pin 25 (GND)
- SDA to the Pi pin 3 (I2C1 SDA)
- SCL to the Pi pin 5 (I2C1 SCL)

Once the wiring is complete, we can now configure the software for the BMP180 sensor:

1. Edit the /etc/modules file to enable the kernel modules that will allow us to use the I2C interface bus on the GPIO header:

   ```
   sudo nano /etc/modules
   ```

2. Add the following lines to the file:

   ```
   i2c-bcm2708
   i2c-dev
   ```

The output should look like the following screenshot:

3. Install some packages that will allow us to use the I2C bus from Python and a tool that we can use to detect which devices are currently connected to the bus:

```
sudo apt-get install i2c-tools python-smbus
```

4. Next, we need to check whether the /etc/modprobe.d/raspi-blacklist. conf file exists, and if so, there are some lines that must be commented out. We can check whether it exists by opening the file in nano; if it does not exist, the nano editor window will be empty:

```
sudo nano /etc/modprobe.d/raspi-blacklist.conf
```

5. If the file is empty, you can skip the next step, otherwise, comment out the following lines:

```
blacklist spi-bcm2708
blacklist i2c-bcm2708
```

The file should look similar to the following screenshot:

6. At this point, we need to reboot the Pi to load the new drivers:

```
sudo reboot
```

7. Once the Pi reboots, use the following command to check whether the BMP180 sensor has been detected by the Pi correctly:

```
sudo i2cdetect -y 1
```

If so, you should see an output similar to the following screenshot:

```
pi@raspberrypi ~ $ sudo i2cdetect -y 1
     0  1  2  3  4  5  6  7  8  9  a  b  c  d  e  f
00:          -- -- -- -- -- -- -- -- -- -- -- --
10: -- -- -- -- -- -- -- -- -- -- -- -- -- -- -- --
20: -- -- -- -- -- -- -- -- -- -- -- -- -- -- -- --
30: -- -- -- -- -- -- -- -- -- -- -- -- -- -- -- --
40: -- -- -- -- -- -- -- -- -- -- -- -- -- -- -- --
50: -- -- -- -- -- -- -- -- -- -- -- -- -- -- -- --
60: -- -- -- -- -- -- -- -- -- -- -- -- -- -- -- --
70: -- -- -- -- -- -- -- 77
pi@raspberrypi ~ $ 
```

8. Assuming that the device is now being detected correctly on the I2C bus, we can clone the repository for the driver that will interface with it over the bus with the following command:

```
git clone https://github.com/adafruit/Adafruit_Python_BMP.git
```

9. Change to the directory for the driver we just downloaded and run the setup script:

```
cd Adafruit_Python_BMP
sudo python setup.py install
```

10. To ensure that the driver is communicating with the sensor correctly, change to the `examples` directory and run the example Python script:

```
cd examples
sudo python simpletest.py
```

This should give an output similar to the following screenshot with the readings taken from the sensor:

```
pi@raspberrypi ~/Adafruit_Python_BMP/examples $ sudo python simpletest.py
Temp = 18.50 *C
Pressure = 99319.00 Pa
Altitude = 168.62 m
Sealevel Pressure = 99313.00 Pa
pi@raspberrypi ~/Adafruit_Python_BMP/examples $ 
```

If you did not get this output, then you may need to double-check the wiring between the sensor and Pi. If that looks OK, then it is worth rebooting the Pi and trying again.

The weather station web application

To make the data we record from the weather sensors a bit more accessible, we will use a web application written in Python to display the current and historical data recorded from our weather station.

To do this, we will make use of a Python web application framework called Flask (`http://flask.pocoo.org/`), an application server called Gunicorn (`http://gunicorn.org/`), and a reverse proxy server called Nginx (`http://nginx.org/`).

The web application will have two pages, one will show the current weather conditions and the other will show the history of the weather conditions over a given time range. To help visualize the data on both the pages, we will use the Google Charts API (`https://developers.google.com/chart/`). This is a JavaScript API that allows the creation of interactive charts on a web page.

Deploying the app on the Pi

It's now time to deploy our web application on the Pi. To do this, we will use the Nginx reverse proxy server and the Gunicorn web application server to host the application. Here, Gunicorn is the server that actually hosts the application and related files, and Nginx is an intermediate server between the Gunicorn and the client that is used to forward requests from a client to the correct web server.

After logging in to the Pi over SSH and uploading `config_files` and `weather_station_webapp` to the `/home/pi` directory, the process to configure the web application is as follows:

1. Install some prerequisite packages:

    ```
    sudo apt-get install python-pip python-dev gunicorn supervisor
    nginx
    ```

2. Clone the repository for Flask, the Python web application framework that our web app is built with:

    ```
    git clone https://github.com/mitsuhiko/flask.git
    ```

3. Change to the directory for the repository we just cloned and install Flask on the Pi:

    ```
    cd flask
    sudo python setup.py install
    ```

4. Copy the configuration file for Nginx to the directory of all the available sites:

```
sudo cp config_files/nginx/weather-station.conf /etc/nginx/sites-available/weather-station.conf
```

5. Create a symbolic link to the site configuration from the `sites-enabled` directory. This tells Nginx that it should handle requests for this site:

```
sudo ln -s /etc/nginx/sites-available/weather-station.conf /etc/nginx/sites-enabled/
```

6. Remove the default site that Nginx hosts when it is first installed:

```
sudo rm /etc/nginx/sites-enabled/default
```

7. Once all the configuration is done, it can save a lot of debugging time to have Nginx. Verify its configuration, which can be done by using the following command:

```
sudo nginx -t
```

Assuming that the configuration was validated correctly, you should see a result similar to the following screenshot. If not, go back through the configuration steps and ensure that the configuration is performed correctly:

```
pi@raspberrypi ~ $ sudo nginx -t
nginx: the configuration file /etc/nginx/nginx.conf syntax is ok
nginx: configuration file /etc/nginx/nginx.conf test is successful
pi@raspberrypi ~ $
```

8. Assuming that the configuration is validated successfully, you can now restart the Nginx service for it to start handling requests for our web app:

```
sudo service nginx restart
```

9. Next, change to the directory for the web app:

```
cd ~/weather_station_webapp
```

10. Before we start to serve the web app, we need to initialize an empty database to record measurements. This can be done using the following command:

```
flask --app=weather_station_webapp initdb
```

11. Now, we are ready to test the web application by running Gunicorn, which can be run using the following command:

```
gunicorn -b 127.0.0.1:5000 weather_station_webapp:app
```

Here, Gunicorn is serving the web application on port 5000 on the local loopback network interface, which is only available to the Pi. Then, a request comes in from an external client on port 80 (the standard port for web pages to be served). Nginx forwards this traffic to `127.0.0.1:5000`, where the request is then processed by Gunicorn.

To test whether this is working properly, browse to the IP address of the Pi from another computer on the same network as the Pi. You should be greeted with a page similar to the upcoming screenshot.

If you receive a page with a **Bad Request** error message, then you may need to reboot the Pi and try the last step again. If you receive **Internal Server Error**, then you may need to run the command to initialize the database again.

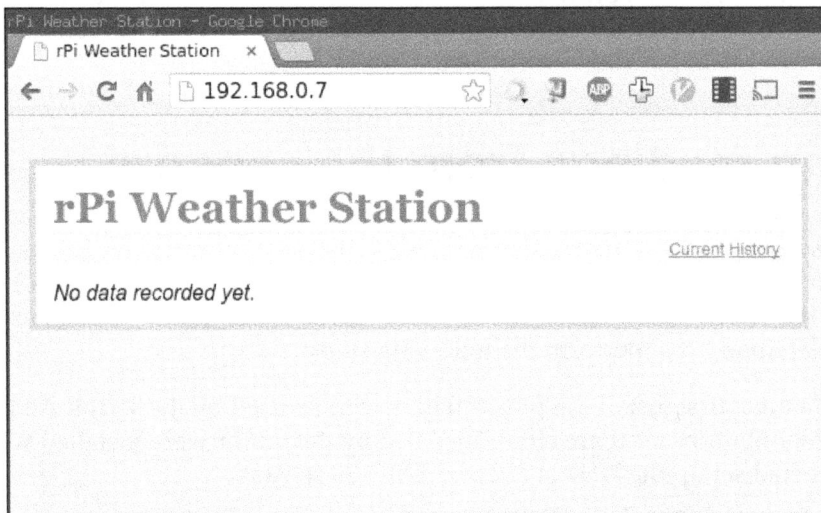

Assuming that the web app is loaded correctly, we can now perform the final step, which will start the Gunicorn server automatically when the Pi boots. To do this, we will use the Supervisor (`http://supervisord.org/`) application, which is a process control tool that makes the creation of daemon instances of programs very easy, and perform the following steps:

1. First, we need to copy the configuration entry for the web application into the Supervisor configuration directory:

```
sudo cp config_files/supervisor/weather-station-webapp.conf /etc/
supervisor/conf.d/weather-station-webapp.conf
```

2. Next, run this set of commands to update the superuser configuration and start the web application as a background process:

```
sudo supervisorctl reread
sudo supervisorctl update
sudo supervisorctl start weather-station-webapp
```

You may receive what looks to be an error message when running the final command here. However, this simply states that the process is already running and can safely be ignored.

3. Finally, reboot the Pi to finish the deployment:

```
sudo reboot
```

Once the Pi has rebooted, browse once again to the IP address of the Pi and you should be able to see the same page as before. If so, you have successfully deployed the web application on your Pi.

Taking readings from the sensors

Now that our app is set up, we need to configure the Pi to regularly take readings from the sensors and update the database with the latest weather conditions. To do this, we will use a Python script that will communicate with the DHT11/22 and BMP180 sensors using their Adafruit libraries and the Maplin sensors using the pySerial library and perform the following steps:

1. We must first install the pySerial library to be used by the script. All the other libraries used are either installed by default or were installed when we had set up the DHT11/22 and BMP130 sensors:

```
sudo pip install pyserial
```

2. Next, we will modify the rc.local file to perform the script run when the Pi boots:

```
sudo nano /etc/rc.local
```

3. Here, add the following line to the file:

```
python /home/pi/sensor_manager.py --database
/home/pi/weather_station_webapp/weather.db --poll-interval
10 --submit-interval 600 &
```

The output should look as shown in the following screenshot:

```
pi@raspberrypi:~
  GNU nano 2.2.6                              File: /etc/rc.local

#!/bin/sh -e
#
# rc.local
#
# This script is executed at the end of each multiuser runlevel.
# Make sure that the script will "exit 0" on success or any other
# value on error.
#
# In order to enable or disable this script just change the execution
# bits.
#
# By default this script does nothing.

# Print the IP address
_IP=$(hostname -I) || true
if [ "$_IP" ]; then
  printf "My IP address is %s\n" "$_IP"
fi

python /home/pi/sensor_manager.py --database /home/pi/weather_station_webapp/weather.db --poll-interval 10 --submit-interval 600 &

exit 0
```

> The interval at which the script takes readings from the sensors
> and stores them in the database can be configured by changing
> the --poll-interval and --submit-interval arguments.
> Note that if the --submit-interval setting is set any lower
> than 300 seconds (5 minutes), then this can make the history
> view in the web application slow to load.

4. Finally, reboot the Pi and try to access the web interface to check whether the
    data update after the submit interval has elapsed.

Assembling the weather station

Now that our weather station is set up and takes the readings correctly, it's time to
assemble the weather station and set it up outside.

Before we do this, you may want to consider how the Pi will connect to your network
and receive power. Here, I would recommend you use Wi-Fi for networking. This
can be set up by following the same procedure that we used in *Chapter 2, Portable
Speaker System*. For power, I used a 10 foot micro USB cable, which was long enough
to reach as far outside as I had located the weather station.

For the Maplin weather sensors, simply assemble the two masts and fix both the
anemometer and wind direction sensor at the top of their own masts by using a 30 mm
M3 screw. These masts can then be pushed relatively easily into the soil. Since they are
not particularly tall, it is better to place them in an area as open as possible to improve
the accuracy of the readings taken from them.

As an enclosure for the remaining sensors, the Arduino, and the Pi, the easiest thing to use is a Tupperware (or sandwich) box. This should be at least 6 inches wide by 4 inches deep, around 3 inches tall, and either clear or very lightly translucent, so that the light intensity does not fall too much between the outside and inside of the box (as the light sensor will be mounted on the inside).

There are a few modifications that must first be made to the box to make it suitable for use as an enclosure for the weather sensors. Firstly, there must be some way to maintain the airflow through the box to ensure that the DHT11/22 and BMP180 sensors get accurate readings. This can be done easily by drilling a pattern of six holes on either side of a corner of the box, as shown in the following image. This provides a path for air to flow through the corner of the case without allowing moisture and water to get to the Pi and Arduino (which will be located at the opposite end of the box).

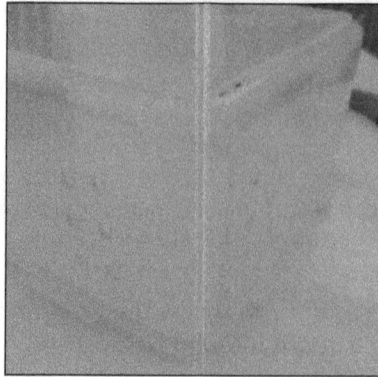

The next thing we will need is a way to run cables inside the box. This can be done by removing the lip on one side of the box, so that when the lid is replaced, there is a gap large enough to run the wires through. The lip can be removed by using a pair of wire/side cutters to create a gap wide enough for the cables from the rain gauge, wind direction sensor, and a micro USB cable, as shown in the following image:

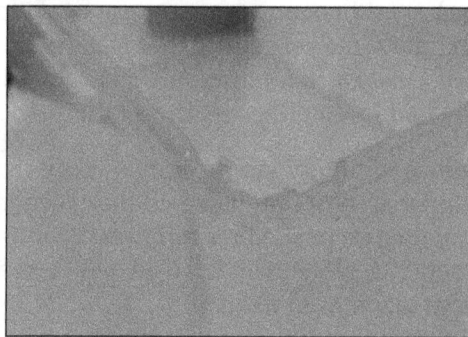

[Be very careful while cutting away the lip of the box like this. Using too much force or trying to cut away too much at once can cause parts of the box to chip away at high speed. Eye protection gear should be worn while doing this.]

Next, we need to assemble the electronics and sensors in the box. The only requirement here is that the LCD faces directly upwards and that the DHT11/22 and BMP180 sensors are close to the path of air which goes through the corner of the box where the holes were drilled.

You should use an adhesive or glue to keep the electronics from moving. You can use anything from a temporary fixing, such as Blu-Tack, to a more permanent (but still removable) adhesive, such as hot glue. Whichever you decide to use, it is important to keep adhesives away from sensitive areas of the electronics, such as the metallic sensor chip on the BMP180 PCB or the surface mount components on the back of the Pi.

The following image shows the assembled electronics and sensors in the box:

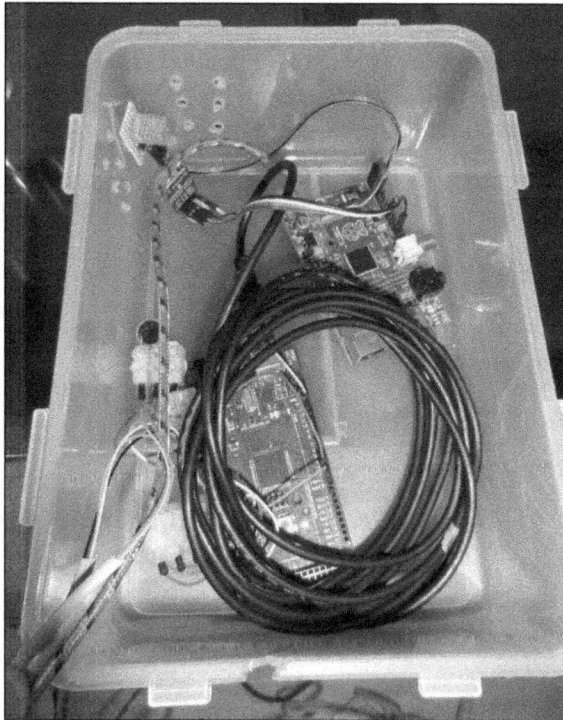

Finally, all that is left to do is to replace the box lid, set up the weather station outside, and apply power. We can now move on to test the weather station and look at some data from it.

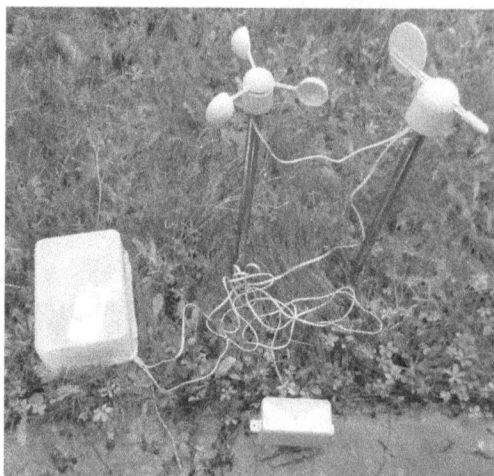

Note that while installing the wind direction sensor, it is important to alight it properly with the north direction. It must be installed such that when the arm is in position, as shown in the following image, the vane must point to north and the round point opposite the vane must point to south:

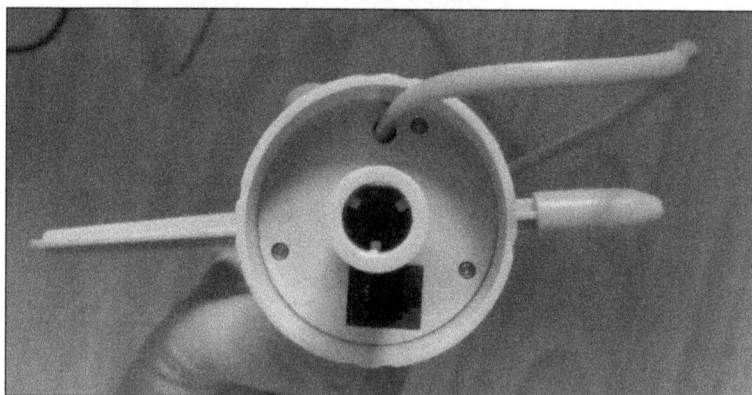

Using the web application

When you first browse to the IP address of the Pi, you are greeted by a page that will look similar to the following screenshot. This shows the current weather conditions that have been recorded over the last measurement period (that is, the period specified by the `--submit-interval` parameter to the `sensor_manager.py` script).

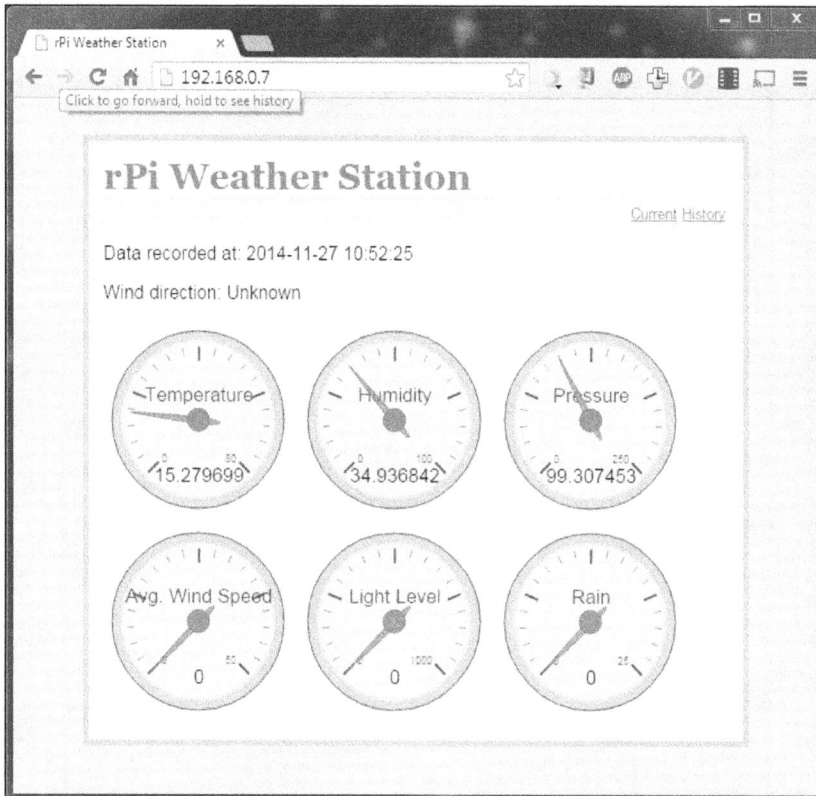

By clicking on the **History** link in the top-right corner of the page, you are able to browse through all the recordings that have been taken by the weather station.

By default, it displays the history for the previous week. This can be changed by using the two options at the top of the page (note that these options may only render correctly in Chrome, Opera, or Safari web browsers).

You can also change which recorded values are to be displayed on the graph by using the selection of checkboxes at the top of the page. Note that some measurements may not be suited to be displayed at the same time as they have different ranges, for example, rainfall and the light level.

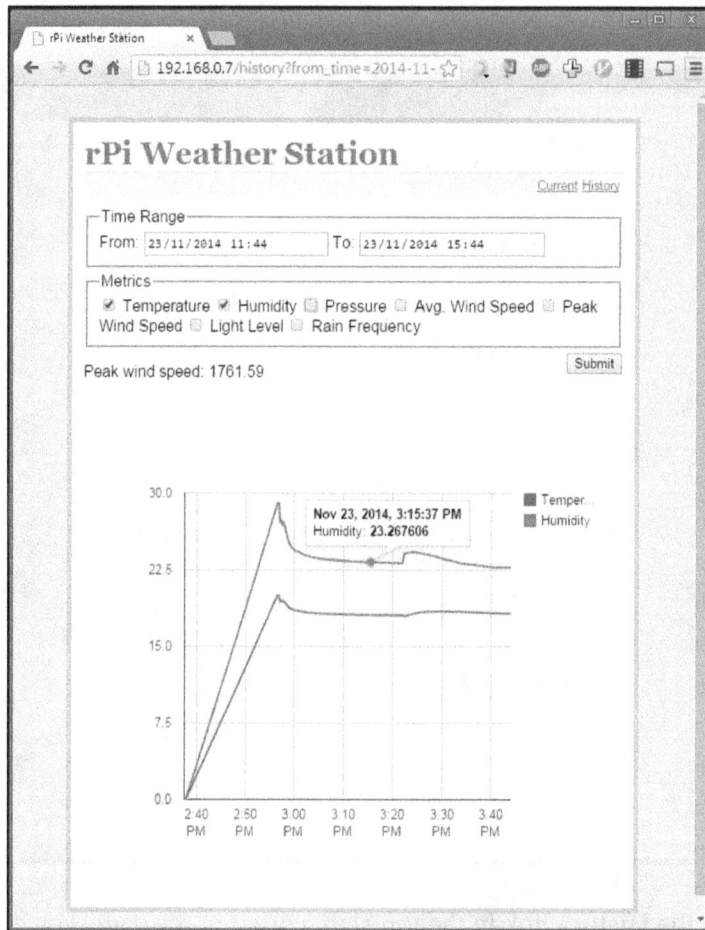

If you ever want to take a backup of the weather data, you can do so by taking a copy of the `weather.db` file in the `/home/pi/weather_station_webapp/` directory. If you want to erase all the recorded data, you can simply run the initialize database command again.

Note the units for the measurements:

- **Wind speed**: This is measured in miles per hour (MPH)
- **Temperature**: This is measured in degrees Celsius
- **Humidity**: This is measured in percentage RH (relative humidity)
- **Pressure**: kPa (kilopascal), where 1 kPa = 10 mb (millibar)
- **Light level and rain**: Arbitrary units

Summary

In this chapter, we looked at the steps needed to design and deploy a Python-based web application on the Pi using the Flask framework. This is a technique we will be using in a couple of chapters later in the book, where we will create web-based control panels and information displays.

We also looked at yet more ways to interface devices to the Pi, both directly via the GPIO port and by using an intermediate device; in our case, an Arduino. We also looked at the advantages this can bring with certain types of sensor.

In the next chapter, we will further explore the use of sensors, as we create a home security system that connects several sensors using a wireless network.

7
Home Security System

In this chapter, we will look at how to create a simplistic security system that will be able to monitor basic security sensors, such as door position sensors and **passive infrared (PIR)** sensors. These are common for standard home security systems and send e-mail alerts when certain combinations of sensors are triggered.

What you will need

This is the list of the minimum parts you will need to complete this project by following the sample system setup, which is described in the first section of this chapter:

- The Raspberry Pi
- At least two nRF24L01 modules (http://imall.iteadstudio.com/im120606002.html)
- At least one Arduino Uno
- 0.1 inch female-to-female pin jumper wires
- 0.1 inch male-to-female pin jumper wires
- A selection of security sensors:
    - The PIR sensor (www.rapidonline.com/Electronic-Components/Pir-Module-61-1516)
    - Magnetic door sensors or reed switches (www.rapidonline.com/Electronic-Components/Surface-Mounting-Proximity-Switch-78-1672)

The number of sensors, Arduino boards, and RF modules you will need for this project will greatly depend on how many rooms you want the security system to cover and how many sensors will be used in each room. In this chapter, it would be worth reading at least the section on how to design your security system before you order any parts. Do this to ensure that you have enough requirements to build a system that will work well for your scenario.

The security system structure

The security system will be divided into five main parts: the Arduino sensor nodes, the RF network that connects each node to the Raspberry Pi, the MQTT broker that connects the RF network to the web application, the web application that manages the senor events and alerts, and the database that stores the configuration of the sensors and alarms and the history of each sensor.

Each sensor node is comprised of an RF module that allows communication between the network of sensor nodes and several security sensors, such as PIR motion detectors and reed switch doors or window sensors, and both the standard sensors used on the standard home security systems. While these nodes can be battery powered for better reliability, we will power ours by using a USB port and USB power supply.

The Raspberry Pi will serve as both the host server for the web application and database and the base node in the RF network. This will use the same RF modules and software libraries as the Arduino sensor nodes.

Our security system will not use a bell or sounder, such as a conventional security system; instead, it will send e-mail alerts to an address configured via the web interface. It will also allow alarms to be configured much more freely than a conventional system, allowing you to set several alarms for each different area in a house. It will also allow the alarms to act independent of each other.

Designing your security system

For the rest of the chapter, we will assume that the security system has three sensor nodes; here, all three have magnetic door sensors and only two out of three have PIR motion sensors.

At this stage, you need to think about where each node will be located, as the RF modules can only transmit over a certain distance before the signal either becomes too weak to ensure reliable communication or is lost completely. From my own testing, I have found that the link between two nodes can rarely travel more than one wall or floor.

Therefore, in order to have a longer distance between the base node and sensor node, the sensor node must communicate through a node that acts as a repeater. This is handled by the network protocol library used on the sensor's nodes and the Pi. We will look at this in more detail later in this chapter, but for now, provisioning at least one sensor node in each room you want to have a sensor in as well as any room between nodes will be sufficient.

The following diagram roughly shows the structure of the system we will use for the rest of the chapter:

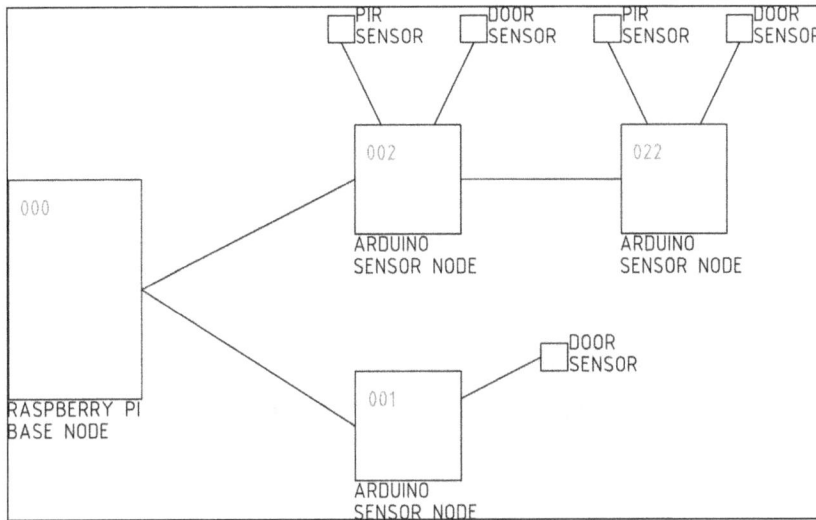

If you are using your own system design, then it helps to make your own diagram similar to this. Make sure to note the sensor node address, location, and MQTT topic of each sensor to help make the programming of each of these sensor nodes and the addition of the sensors to the web application easier.

Web applications

The security system will be based on a web application that will be used to record and view events from the sensors and will allow a configuration of sensors and alarms.

For this, we will use the Flask framework for Python, which was used in the previous chapter, and the MQTT protocol to establish communication between the sensors and web application. This protocol is a publisher and subscriber model, where clients can subscribe to information (topics) they are interested in and receive new data as it is made available (published) by other clients.

An overview of the structure of the web application is shown in the following diagram. As we did in the previous chapter, we will use the SQLite database engine:

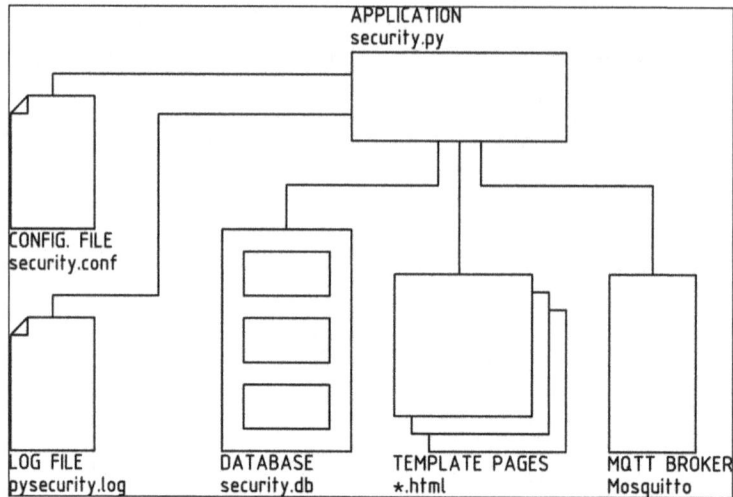

```
                            APPLICATION
                            security.py


 CONFIG. FILE
 security.conf




 LOG FILE          DATABASE        TEMPLATE PAGES    MQTT BROKER
 pysecurity.log    security.db     *.html            Mosquitto
```

Deploying our application

We will first start by deploying the web application on the Pi. This will mostly be the same process as was used in the previous chapter for the weather station web application. However, there are additional steps here as the security application requires an extra configuration file to set options for the login details, MQTT broker, and e-mail alerts:

1. First, we will add an additional source to the list of repositories that APT searches for. When we install new packages, this will allow us to install the up-to-date version of the Mosquitto MQTT broker needed for the security system:

    ```
    wget http://repo.mosquitto.org/debian/mosquitto-repo.gpg.key
    sudo apt-key add mosquitto-repo.gpg.key
    cd /etc/apt/sources.list.d/
    sudo wget http://repo.mosquitto.org/debian/mosquitto-wheezy.list
    cd
    ```

2. Now that the repository has been added, we need to update the local copy of the list of packages that are available and install any updates while we are at it:

    ```
    sudo apt-get update
    sudo apt-get upgrade
    ```

3. Now that the Pi is up to date, we can start installing the packages we will need for the security system. Don't worry if you get a message saying a package is already installed or is up to date, as some of these may or may not be already installed:

```
sudo apt-get install mosquitto mosquitto-clients python-pip git
python-dev gunicorn supervisor nginx
sudo pip install paho-mqtt
```

4. From here on, the procedure will be similar to that used while installing Flash in the previous chapter. However, we will be making a couple of modifications this time, so we will go through the full procedure here. Continue by cloning the Flash code repository and install Flask on the Pi:

```
git clone https://github.com/mitsuhiko/flask.git
cd flask
sudo python setup.py install
```

5. Next, we need to copy the Nginx configuration files for the security web application site. Enable the site configuration and remove the default Nginx site:

```
sudo cp config_files/nginx/security.conf /etc/nginx/sites-
available/security.conf
sudo ln -s /etc/nginx/sites-available/security.conf /etc/nginx/
sites-enabled/
sudo rm /etc/nginx/sites-enabled/default
```

6. Now, we can let Nginx test the configuration and assuming that the test has passed, restart the service. If the test failed, go back to the configuration and ensure that all the files have been copied correctly:

```
sudo nginx -t
sudo service nginx restart
```

7. Next, we can test the web application by running it manually with Gunicorn. Here, it is not important that the application is missing the configuration file, so it can be started with the following commands:

```
cd ~/security_webapp
flask --app=security initdb
gunicorn -b 127.0.0.1:5000 security:app
```

> Note that while initializing the database, you may get an error similar to that shown in the following screenshot; this is caused by the exit of the application while the MQTT client is still running and can be safely ignored.

```
pi@raspberrypi ~/security_webapp $ flask --app=security initdb
Initialized the database.
Exception in thread Thread-1 (most likely raised during interpreter shutdown):
Traceback (most recent call last):
  File "/usr/lib/python2.7/threading.py", line 552, in __bootstrap_inner
  File "/usr/lib/python2.7/threading.py", line 505, in run
  File "/usr/local/lib/python2.7/dist-packages/paho/mqtt/client.py", line 2180, in _thread_main
pi@raspberrypi ~/security_webapp $ 
```

8. Now, browse the IP address of the Pi on a computer of the same network and you should see a page similar to that shown in the following screenshot. As it is, this is the only page of the site that will work, as the application is running without the configuration file:

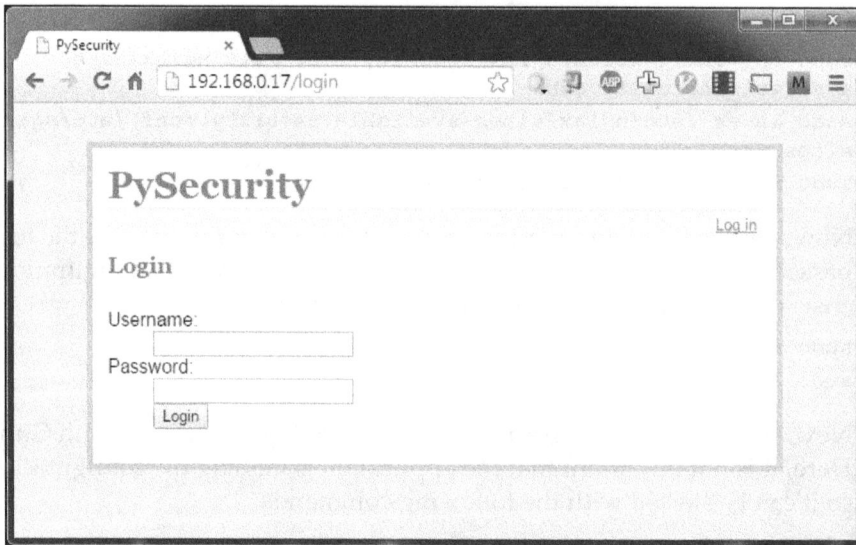

If the web page does not appear, then you may need to reboot the Pi before trying again to flush out any bad configuration, which may still be applied to one of the running services. If this does not work, then go back to the configuration steps and ensure that each file was copied correctly.

9. Next, we will configure the web application that will start automatically when the Pi boots using the supervisor:

```
sudo cp config_files/supervisor/security-webapp.conf /etc/
supervisor/conf.d/security-webapp.conf
sudo supervisorctl reread
sudo supervisorctl update
sudo supervisorctl start security_webappp
```

> Here, you can try to access the web application again. This should give the same login page as before. This will still be the only functional page in the application at this point.

10. Now that the web application is deployed, we need to edit the configuration file to enable login, MQTT broker connection, and e-mail alerts:

```
sudo supervisorctl stop security_webappp
sudo cp config_files/security.conf ~
nano ~/security.conf
```

11. Now, we need to modify the configuration file so that it suits the setup we have for the MQTT broker, e-mail alerts, and the credentials used to login to the web application. Here, we must also set a secret key that allows our application to save information in a browser session.

In the configuration file, you will find that all the configuration entries are already there; they simply need to be populated with customized values. Note that while the SECRET_KEY value will allow you to log in to the application, it should be changed to something unique to your application before you start using the system properly.

The MQTT_BROKER and MQTT_PORT configuration parameters are used to determine which MQTT broker the application should connect to. Here, we are using the broker running on the Pi locally, so these can be left as the parameters' default values.

The USERNAME and PASSWORD parameters are used to set the credentials that you will use on the login page to access the web application. As it is, the web application only supports a single user.

The SMTP_SERVER, SMTP_USERNAME, SMTP_PASSWORD, and FROM_EMAIL parameters are used to configure the sending of e-mail alerts. Currently, only Gmail and Google Apps e-mail accounts have been tested with the application, so it is highly recommended that you use one of these accounts. However, the Python SMTP library (https://docs.python.org/2/library/smtplib.html) is well documented, so modifying the send_mail() function in security.py is always an option if you want to use a different e-mail provider.

Assuming that you will just use a Gmail (or Google Apps) e-mail account for e-mail alerts, the SMTP_SERVER parameter is already set to the correct value. SMTP_USERNAME and SMTP_PASSWORD must be set to your account login details, which are your full e-mail address and password. The FROM_EMAIL parameter is used to set the e-mail address the message is sent from; this should be set to the same as the SMTP_USERNAME parameter.

Once the configuration file is complete, it should look something like what is shown in the following screenshot:

Now that the configuration file has been modified, the last step is to start the web application once more:

```
sudo supervisorctl start security_webappp
```

Once this final step is complete, you can try to access the web application by browsing to the IP address of the Pi on a computer on the same network. This should present you with the same login screen as before.

Configuring sensors and alarms

Now that the web application is deployed correctly, it is time to log in to it and configure the sensors and alarms we will use for the system:

1. Start by browsing to the IP address of your Pi and enter the login details in the page you are taken to. These login credentials are the ones that were configured in the configuration file in the previous section.

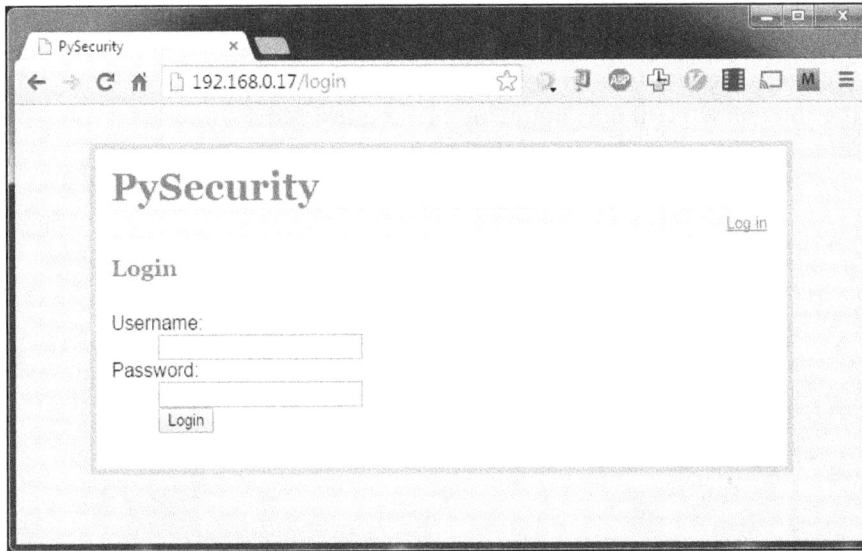

2. Once logged in, you will be greeted with the **Sensors** page. This shows a list of all the sensors that are currently configured on the security system. We will start by first adding a new sensor by clicking on the **Add New Sensor** link at the top of the page.

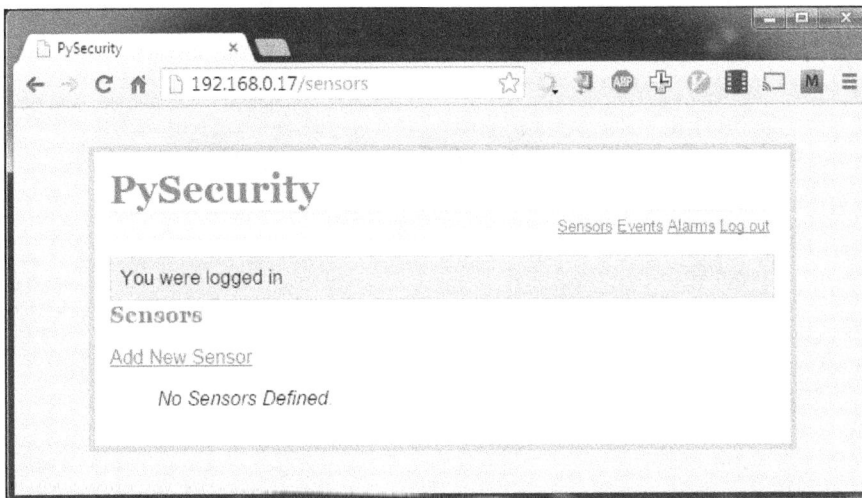

3. Here, we are given options for the name and identification of the sensor, both in relation to the position in the house and the MQTT topic that it maps to. We will set this sensor to be the door sensor on the first sensor node. For all the sensors we will use, the value of **Triggered text** should be 1.

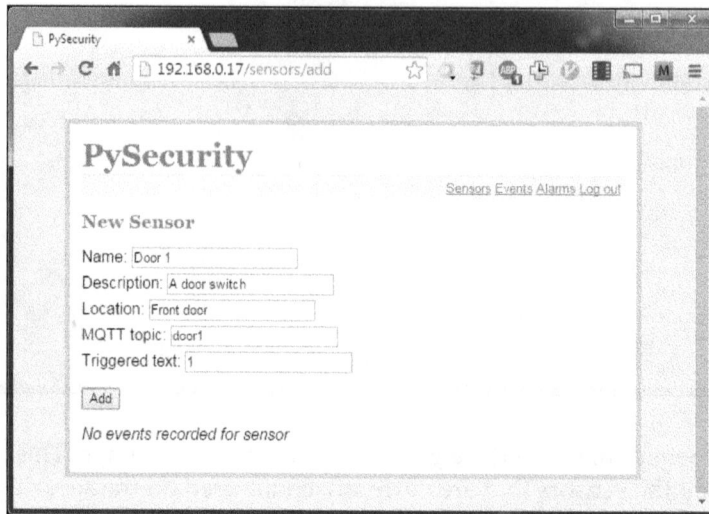

4. Once this is complete, click on **Add** and you will see a message saying that the sensor has been added. At the bottom of this screen, you will see a section that displays the last recorded event for this sensor. Since it has just been added, no events have been recorded yet.

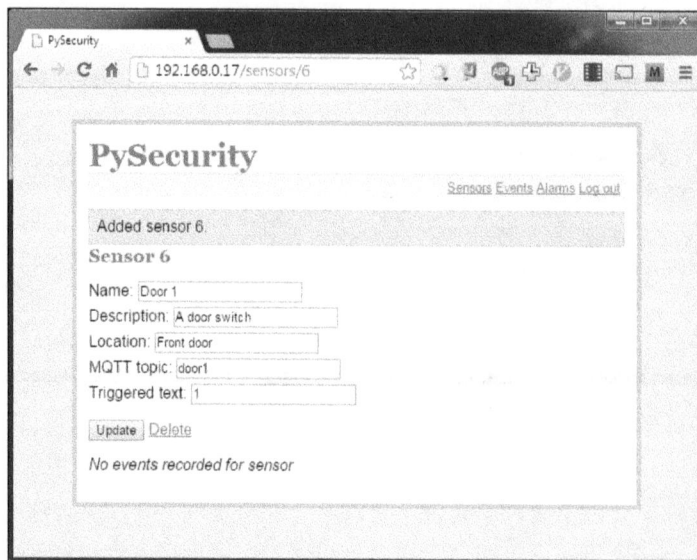

5. Follow this procedure for the remaining sensors in your setup, following the system structure diagram you made earlier in this chapter. Once this is complete, you will have a fair few sensors added to the system, as depicted in the following screenshot:

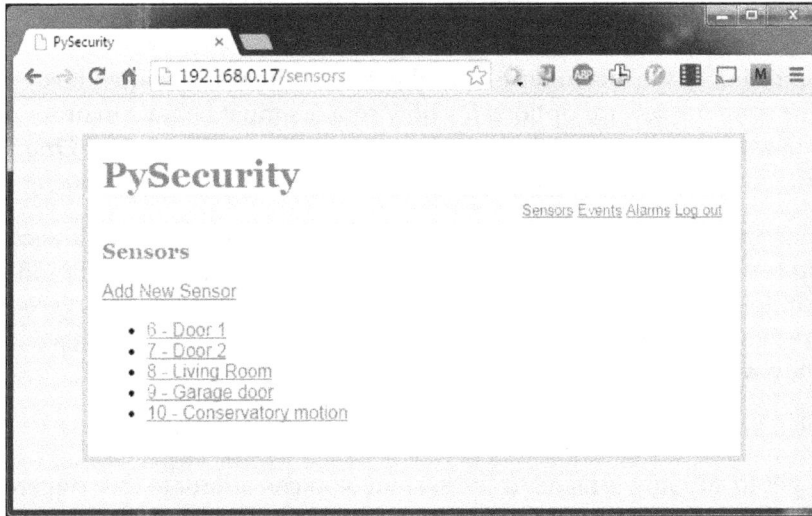

6. Next, we will move on to add an alarm for some of the sensors. This will control how and when you receive alerts when the state of the sensors in the network changes. To start, click on **Alarms** to navigate to the alerts page and add a new alarm.

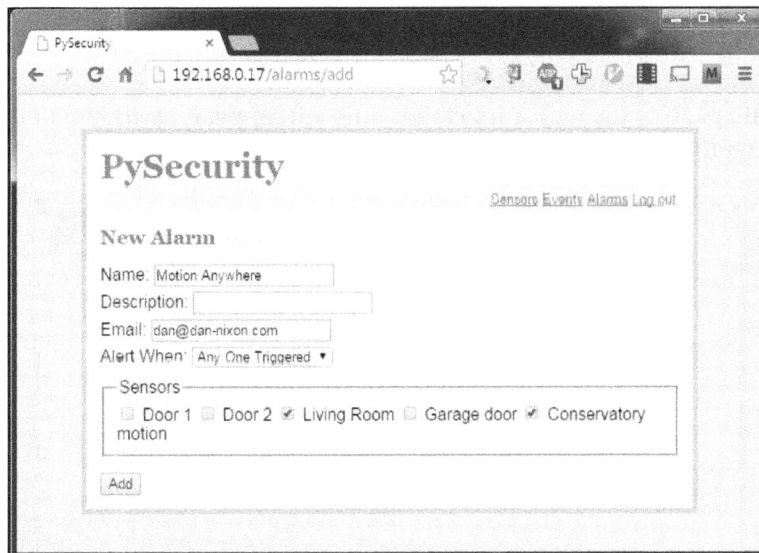

7. On this screen, you will be given the option to give the alarm a name and description to assist identification as well as a field for an e-mail address to send notification e-mails when the alarm is triggered.

8. At the bottom of the screen is a list of all the sensors that have been added to the security system. Check all of them that you want to have an effect on this alarm.

9. Next, choose the alarm type from the **Alert When** drop-down box. This contains several options for how sensors must behave in order to trigger the alarm. Typically, you will usually set this to **Any One Triggered**. There is also an option to disable the alarm if needed.

At this point, the system is sufficiently configured to behave as a simple security system and send alerts when sensors have been triggered. However, should you ever need to look up the history of a sensor to see when it has been triggered, there is an events page, which will display all the recorded sensor events and the time they were recorded at.

This can also be handy to verify that a sensor is functioning correctly.

As we are yet to add any sensors to the system, you can simulate the triggered sensors using the Mosquitto command-line tools. If not already installed, they can be downloaded using the following command:

```
sudo apt-get install mosquitto_clients
```

Once these are installed, you can simulate, for instance, a door being opened and closed using the following two commands, where PI_IP is the IP address of the Pi:

```
mosquitto_pub -h 192.168.0.17 -t door2 -m 1
mosquitto_pub -h 192.168.0.17 -t door2 -m 0
```

On the **Events** page of the web application, this will appear, as shown in the following screenshot:

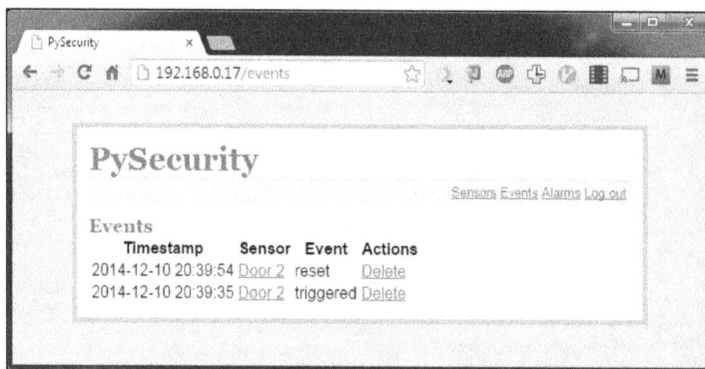

When an alarm is triggered and a valid e-mail address has been set in the configuration page, an e-mail similar to the following will be delivered to the configured e-mail address:

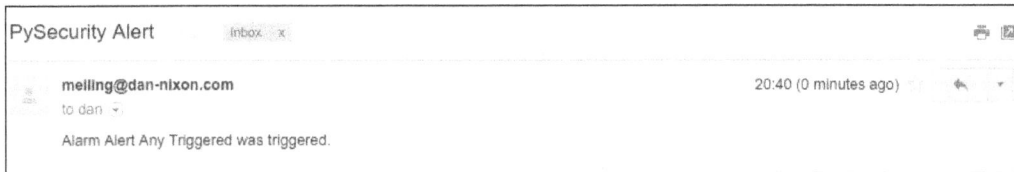

Interfacing sensors

The two sensors we will use in this project are fairly simple to interface with Arduino, as both use a simple digital signal. We will now look at the electrical connection between the sensors and Arduino and the configuration required in the Arduino code for each sensor.

In the code for the sensor nodes (the `rf_network/SensorNode_Arduino` directory), there are two important variables related to the configuration of sensors on a given node: `NUM_SENSORS` and `sensors`. The first is a count of how many sensors are attached to the current sensor node and the second is an array of configurations for each sensor.

The configuration for each sensor is stored in a struct with the following initialization:

```
{"MQTT_TOPIC", PIN, ACTIVE_LOW, PULL_UP}
```

Here, `MQTT_TOPIC` is the MQTT topic where the changes to the state of the sensor will be published, `PIN` is the Arduino IO pin the sensor is connected to, and `ACTIVE_LOW` shows whether the sensor should be considered as triggered when the input is low. If this is the case, this should be set to 1, otherwise 0. `PULL_UP` dictates whether the internal pull up resistor should be activated for the sensor; if so, this should be set to 1, otherwise 0.

The PIR motion sensors

The PIR motion sensors have three wires: ground, power, and signal, where the signal output is high when motion is detected in the field of view of the sensor.

These sensors operate by detecting a relative change in temperature across the field of view of the sensor. This is done by positioning the two infrared detectors at slightly different angles from the lens. When a temperature change occurs, the voltage across the two sensors relative to each other changes, which is then processed on the sensor that is to be converted into a digital output.

If you look from the top of the sensor (that is, with the lens facing towards you), the three wires are ground, power, and signal from left to right. The signal wire is indicated with a grey stripe along it.

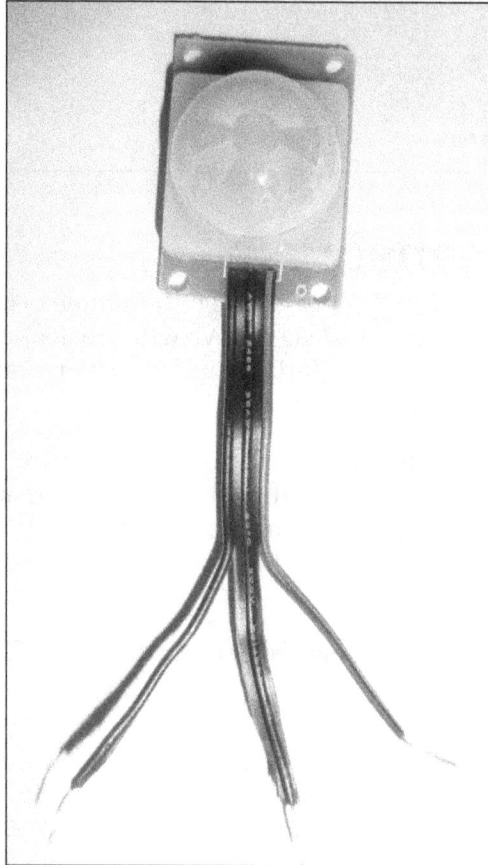

To wire this up to Arduino, connect the ground wire to an Arduino pin marked GND, send power to either the Arduino pin marked as +5 V or Vin and the signal wire to any unused digital input (any, from 2 to 8).

> Note that if you plan to power the Arduino sensor node using a power supply higher then 5 V, then you should connect the PIR sensors power wire to +5 V and not Vin. Supplying the sensor with more than 5 V may cause permanent damage to Arduino or the power supply.

Within the Arduino code, a PIR sensor should be added with the value of ACTIVE_LOW and PULL_UP set to 0.

Magnetic door sensors

This sensor can be used to determine when two objects, commonly a door and its frame, move apart. This is simply a reed switch and magnet, therefore all that is required to use this sensor is to detect when a digital input signal level changes.

Although there are four wires coming from the sensor, only two are needed for our usage. These two have the ends of the wire stripped, revealing a section of the conductor, and are slightly longer than the other two. The two unnecessary wires can be cut off if desired.

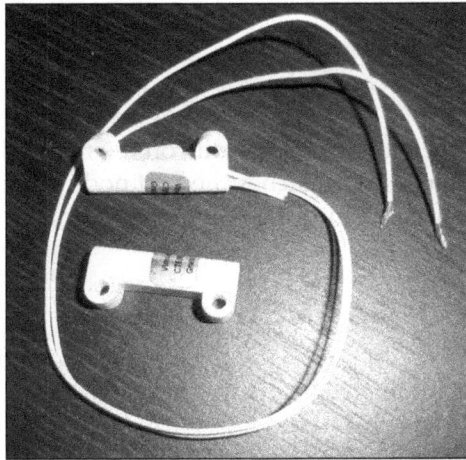

Within the Arduino code, a magnetic door sensor should be added with the value of ACTIVE_LOW set to 0 and PULL_UP set to 1.

The RF network

The RF network that will be used for the sensor nodes is provided by the RF24Network library (https://github.com/TMRh20/RF24Network). This allows RN nodes to be networked in a tree structure in which each node can have up to five child nodes, since each individual node can listen to up to six other nodes at once.

As such, the addresses for the nodes are octal and follow the structure, as shown in the following diagram, where 000 is always the base node, 001 is a child of the base node, 021 is a child node of 001, and so on:

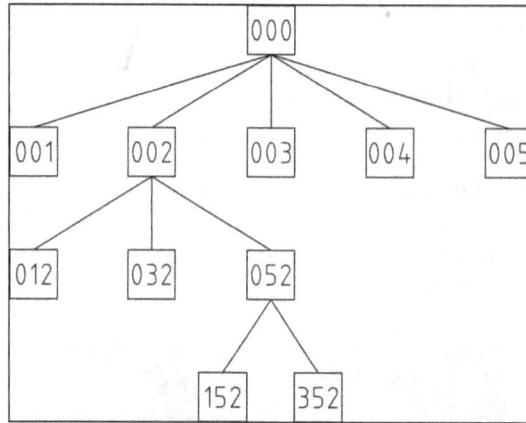

This allows a message to be passed to any node on the network by first transmitting it upwards through the tree until it reaches the first node that is a common path for both the sending and receiving node.

Setting up the Raspberry Pi

To set up the Pi as the base node for the RF network, we must first connect the RF module to the GPIO port and install the drivers that will allow us to receive messages send to it by using a Python script. To do this, perform the following steps:

1. First, start by wiring the module to the GPIO port using the following wiring diagram:

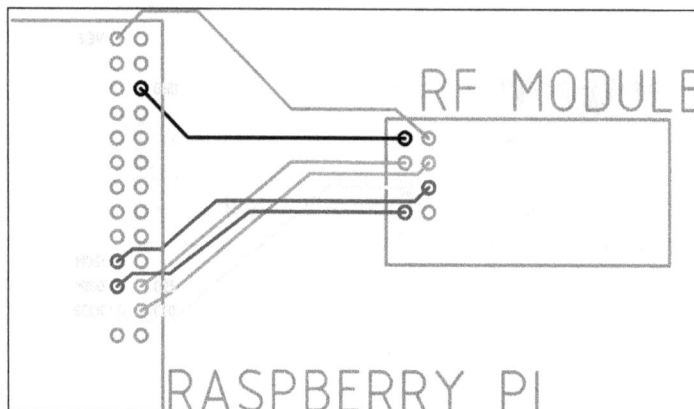

2. Next, install the driver for the RF module. This is the driver that allows basic point-to-point communication using the RF modules:

```
sudo apt-get install libboost-python-dev git
git clone https://github.com/TMRh20/RF24.git
cd RF24
sudo make install
cd RPi/pyRF24
sudo python setup.py install
```

3. Now that the driver is installed, return to the home directory:

```
cd
```

4. Next, we will install the RF network driver. This is the network layer that provides the tree network routing:

```
git clone https://github.com/TMRh20/RF24Network.git RFNetwork2
mv RFNetwork2/RPi/RFNetwork ~
cd RFNetwork
sudo make install
cd RF24Network2/RPi/pyRF24Network
sudo python setup.py install
```

5. Once the two libraries are installed, you will need to copy the BaseNode_RPi.py script from the rf_network directory in the files for this project to the home directory on the Pi.

6. Now that the drivers for both the module and the network layer are installed, we can test the base node script using the following command:

```
sudo python BaseNode_RPi.py localhost 1338
```

This should give an output similar to the following. If you see a repeating pattern in the configuration data or all the bits are set to the same value, then you may have an issue with the wiring between the RF module and the Pi.

```
pi@raspberrypi ~ $ sudo python BaseNode_RPi.py localhost 1883
=============== SPI Configuration ================
CSN Pin               = CE0 (PI Hardware Driven)
CE Pin                = Custom GPIO25
Clock Speed           = 8 Mhz
=============== NRF Configuration ================
STATUS                = 0x0e RX_DR=0 TX_DS=0 MAX_RT=0 RX_P_NO=7 TX_FULL=0
RX_ADDR_P0-1          = 0xf0f0f0f03c 0xf0f0f0f05a
RX_ADDR_P2-5          = 0x69 0x96 0xa5 0xc3
TX_ADDR               = 0xe7e7e7e7e7
RX_PW_P0-6            = 0x20 0x20 0x20 0x20 0x20 0x20
EN_AA                 = 0x3f
EN_RXADDR             = 0x3f
RF_CH                 = 0x5a
RF_SETUP              = 0x07
CONFIG                = 0x0f
DYNPD/FEATURE         = 0x00 0x00
Data Rate             = 1MBPS
Model                 = nRF24L01+
CRC Length            = 16 bits
PA Power              = PA_MAX
```

Assuming that the output of the script was similar to the previous screenshot (such that the values are not all 0x00 or 0xFF), we can go ahead and configure the base node script to start when the Pi boots. To do so, perform the following steps:

1. Open the rc.local file in nano:

   sudo nano /etc/rc.local

2. Add the following line to the end of the file, just before the exit 0 line:

   python /home/pi/BaseNode_RPi.py localhost 1883

   This is shown in the following screenshot:

```
  GNU nano 2.2.6                                            File: /etc/rc.local

#!/bin/sh -e
#
# rc.local
#
# This script is executed at the end of each multiuser runlevel.
# Make sure that the script will "exit 0" on success or any other
# value on error.
#
# In order to enable or disable this script just change the execution
# bits.
#
# By default this script does nothing.

# Print the IP address
_IP=$(hostname -I) || true
if [ "$_IP" ]; then
  printf "My IP address is %s\n" "$_IP"
fi

python /home/pi/BaseNode_RPi.py localhost 1883

exit 0
```

Once this is complete, reboot the Pi to run the base node and web application on boot. This completes the configuration that needs to be done on the Pi.

Setting up Arduino

It's now time to program each of the RF nodes that will be used in the sensor network. We can program these using the code in the `rf_network/SensorNode_Arduino` directory in the files for this project and the Arduino IDE.

You should already have the Arduino IDE installed from when it was used in a previous chapter. However, we first need to download some additional libraries for the RF module:

1. The two libraries needed can be downloaded from `https://github.com/TMRh20/RF24` and `https://github.com/TMRh20/RF24Network`. You will see the **Download ZIP** option at the right-hand side bar of the website.

2. Once these are downloaded, extract both the archives and place them into the `sketchbook/libraries` directory. The sketchbook directory is where the Arduino IDE stores saved code files by default and where it searches for third-party libraries. By default, this folder is in your home directory.

   When doing this, ensure that the program used to unzip the archives does not create an additional directory (this is known to happen when you unzip them with Windows Explorer). The directory structure should be similar to that shown in the following screenshot:

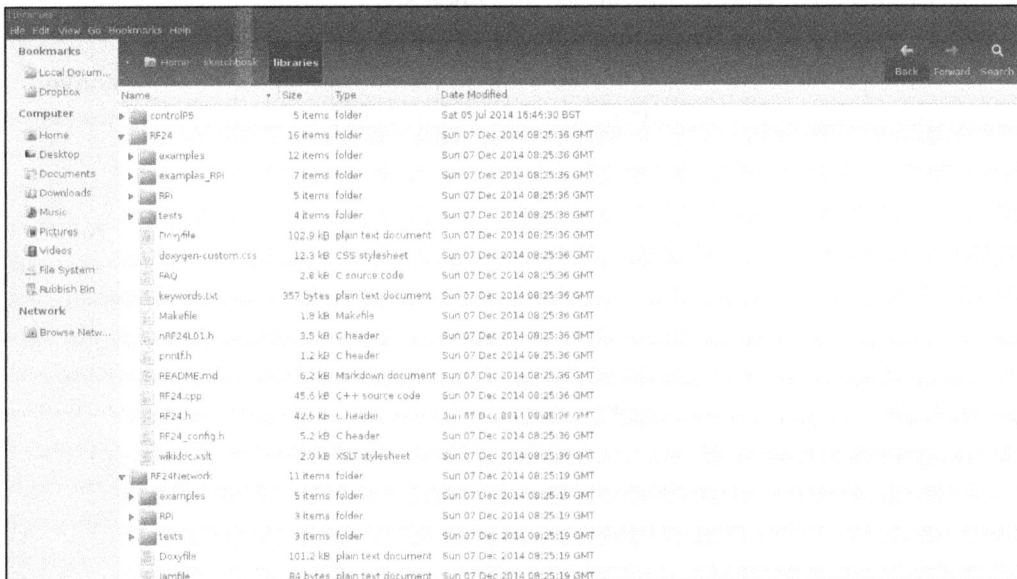

3. Next, we will connect an RF module to each Arduino that we will use as a sensor node. This should be done by following the next diagram and when the Arduino is not powered:

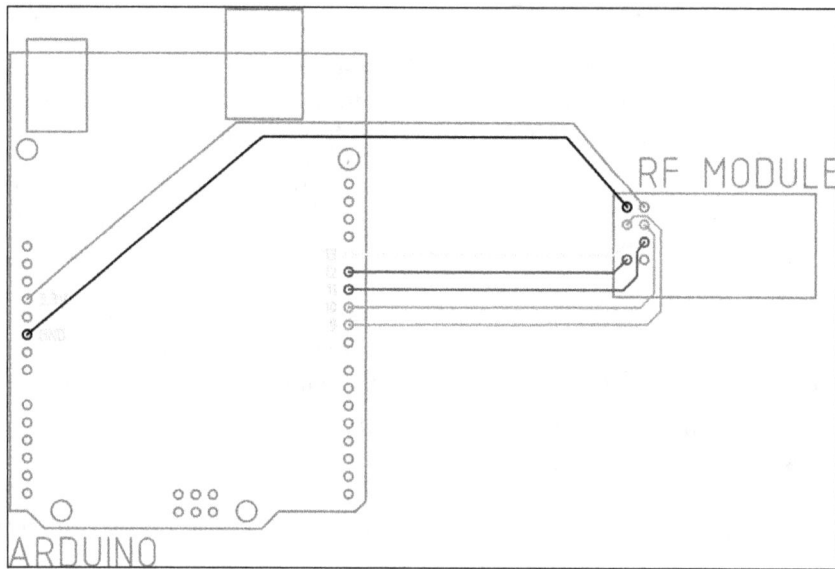

Next, using the following steps, program each Arduino by using the sensor node code based on the system structure diagram given earlier in this chapter:

1. Connect the Arduino to your PC and open an unmodified version of the `SensorNode_Arduino.ino` code in the Arduino IDE.

2. Change the `THIS_NODE_ADDR` variable to the address of the node you have connected. Note that having `0` at the start of the address is required, that is, if the address is 23, you must use `023` as the value.

3. Set the NUM_SENSORS and sensors variables as described in the *Interfacing sensors* section.

4. If you program the nodes in order of their position away from the base node (for example, 002, 012, and 003), you will be able to test each node as you program it. This is as simple as opening the events page on the web application and verifying that new events show up for the sensor when it is changed. If this does not happen, refer to the *Troubleshooting* section

5. Assuming that the sensor node works as intended, you can now disconnect the node from your PC. Although, if you wish to keep testing additional nodes, you will need to power the node externally.

Once all the sensor nodes are programmed and tested, they can be installed in their intended positions. I found that Blu-Tack is a good temporary fix for the nodes that are to be placed above the doors.

The sensor node with a door switch and PIR sensor installed above a door frame using Blu-Tack

Troubleshooting

If you find that a sensor node is not updating the security web application when the sensors are triggered, you may need to first check the wiring and configuration of the sensor node. Do this to check whether the sensor node has a valid address and that it is trying to connect to a parent node that exists on your network (refer to the start of *The RF network* section).

If this does not seem to be the issue, then you may simply be out of range of the sensors or have a signal integrity issue caused by other devices using the same frequency range. If you suspect this to be the case, you can try changing the value of the CHANNEL variables in the BaseNode_rPi.py and SensorNode_Arduino.ino code files. This value sets the frequency that the RF module operates on. The frequency can be derived by $f = 2400 + CHANNEL\ MHz$.

Hence, the default value of 90 gives a frequency of 2.49 GHz. The RF module can operate anywhere between 2.4 GHz and 2.525 GHz.

Summary

In this chapter, we gained more experience with expanding the Pi's hardware capability by adding additional means of communication to it and adding hardware using a new protocol, that is, SPI.

Arduino also played a large part in this chapter and has helped to provide an example of a wide range of hardware that could possibly be used with the Pi. Even if a sensor, motor, or other device cannot be controlled directly from the Pi, it is almost guaranteed that there is an additional piece of hardware that can sit between the Pi and the device and allow control of the device from the Pi.

We also had a more in-depth look at the type of web applications that can be created using Python and Flask and introduced quite a few new features into the security web application over the application made in the previous chapter.

We will continue to explore the way web applications can be used as an input method for the Pi and control physical hardware in the later chapters in this book by using several new ways of interfacing custom electronics.

8
Remote-operated Robotic Arm

In this chapter, we will use the Raspberry Pi to create a simple robotic arm actuated with several micro servos mounted on a movable base using two motors. All of these will be controlled through a web interface via the Pi GPIO port.

We will also mount the camera module at the front of the base and stream it to the web interface, enabling a full remote operation.

What you will need

This is a list of the parts that you will need to complete this project. Most of them will be available at either a local electronic components store or an online retailer:

- The Raspberry Pi
- A 3 mm MDF (600 x 600 mm)
- M3 and M4 screws, washers, and nuts
- The M3 threaded bar
- 4x micro servos (www.amazon.co.uk/Vktech-MG90S-Geared-Helicopter-Airplane/dp/B00FF26480)
- Servo extension cables (www.amazon.co.uk/300mm-Servo-Extension-Cable-Futaba/dp/B009REWWGU)
- A relay board (www.ebay.co.uk/itm/New-8-Channel-5V-Relay-Module-Board-for-Arduino-PIC-AVR-MCU-DSP-ARM-UK-/151105724470)
- Geared motors (www.rapidonline.com/Electrical-Power/950d5001-Gearbox-and-Motor-500-1-6mm-Shaft-6-15v-37-1114)

- 0.1 inch pin headers
- 0.1 inch female-to-female pin jumper wires
- 0.1 inch male-to-female pin jumper wires
- A 18 AWG wire
- Thick copper wire
  (www.clasohlson.com/uk/Copper-Wire-1.2-mm/30-5028)
- A small section of a prototyping board
  (www.maplin.co.uk/p/veroboard-copper-stripboard-100x160mm-a62rl)
- A 9 V battery
- A 9 V battery clip (www.maplin.co.uk/p/pp3-snap-battery-clip-hf28f)
- A USB power bank (www.maplin.co.uk/p/lithium-ion-6000mah-portable-power-bank-n481k)
- The 38 mm version of a castor (www.clasohlson.com/uk/Swivel-Castors/Pr309743000)
- An old USB cable
- The Raspberry Pi camera module

Drive electronics

The first step is to wire up and configure the drive electronics and motors that will move the various parts of the robot arm; this will consist of four micro servos that will move the arm, and two geared motors that will provide drive to the chassis.

The servos are powered by a 5 V power supply and can be driven using a pulsed digital signal (through **Pulse Width Modulation (PWM)**) from the Pi GPIO ports, which define the position that the arm of the servo is to be kept in.

The motors will be driven using a relay board, which allows the Pi GPIO port to switch the higher currents needed to power the motor. This is just one of the many ways this can be done. Another possibility is to use a MOSFET H-bridge, which will also allow control of the speed of the motors. However, the relay solution is simpler in both code and electronic construction, so it will be used here.

The wiring for the drive electronics is shown in the following diagram:

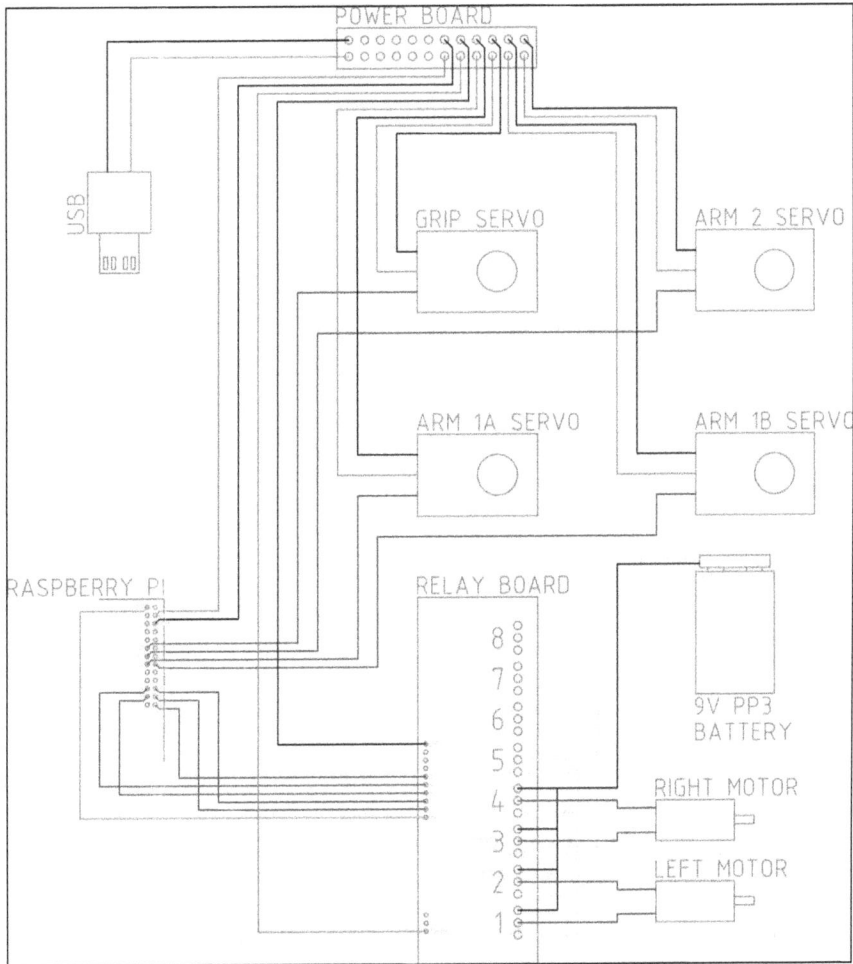

The wiring of the Pi GPIO header is shown in greater detail in the following diagram:

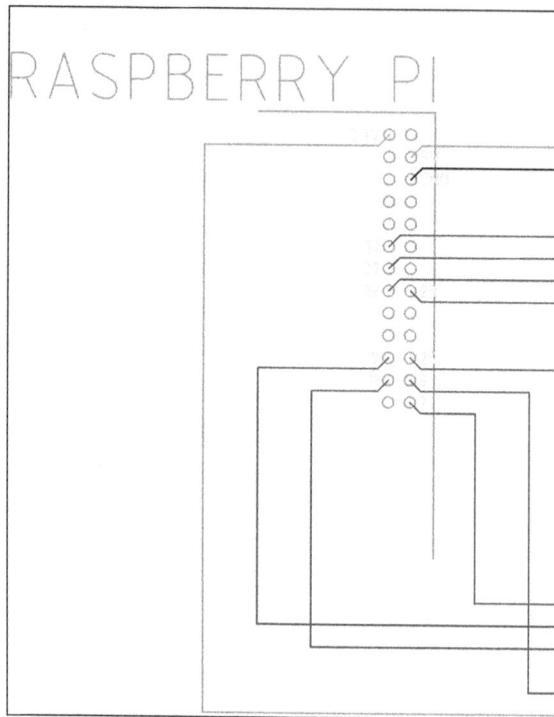

We will start by constructing the power board; this is simply two sets of 0.1 inch pin headers on a small section of the stripboard that will distribute the 5 V and ground power rails. We will need at least seven headers for both the 5 V and ground rails; however, adding more headers will allow possible expansion later.

The board should be laid out as shown in the following diagram:

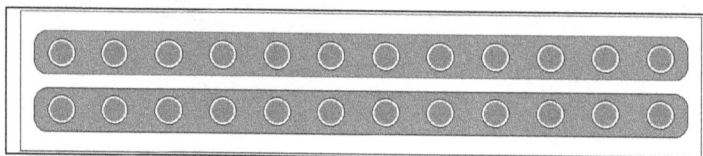

Now that we have all the parts needed for the drive electronics, we can start assembling them to test with the web application, later in the chapter:

1. Solder a 18 AWG wire on to each terminal of both motors, as shown in the following image:

2. Take some more 18 AWG wires and wire up the relay board, as shown in the diagram earlier in the chapter.

3. Connect the motors and PP3 battery clip to the relay board. By now, the board wiring should look something like what is shown in the following image:

4. Remove the small orange pin jumper on the three-pin connection on the relay board; it can be stored by connecting one side of it to the middle pin of this header, as shown in the following image:

5. Now, take the power board and connect the four servos to it, as shown in the following image, to provide them with power and leave the signal pin accessible from the side of the board:

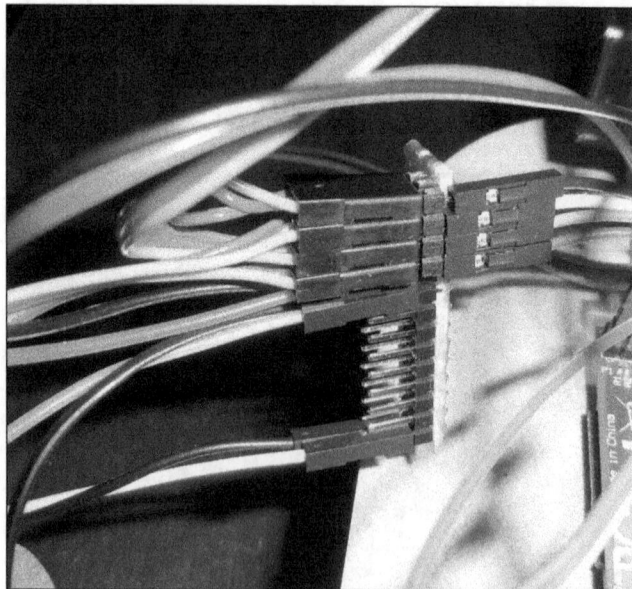

6. Next, take four male-to-female pin jumper cables and connect the servos to the GPIO header, as shown in the preceding diagram.

7. Take the USB cable and cut the cable 10 cm away from the USB A connector.

8. Strip the outer insulation and shielding to reveal four wires.

9. Strip the red and black wires. These are the 5 V and ground power connections that we will use to power the robot arm from the USB power bank.

10. Connect the wires to the two male-to-female pin jumpers using a strip of two terminal blocks, as shown in the following image:

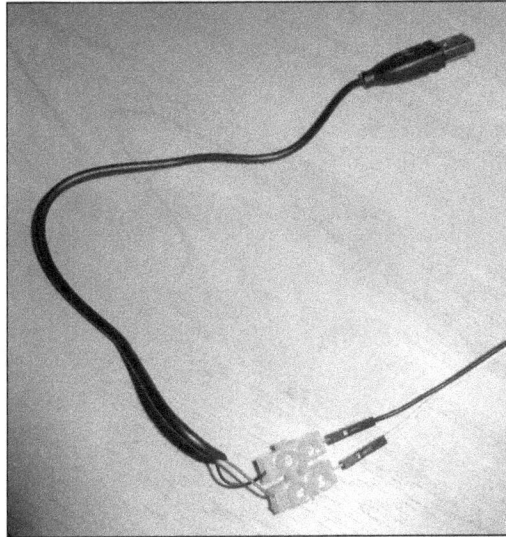

11. Finish off any remaining wiring by following the wiring diagram shown earlier.

Now that the wiring is complete, attach the USB power bank to the USB cable to provide power to the Pi and servos. Ensure that you use the higher output current port on the bank (usually marked as either 2.1 A or used for tablet charging) and connect a 9 V PP3 battery to the battery clip attached to the relay board.

Setting up the camera

There are a few ways in which we could stream a video from the Raspberry Pi camera module to a web page. The easiest of which is to use the **Video for Linux 2 (V4 L2)** driver (which is documented in greater detail at www.linux-projects.org/modules/ sections/index.php?op=viewarticle&artid=14), which includes a server that allows the camera to be controlled and streamed over a network connection.

First, we will connect and configure the camera in the Raspbian OS and perform the following steps:

1. With the power disconnected, connect the camera module to the **Camera Serial Interface** (**CSI**) port on the Pi just behind the Ethernet port. You can do this by lifting the cable clip, inserting the flat, flex cable, as shown in the next image, and pressing down on the clip such that the cable is firmly held in place:

2. Next, boot into Raspbian and run the configuration utility:

    ```
    sudo raspi-config
    ```

3. Select the **Enable Camera** option using the arrow keys and press *Enter*:

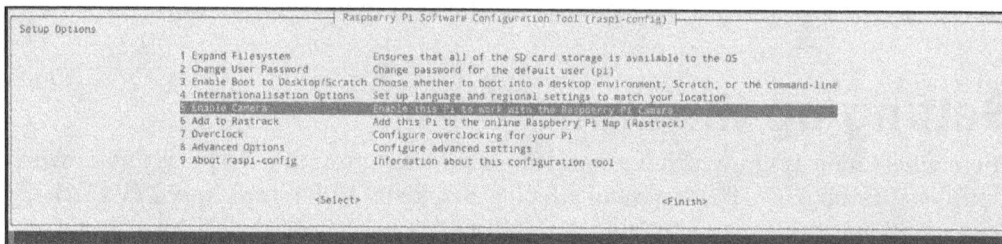

4. Select the **Enable** option and press *Enter*:

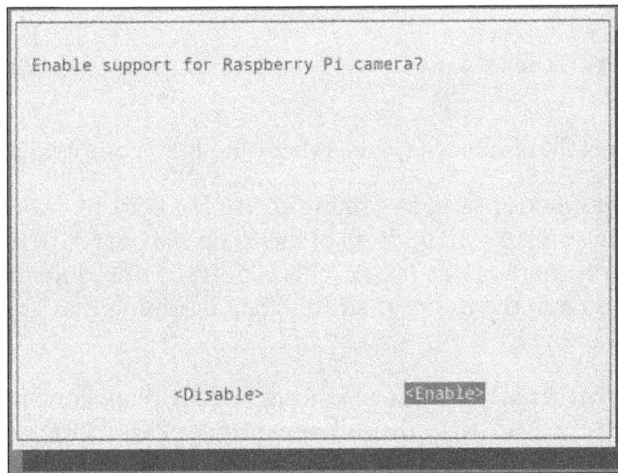

```
Enable support for Raspberry Pi camera?




                        <Disable>              <Enable>
```

5. Exit the configuration utility by selecting the **Finish** option and reboot the Pi.

The Pi camera is now enabled within the OS. We will now install the V4L2 driver with the following steps:

1. Before installing the driver, we first need to add an additional repository to the APT package manager. This manager requires you to download and add an APT key, which is done using the following two commands:

   ```
   wget http://www.linux-projects.org/listing/uv4l_repo/lrkey.asc
   sudo apt-key add ./lrkey.asc
   ```

2. Next, we must add the repository to the list of sources used by APT. This is done by editing the sources.list file using nano:

   ```
   sudo nano /etc/apt/sources.list
   ```

3. Next, add the following line to the sources.list file:

   ```
   deb http://www.linux-
   projects.org/listing/uv4l_repo/raspbian/ wheezy main
   ```

   This looks similar to what is shown in the following screenshot:

```
GNU nano 2.2.6            File: /etc/apt/sources.list

deb http://mirrordirector.raspbian.org/raspbian/ wheezy main contrib non-free rpi
deb http://www.linux-projects.org/listing/uv4l_repo/raspbian/ wheezy main
```

4. Now, we need to refresh the list of packages known to APT and finish by installing the required packages:

```
sudo apt-get update
sudo apt-get install uv4l uv4l-raspicam uv4l-raspicam-extras uv4l-server
```

5. Once the installation is complete, reboot the Pi to complete the setup.

Now that the camera module and streaming server are both setup, the camera can be tested by browsing the IP address of the Pi on the port 8080 using a PC connected to the same network as the Pi. This is done by entering, for example, `192.168.0.56:8080` into the browser address bar assuming that `192.168.0.56` was the IP address of the Pi.

Assuming that the server setup went according to your plan, you should see a web page similar to that shown in the following screenshot. Here, you will see two links: one to view the video stream from the Pi camera and one to configure the camera settings.

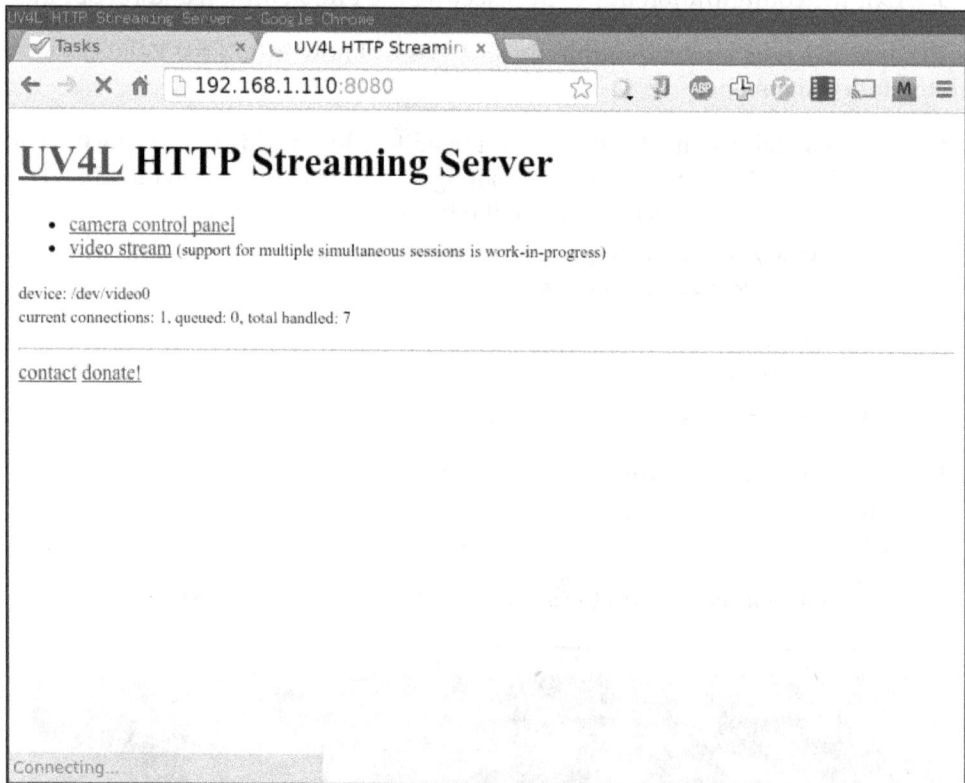

Although we will be able to view a stream straightaway, we will go to the settings page first (shown in the following screenshot) in order to change the capture resolution to increase the frame rate of the video stream.

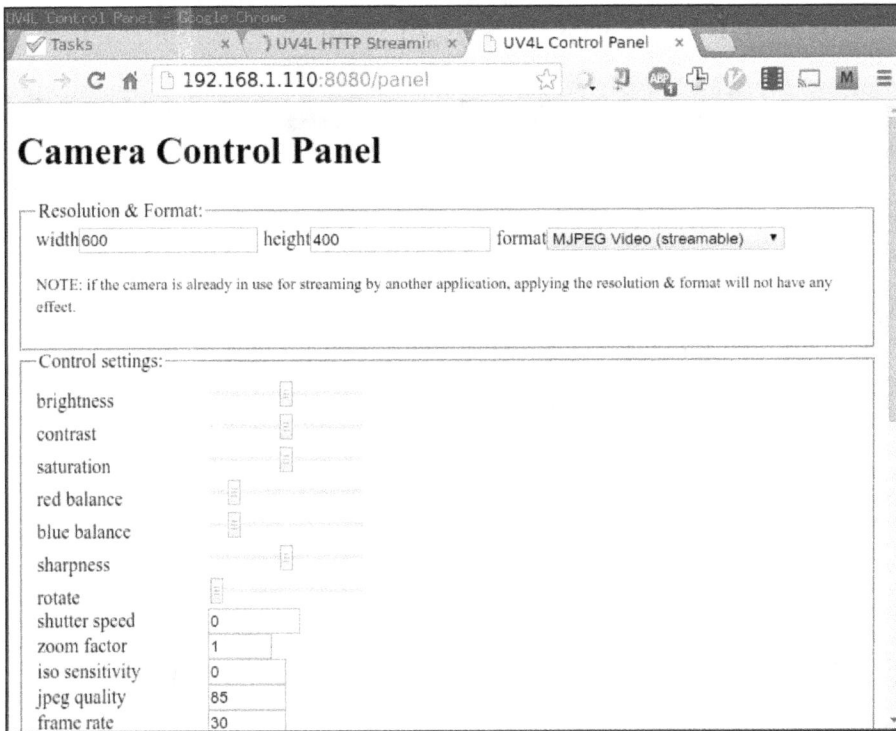

Here, we will change the image width and height options at the top of the page. The optimal values will depend on the network connection being used. However, I have found that 600 x 400 is a reasonable starting point, as this streams well on most connections and gives an image of sufficient quality for which we will use the camera.

To set this, enter the corresponding options in the **height** and **width** fields at the top of the page and click on the **Apply** button towards the end of the page as shown in the following screenshot. Once this is applied, you will be redirected back to the settings page. To get back to the main page, either use the **home** link at the bottom of the page or navigate to the page manually by using the same address we used previously.

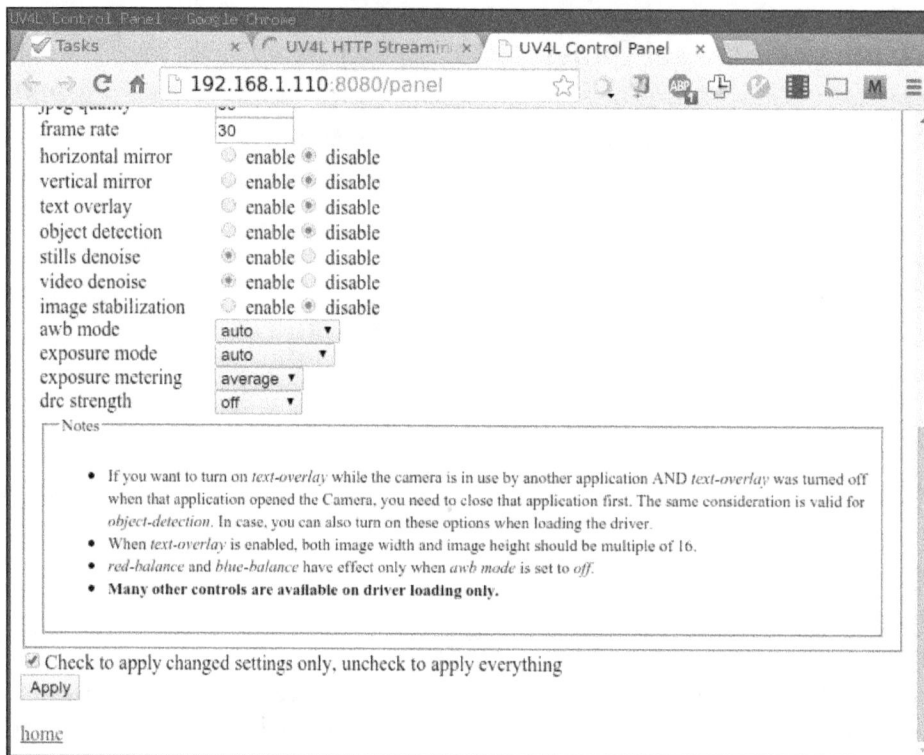

Once you're back on the main page, select the **video stream** link to view the live feed from the Pi camera. The following screenshot displays the main page on which the video is streamed:

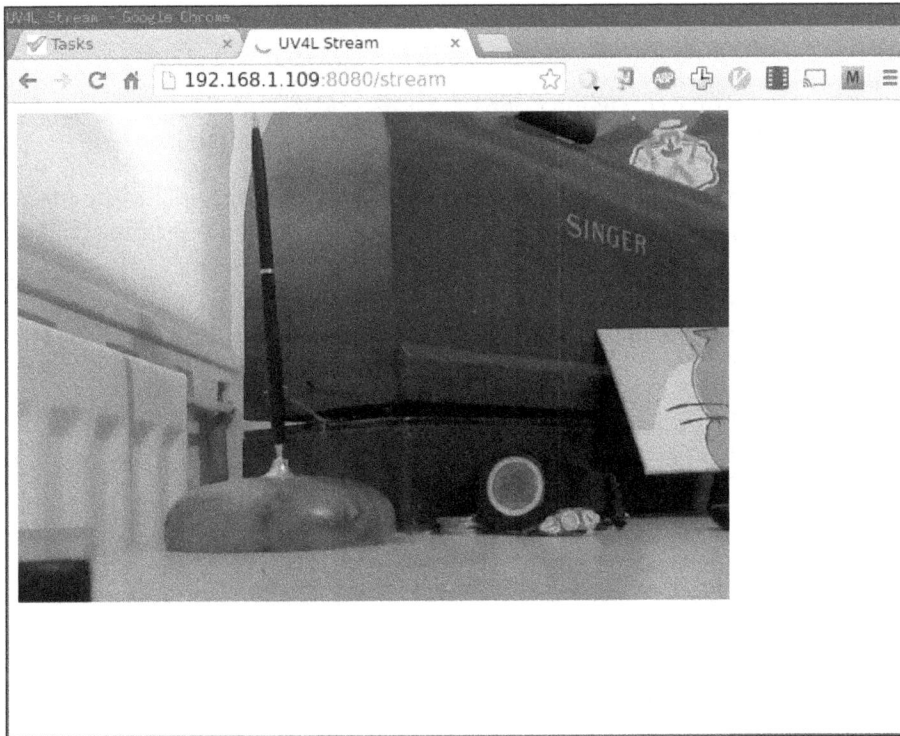

You will notice some delay between the movement in the front of the camera and it being displayed on the web page. This is caused by overheads in the streaming protocol and the network the Pi and computer are connected to. Unfortunately, there is little that can be done about this, however, I have only ever managed to measure at most three seconds of delay.

Deploying web applications

Next, we will deploy the web application that will allow us to control the arm and chassis remotely and view the video stream from the Pi camera. Since this web application is also built using the Flask framework, the process of deploying it will again be similar to that used in the previous chapters.

Before we start, be sure to copy the `config_files` and `robot_arm_webapp` directories from the project files to the `/home/pi` directory on the Pi:

1. First, we will install the required packages and libraries, including the RPIO Python library used to control the GPIO pins from Python:

   ```
   sudo apt-get update
   sudo apt-get upgrade
   sudo apt-get install python-pip git python-dev gunicorn supervisor
   nginx
   sudo pip install RPIO
   ```

2. Next, download and install the Flask framework:

   ```
   git clone https://github.com/mitsuhiko/flask.git
   cd flask
   sudo python setup.py install
   cd
   ```

3. Now, copy the Nginx configuration and perform the configuration self-test:

   ```
   sudo cp config_files/nginx/robot_arm.conf /etc/nginx/sites-
   available/robot_arm.conf
   sudo ln -s /etc/nginx/sites-available/robot_arm.conf /etc/nginx/
   sites-enabled/
   sudo rm /etc/nginx/sites-enabled/default
   sudo nginx -t
   sudo service nginx restart
   ```

4. Copy the supervisor configuration and tell the supervisor to reread the configuration files:

   ```
   sudo cp config_files/supervisor/robot_arm_webapp.conf /etc/
   supervisor/conf.d/robot_arm_webapp.conf
   sudo supervisorctl reread
   ```

5. Copy the web application configuration file to the home directory. This defines the calibration settings for the servo positions and the GPIO pins each device is connected to. The GPIO settings should not be changed if the electronics were built by following the wiring diagram. We will look at the calibration values in greater detail later in this chapter. However, it would be useful to open the file and be familiar with the options that are available there.

```
sudo cp config_files/robot_arm.conf ~
nano ~/robot_arm.conf
```

6. Finally, tell the supervisor to start the web application:

```
sudo supervisorctl update
sudo supervisorctl start robot_arm_webappp
```

Now that the web application has been deployed, we can test the electronics and camera streaming through the web application.

The main page of the web application shows the movement controls for the chassis and **piArm**:

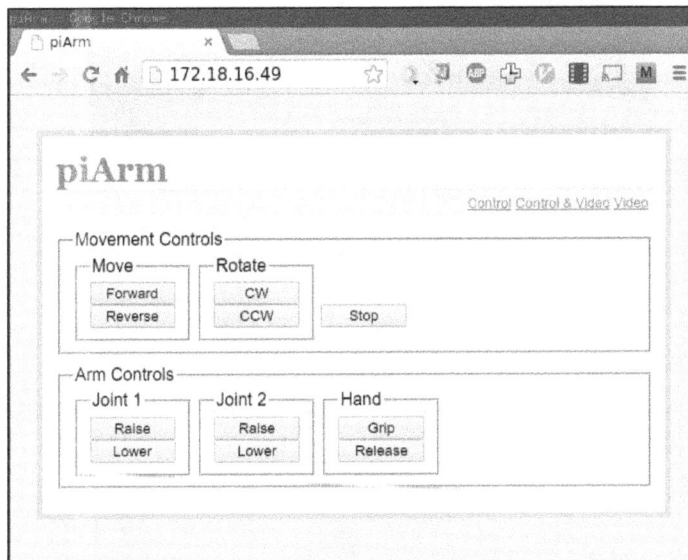

7. First, test the movement controls and ensure that both the motors rotate in the same direction when you select **Forward** and in the opposite direction when you select **Reverse**.

8. Next, ensure that the arm controls move the servos correctly. For **Joint 2** and **Hand**, a single servo should move and for **Joint 1**, two servos should move in the opposite direction.

The video page (accessed using the **Video** link in the top-right corner of the web application) shows the live video stream from the Pi camera module. Below the stream, there is a link to the camera settings page provided by the streaming server. Note that there is no link back to the web application from the camera settings page, so you must navigate back to it manually after following this link.

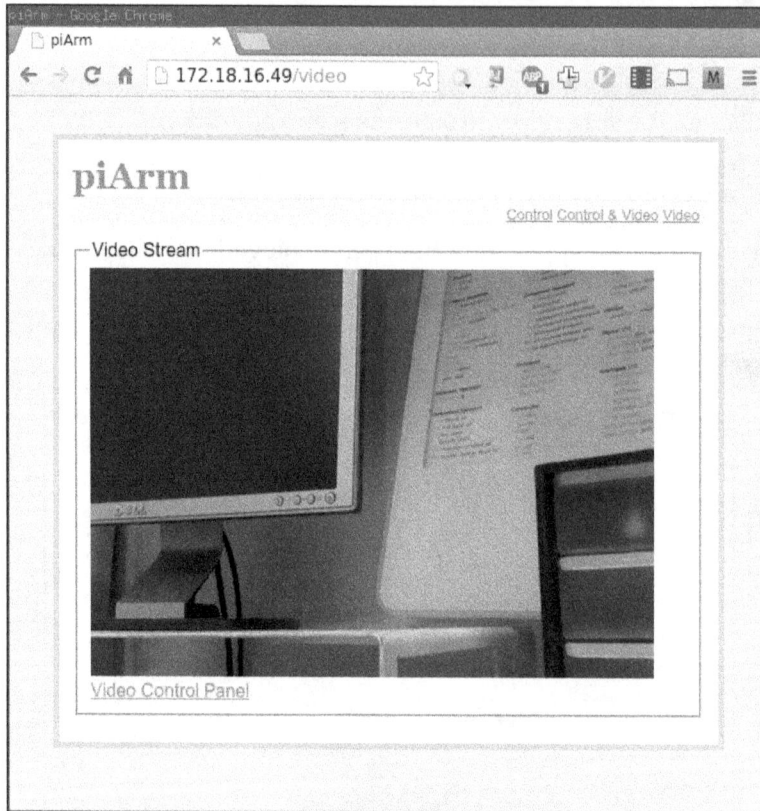

There is also a page that shows both the video stream and controls accessed using the **Control & Video** link in the top-right corner of the web application.

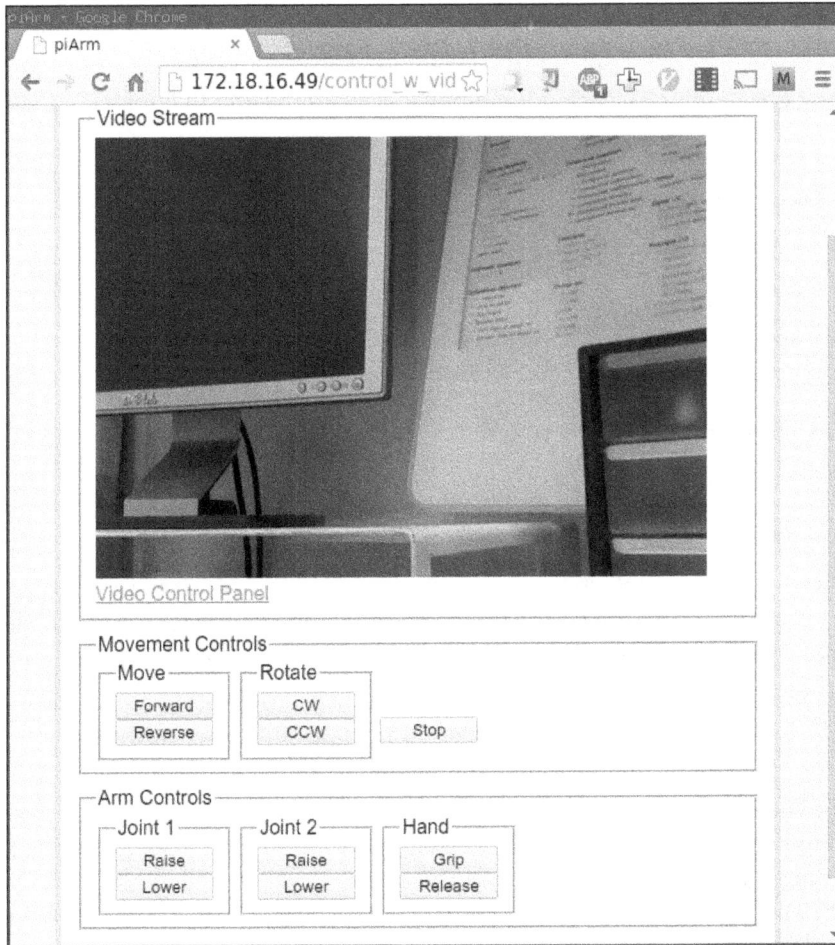

The arm and chassis construction

Now that the electronics are assembled, it is time to assemble the robotic arm and chassis. Firstly, we will go over what parts are needed to construct the robot.

In the `cad` directory in the project files, there are several DXF files for parts that are needed; the following is a list of all the parts that are needed to construct the robot:

- 1 x `Arm1_Main.dxf`
- 2 x `Arm1_ServMount.dxf`
- 1 x `Arm2_Main.dxf`
- 2 x `Wheel.dxf`
- 1 x `Spacers.dxf`
- 1 x `CameraMount.dxf`
- 1 x `Claw_ServoAttachment.dxf`
- 1 x `BaseLayer.dxf`

Once all of the parts are machined, we can start the assembly:

1. First, we need to attach the two geared motors and castor to the chassis base. This is done using four M3 screws and nuts for each motor and four M4 screws and nuts for the castor.

2. Next, we can attach the relay board and the Pi to the chassis base using M3 screws and nuts as well as two of the spacers between the chassis base and PCBs.

3. Next, we will attach the claw attachment to one of the servos, which will be mounted at the end of the second arm assembly. First, use one of the plastic attachments supplied with the servo to manually move the servo to half of its travel (this is to allow plenty of travel on either side of the current position for the calibration step later on).

4. Once the servo shaft is in the correct position, we can remove the plastic attachment and attach the MDF claw attachment. This is done by pushing the servo shaft into the hole in the center of the circle. This will take some force, but will ensure that the MDF has a good grip of the servo shaft.

5. Once the claw attachment has been attached to the shaft, use an M3 washer and the screw that came with the servos to fasten the attachment onto the servo shaft using the tapped thread at the end of the servo shaft.

6. Next, we will attach the servo to the arm 2 section; this is done by first threading the cable through the square cutout in one of the arm sections and using some hot glue to fix the servo into the cutout, as shown in the following image:

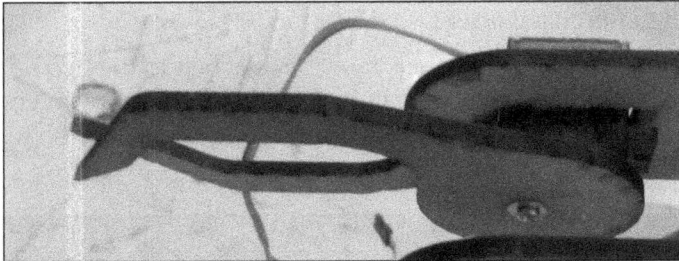

7. Next, we need to cut six 50 mm lengths of M4 threaded bar, which will later be used to assemble the two arm sections.

8. Next, we will assemble the upper arm assembly. Start by assembling the two sections of the upper arm by using two sections of the M4 bar in the first two holes nearest to the claw and space the gap using nine of the MDF spacers.

9. Insert a section of the M4 threaded bar through the two holes at the end of the upper arm section; this will be used to connect to the servo, which will move the upper arm section.

10. Next, we will attach the servo that will move the upper arm section to the lower arm section; again, the servo must first be set to 50 percent of its travel before you do this.

11. Now, attach a single arm to the servo and screw it onto the servo shaft.

12. Attach the servo onto the lower arm panel in the same way as was done with the previous servo, as shown in the following image:

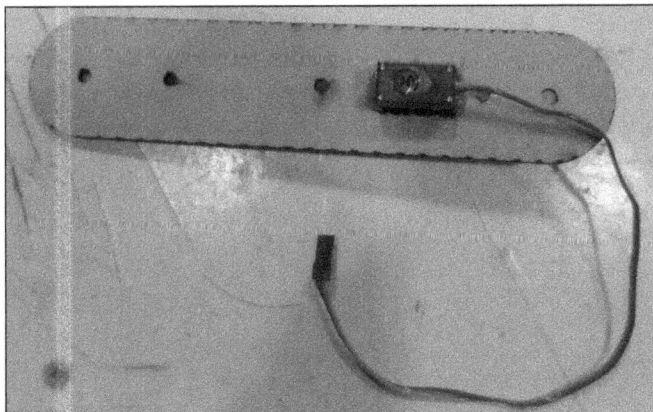

13. Next, we will take the remaining two servos and attach them to the two mounting brackets that are attached to the chassis base. These servos should both be set to 50 percent travel and aligned such that one servo is in the top-right corner of the cutout and the other is in the top-left corner. This is to ensure that the shafts have the best chance of lining up when they are attached to the chassis base.

14. Next, the two lower arm panels must be attached to the two servos. This is done by pressing the shaft into the holes in the lower end of the arm panels and fastening the shaft with M3 washers and the screws supplied with the servos.

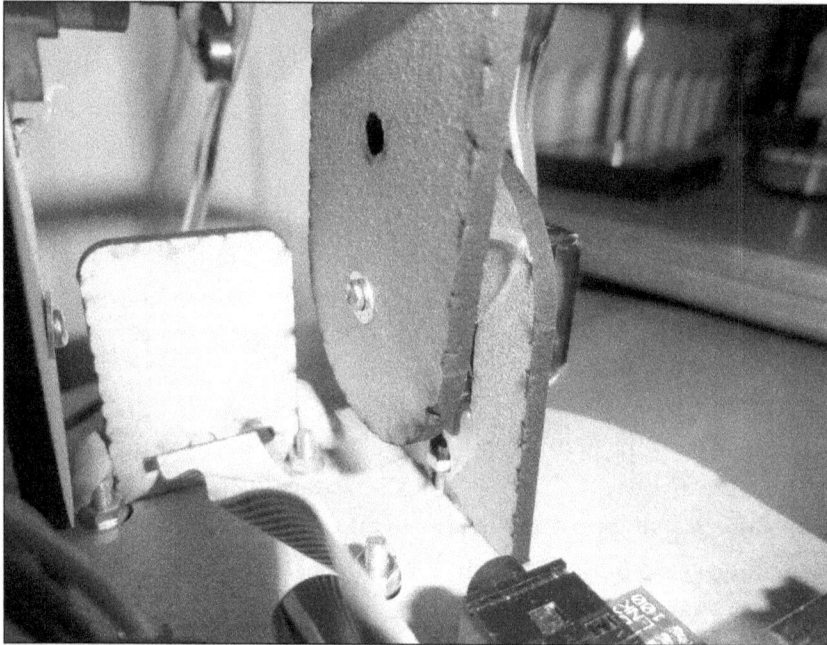

15. Now, the lower arm assembly can be assembled in the similar way to the upper-arm section by fastening the two panels together using two of the M4 threaded bar sections and eleven of the MDF spacers.

16. The upper and lower arm sections can now be joined using a section of the M4 threaded bar, as shown in the following image. Note that this should be a fairly loose fastening to reduce the friction in this joint and therefore reduce the load on the servo.

17. Now, we can attach the entire arm assembly to the chassis base by using an M3 screw on each of the servo brackets, as shown in the following image:

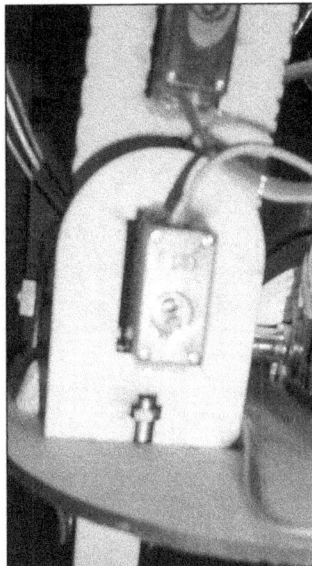

18. Now, we can connect the servo mounted in the lower-arm section to the bar across the upper-arm section using a piece of rigid copper wire. This should be attached to get the desired field of movement on the upper-arm section, which can be measured by manually moving the servo arm.

19. The final step of the assembly is to attach the camera to the mounting bracket; the camera should first be disconnected to feed the flat, flex cable through the slot at the bottom of the bracket, as shown in the following image:

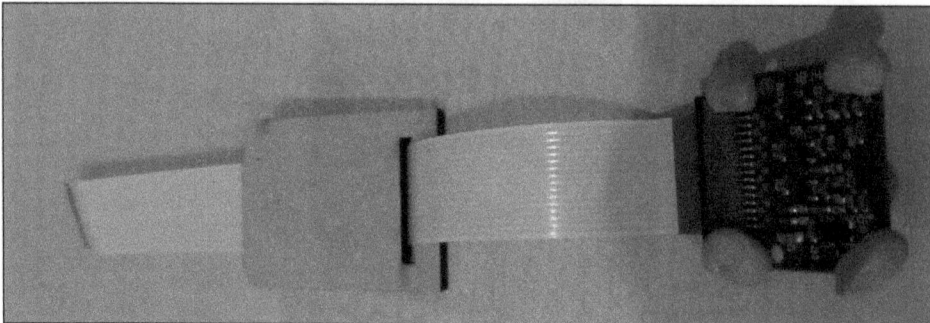

20. Next, attach the camera to the bracket by using small sections of Blu-Tack (this allows us to adjust the angle of the camera to the optimal angle) and place the camera attachment into the slot in the chassis base.

Once fully assembled, the robot should look something like what is shown in the following image:

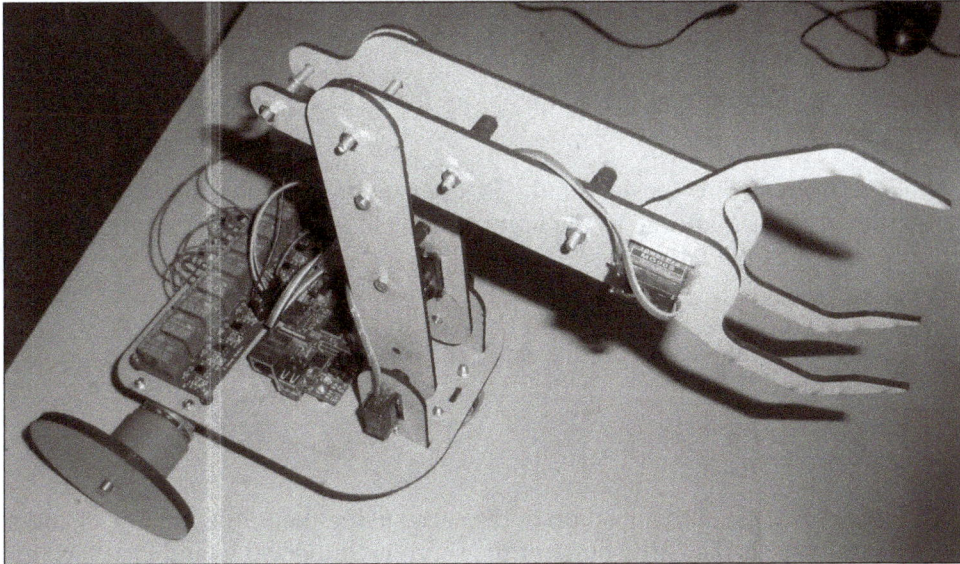

Calibration

Now that the arm and chassis are built, we need to calibrate the motors and servos to ensure that they react in the correct way to the commands from the web application. In the case of the servos, do not attempt to move them too far as this will cause damage to them or other parts of the robotic arm.

Chassis motors

Firstly, we will ensure that the chassis motors behave correctly. This is simply a case of running the motors in each of their directions to ensure that the chassis moves in the direction intended.

When running in forward or reverse motion, if one motor is running in the wrong direction, this can be corrected by swapping the polarity of the motor. You can swap the polarity by swapping the connections on the two wires leading to it from the relay board.

When the motor runs in the clockwise or counter clockwise rotation, if the base rotates in the wrong direction, then both motors need to have their polarity swapped.

Arm 2 and hand servos

Since these two servos operate independently, they are fairly simple to calibrate, as all that needs to be done is to find the limits of the range you want the servos to move in.

To find this, we will use the RPIO library from the Python console to set different values on the servo:

1. First, from an SSH session on the Pi, open a new Python console as root (root access is required as the library needs to access memory directly to control the GPIO pins):

```
sudo python
```

2. Next, import the RPIO library using the following line and create a Servo object:

```
import RPIO.PWM as pwm
s = pwm.Servo()
```

3. Now, you can set the position of the servo using the following line of code, where GPIO is the GPIO number the servo is connected to and VALUE is the timing value for the PWM signal sent to the servo (this should be between 500 and 2500):

```
s.set_servo(GPIO, VALUE)
```

4. Repeat the last step until you find good values for the maximum and minimum values of the servo that give reasonable limits to the motion of the servo.

Once the optimal value has been found, it should be entered in the robot_arm.conf configuration file in the appropriate _MAX and _MIN configuration options.

The arm 1 servos

Since these two servos operate parallely with each other, the calibration procedure is slightly more complex. We must first determine a point on both the servos where they are in equal positions and are not moving to try and cancel each other out.

1. Firstly, open a Python console as before:

```
sudo python
```

2. Import the GPIO library:

```
import RPIO.PWM as pwm
```

3. Next, create two servo objects, one for each servo:

```
s1 = pwm.Servo()
s2 = pwm.Servo()
```

4. Now, set a starting value (VALUE) for the first servo (on GPIO number, GPIO) that is within the range of movement for the lower section of the arm (1500 is a good starting value; however, you may need to experiment to find the best value):

```
s1.set_servo(GPIO, VALUE)
```

5. Now, we need to find a value (VALUE) on the second servo (on GPIO number, GPIO) at which both servos are at rest and not trying to move. This indicates that the two servos are in the same position. Note that you may need to move the arm slightly to stop the servos from trying to move. The weight of the arm may keep the servos in motion even though they are in the same position:

```
s2.set_servo(GPIO, VALUE)
```

6. Once the two servos are in the same position, make a note of the two values (for example, 1400 and 1600) and calculate the midpoint of the two (1500). This value should also be a position in which both the servos will be in the same position.

7. Now that we know this value, we can define the sets function, which will set both the servos to a given offset, allowing us to derive the upper and lower limits for both servos. Here, GPIO_1 and GPIO_2 are the GPIO numbers that each servo is connected to and VAL is the midpoint value calculated in the previous step:

```
def sets(position_delta):
    s1.set_servo(GPIO_1, VAL + position_delta)
    s2.set_servo(GPIO_2, VAL - position_delta)
```

8. We can now use trial and error, as with the previous servos, to find the optimal maximum and minimum servos positions by making calls to the sets function:

```
sets(-300)
sets(0)
sets(1000)
...
```

9. Now that we have the maximum and minimum values that can be passed to the `sets` function, we can easily derive the values that need to be set in the configuration file as (where *VAL* is the calculated midpoint, *SETS_MIN* and *SETS_MAX* are the maximum and minimum values passed to the `sets` function, *SETS_MIN* is negative, and *SETS_MAX* is positive):

   ○ `ARM_1_A_SERVO_MIN` = *VAL* + *SETS_MIN*
   ○ `ARM_1_A_SERVO_MAX` = *VAL* + *SETS_MAX*
   ○ `ARM_1_B_SERVO_MIN` = *VAL* - *SETS_MAX*
   ○ `ARM_1_B_SERVO_MAX` = *VAL* – *SETS_MIN*

Once these values are derived, they can be entered into the `robot_arm.conf` configuration file.

Troubleshooting

The following are a few issues you may come across while building and using the robotic arm, where the causes of the issues and information on how the problem can be fixed.

The video stream has a substantial delay

This delay can be caused if you attempt to stream at too high of a resolution. The first thing to do is to try and reduce the resolution you are streaming at (note that this has to be done every time the Pi is rebooted).

If the issue is still there, then you may want to try reducing the JPEG quality and frame rate options on the streaming server configuration page (which is accessible via the link on the video stream page of the web application).

The servos make a loud humming noise

The servos can often make a loud humming sound when they are under substantial load. Usually, this is the case when the arm is fully extended or is attempting to lift a load. If this continues, an extended length of time will consume more battery power and could lower the expected lifetime of the servos; however, in this project, this behavior is normal operation.

Control of the robot is lost

If the control of the robot is lost, the most likely cause is the loss of the Wi-Fi signal. However, other causes can include low power in the USB battery bank or additional load on the servos that causes them to draw more power than usual (however, this should only ever cause an issue when the battery bank is running low).

The arm jumps to new positions

This can be caused by too many requests to move an axis of the arm in a given direction being sent in a period of time. If you find that it takes too long to move the arm, then consider increasing the value of SERVO_DELTA in the web application configuration file.

Summary

In this chapter, we had a look at yet more ways to interface with hardware over the GPIO port that includes using pulse width modulation, which can be used to drive devices such as the servos used in this chapter. We also took a look at how to emulate an analog signal, which can then be used, for example, to control the brightness of an LED.

We also took a look at the ways in which the Raspberry Pi camera can be accessed remotely using the V4 L streaming server. In the server, the same control and streaming options that are available to the local applications are made available to the devices on the same network.

In the next chapter, we will look at how to use the Pi for a true ubiquitous computing project, which will combine an information display into a fairly standard mirror.

9
Magic Mirror

In this chapter, we will create a mirror that is capable of being both a reflective surface and an information display that can be used to show customized information.

This will be done by taking advantage of the properties of a two-way mirror (commonly used for shop security), which will allow light to pass through it as if it was a glass when the other side is darker and behave like a regular mirror otherwise.

This project is based on the Magic Mirror project by Michael Teeuw. More information about his original version can be found at `http://michaelteeuw.nl/tagged/magicmirror`.

What you will need

The following is a list of things that you'd need for this project:

- The Raspberry Pi
- A USB keyboard (for setup only)
- A VGA monitor
- A 6 mm plywood
- A 12 mm plywood
- A sheet of two-way mirrored acrylic (`www.cutplasticsheeting.co.uk/mirrored-sheeting/two-way-acrylic-mirror`)
- M4 machine screws and washers

Tools you will need

The following is a list of tools you will need to construct the plywood enclosure for the mirror:

- A 25 mm Forstner drill bit
- A large electric drill or drill press
- A jigsaw
- A router and table
- A straight, top bearing, and guided router bit (www.screwfix.com/p/titan-flush-trim-bit-with-bearing-shank-12-7-x-25mm/72588)
- A 4 mm rebate router bit (www.screwfix.com/p/biscuit-router-cutter-no-20-shank-41mm/86179)

Note that here, a router and table are required to machine the plywood enclosure for the mirror, which are both tools that you may not have easy access to. If this is the case, as with laser cutting in the previous chapters, a good place to start would be to look for a local hacker space, which would likely have these tools and members who would be happy to help you use them.

The router bits I have lined here are for a 1/2 inch shank, which must fit the router you intend to use. If your router can only find 1/4 inch shank, then you will need to find alternative cutters.

If you still have trouble getting access to one, there is an alternative way to build this project that will forgo the plywood enclosure at the expense of some aesthetic appeal of the mirror.

The monitor you select should preferably be widescreen if you intend to use the monitor in portrait mode (as will be done in this chapter). Although it is not required, the build process is made easier if the control buttons for the monitor are mounted on the back of the display.

Theory

The two-way mirror that will be used in this project has an important property. When one side of the mirror is exposed to a brighter ambient light than the other, this light is reflected in the mirror surface and is allowed to pass through to the other (darker) side of the mirror.

Typically, this property is used to control how the mirror is used in security applications, for example, a shop may fit such a mirror between an office and the shop floor so that those in the office can still see what is happening on the shop floor. For this to happen, the office must have very minimal lighting to ensure that the bright light from the already well-lit shop floor passes through to the office and that no light from the office leaks through the mirror, exposing it to the shop floor.

In our project, we will use this property to create a display that shows white text and graphics on a mirrored background by placing a section of the mirror in front of an LCD monitor.

This is possible if you keep the display dark in the areas where the mirror surface should be preserved and use bright white text and graphics where they should be shown instead of the mirror surface. By doing this, you can allow them to pass through the mirror surface provided that the brightness of the display is greater than that of the ambient light in the room the project is in.

For this reason, it is worth noting that this project will not work if the mirror surface is subject to bright sources of light, so it is best to keep the mirror pointed away from large windows or lights.

While searching for a suitable monitor, it is also better to get the highest combination of brightness and contrast ratio possible, as this will allow you to get brighter text and graphics from the display. This in turn will improve the quality of the image on the mirror surface while maintaining a dark background so as not to cause any light leakage where the display should remain a mirror.

The web application

The web application we will use for the mirror is essentially a framework built using Flask, which provides a common interface for individual widgets displayed on the mirror. In order to get the desired effect where the widgets are visible through the mirror, the page must have a black background with white text and graphics. For best results, the text should be as large as possible so that it allows maximum light to pass through the mirror's surface.

Developing a new widget

Each type of widget that can be shown on the mirror is comprised of four files:

- A server-side (Python) script file (`widgets/CLASSNAME.py`)
- A Jinja-style template file (`templates/widgets/CLASSNAME.html`)

- A CSS file (`static/widgets/CLASSNAME/style.css`)
- A client-side (JS/jQuery) script file (`static/widgets/CLASSNAME/script.js`)

Here, `CLASSNAME` is the class name given to the widget that is used in the widget configuration files to create an instance of the widget on the mirror display. Templates for these files can be generated using the following script (assuming that you are currently in the `mirror_webapp/` directory):

```
./make_new_widget CLASSNAME
```

We will now take a look at the demo widget to see what needs to be done if you want to implement your own widgets.

The Python code

The first step to develop a new widget is to create a Python script that will provide the web application with the data it needs to operate. This will have access to the configuration options that are set under the `[widget]` section of the configuration file. The main part of the Python script is the `get_data` function which must return a dictionary that will be made accessible from the widget data web service and translated into **JavaScript Object Notation (JSON)**:

```
from AbstractWidget import AbstractWidget
class DemoWidget(AbstractWidget):
    def get_data(self, config):
        self.logger.info('Getting data for demo widget')
        data = { 'greeting':'No Text Set!' }
        if 'text' in config:
            data['greeting'] = config['text']
        return data
```

Here, you can see the `get_data` function, which takes the widget configuration as a dictionary parameter and returns a dictionary. This is only a simple example that returns a text string taken from the configuration file. However, there is a lot of scope for the additional processing that can be done here (refer to the code for some of the other widgets, for example).

You will also notice that the first line of the function is used to log information. This can be very useful for debugging the application. The log is kept in the `/home/pi/mirror_webapp/mirror_app.log` file and contains the log output from the framework application and each configured widget.

Text can be output to the log at several levels, from least severe to most severe: `debug`, `info`, `warning`, `error`, and `critical`.

The data returned by the `get_data` function is made available on the widget data web service available at `[PI_IP]/widget_data/[widget_id]`. Here, `PI_IP` is the IP address of the Pi and `widget_id` is the widget ID that is given by the filename of the configuration file (that is, a widget with the configuration filename `clock.conf` will have the widget ID `clock`).

The Jinja page template

The web page for the application is generated by Flask using Jinja2 templates. This allows a very simple and clean way of building an HTML structure dynamically.

The first thing required in the file is the `extends` statement, which takes a common section of code used for each widget and adds the contents block to it based on the rest of the file:

```
{% extends "widget.html" %}
```

The next section is the `widget_contents` block. This is where the actual contents of the widget should be written.

Here, you have access to a `data` variable that contains the data returned by the `get_data` function in the Python code for the widget:

```
{% block widget_contents %}
  <p>{{ data.greeting }}</p>
{% endblock %}
```

Typically, you will find that a lot of dynamic content is handled by JavaScript, as once the Pi has booted, the web page will never be refreshed under normal operation. Hence, this HTML generation step is only ever performed once.

> For more information on the Jinja template language, refer to the documentation at http://jinja.pocoo.org/docs/dev/.

The JavaScript code

Since the demo widget does not have any dynamic content, the functions in the JavaScript file are just empty placeholders. However, the main point to be shown here is how the functions are called by the framework.

Firstly, there is a **closure** (a way of limiting scope in JavaScript to get something that behaves similar to a class in object-oriented languages) that defines the widget. This can be used to store instance-specific variables for the widget:

```
var DemoWidget = function() {
}
```

Next, there is a public function that is executed when the page first loads. This is used to get the widget into its initial state (for example, populating a list of RSS items before the next update or setting the time of a Date object):

```
DemoWidget.prototype.init = function(widgetDOM) {
    return;
};
```

The next function is called at intervals of the update_time variable set in the widget configuration file (refer to the *Configuration* section later in this chapter). This should be used to update the contents of the widget so that the mirror keeps displaying new information, for example, refreshing a list of news stories or incrementing the second hand of a clock:

```
DemoWidget.prototype.update = function(widgetDOM) {
    return;
};
```

The widgetDOM parameter given to both the functions is the **Document Object Model (DOM)** of the widget container element. This provides a safe and easy way to access the elements of your widget without having to rely on ID attributes in the HTML.

For instance, to access a certain paragraph element of the widget, you would first assign a class to the element in the HTML template, shown as follows:

```
<p class="news-story-title"></p>
```

Then, you can easily access the element and change its test using the following line of JavaScript:

```
widgetDOM.getELementsByClassName("news-story-title")[0].innerText
= "Hello, World!"
```

> For more information on JavaScript development, refer to the w3schools reference pages at www.w3schools.com/jsref.

The Pi setup

The initial steps to set up the Pi are to get a copy of Raspbian installed on an SD card of at least 4 GB (although 8 GB or larger is preferable), as described in *Chapter 1, Raspberry Pi Pirate Radio,* and if desired, connect the Pi to your Wi-Fi network. This project will keep the Pi outside the display enclosure so that Wi-Fi is only really needed if a wired connection is not available.

Rotating the display

You may wish to rotate the display to use the mirror in a portrait orientation, in which case the video output of the Pi will also need to be rotated. Fortunately, this is done by a simple change to a configuration file:

1. Open the boot configuration file using:

    ```
    sudo nano /boot/config.txt
    ```

2. Add the following line and replace N with one of the options described in the next screenshot:

    ```
    display_rotate=N
    ```

The configuration file looks similar to the following screenshot:

```
GNU nano 2.2.6                                              File: config.txt

# For more options and information see
# http://www.raspberrypi.org/documentation/configuration/config-txt.md
# Some settings may impact device functionality. See link above for details

# uncomment if you get no picture on HDMI for a default "safe" mode
#hdmi_safe=1

# uncomment this if your display has a black border of unused pixels visible
# and your display can output without overscan
#disable_overscan=1

# uncomment the following to adjust overscan. Use positive numbers if console
# goes off screen, and negative if there is too much border
#overscan_left=16
#overscan_right=16
#overscan_top=16
#overscan_bottom=16

# uncomment to force a console size. By default it will be display's size minus
# overscan.
#framebuffer_width=1280
#framebuffer_height=720

# uncomment if hdmi display is not detected and composite is being output
hdmi_force_hotplug=1

display_rotate=1

# uncomment to force a specific HDMI mode (this will force VGA)
#hdmi_group=1
#hdmi_mode=1

# uncomment to force a HDMI mode rather than DVI. This can make audio work in
# DMT (computer monitor) modes
#hdmi_drive=2

# uncomment to increase signal to HDMI, if you have interference, blanking, or

^G Get Help      ^O WriteOut      ^R Read File
^X Exit          ^J Justify       ^W Where Is
```

3. Save the file and reboot the Pi to see the changes:

    `sudo reboot`

    The possible options that can be given for N are:

    - ° 0: Normal display
    - ° 1: Rotate 90 degrees clockwise
    - ° 2: Rotate 180 degrees clockwise
    - ° 3: Rotate 270 degrees clockwise

Deploying the web application

Now that the Pi is set up, we can go ahead with the deployment of the web application on the Pi. Once again, this is a Flask application, so the procedure will be very similar to that used in the previous projects:

1. First, start by copying the `config_files` and `mirror_webapp` directories to the `/home/pi` directory on the Raspberry Pi.

2. Now, we will ensure that the software on the Pi is up to date and install the required software to run the web application (note that the last lines here are Python libraries required by some of the widgets):

    ```
    sudo apt-get update
    sudo apt-get upgrade
    sudo apt-get install python-pip git gunicorn supervisor nginx
    sudo pip install requests pytz feedparser
    ```

3. Next, we will download the Flask code repository and install it:

    ```
    git clone https://github.com/mitsuhiko/flask.git
    cd flask
    sudo python setup.py install
    cd
    ```

4. Now, we will copy the Nginx configuration for the mirror web application, enable it, and restart Nginx so that it starts handling requests for the mirror web application:

    ```
    sudo cp config_files/nginx/mirror.conf /etc/nginx/sites-available/mirror.conf
    sudo ln -s /etc/nginx/sites-available/mirror.conf /etc/nginx/sites-enabled/
    sudo rm /etc/nginx/sites-enabled/default
    sudo nginx -t
    sudo service nginx restart
    ```

5. Next, we will copy the supervisor configuration for the application, which will allow the web application to be served by the Pi, as soon as it boots:

    ```
    sudo cp config_files/supervisor/mirror_webapp.conf /etc/supervisor/conf.d/mirror_webapp.conf
    ```

6. Next, copy the default widget configuration files. For now, we will just use the defaults until the mirror is fully set up and go over the steps to configure widgets and styles later in the chapter:

    ```
    cp config_files/mirror_app.conf ~
    cp -r config_files/widgets/ widget_configs/
    ```

7. Finally, update supervisor to enable the web application:

```
sudo supervisorctl reread
sudo supervisorctl update
sudo supervisorctl start mirror_webappp
```

Once this has been done, you should be able to browse the web application using the IP address of the Pi from any PC on the same network. On doing so, you should be greeted with a page similar to that shown in the following screenshot:

Don't worry if the page looks badly rendered, as the default widget configuration is designed to be shown on a portrait monitor and the font sizes are set relative to the width of the screen. When displayed on the Pi, this looks a lot better.

Setting up Chromium

Now that we have the web application set up, we can move on to install the Chromium browser. We will use the browser in the kiosk mode to display the web application on the PI automatically, when it boots. To set up Chromium, perform the following steps:

1. Firstly, we must configure the Pi to boot straight into LXDE (the default window manager used on Raspbian) instead of a console. This can be done using the Pi configuration utility:

```
sudo raspi-config
```

2. Next, select the **Enable Boot to Desktop/Scratch** option and hit *Enter*.

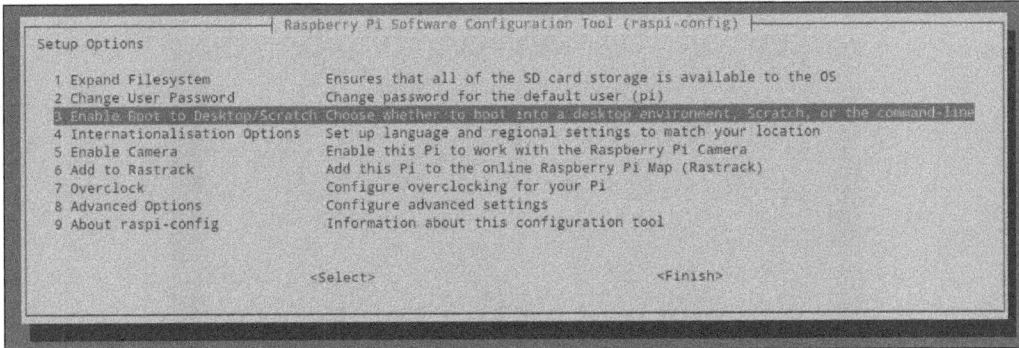

3. Now, select the **Desktop Log in as user 'pi' at the graphical desktop** option and hit *Enter*.

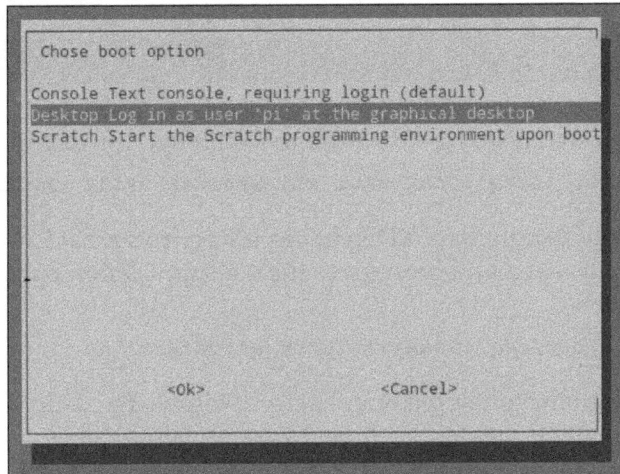

4. Next, select the **Finish** option and when asked whether you would like to reboot now, select **No**.

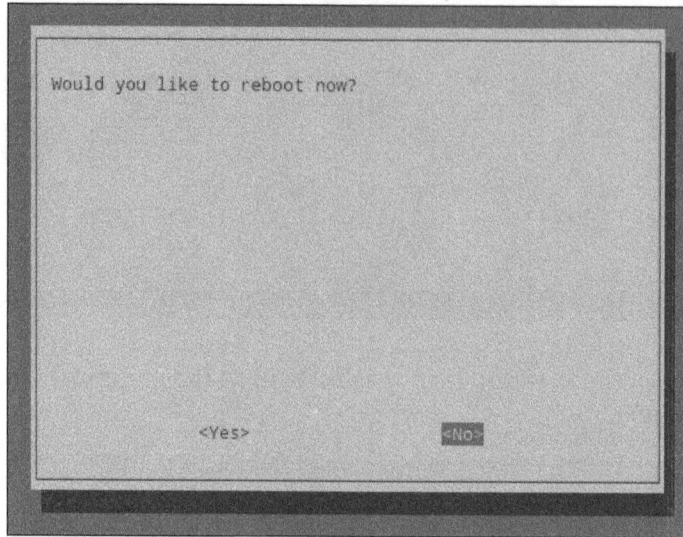

5. Once that is complete, we now need to install the Chromium browser:

```
sudo apt-get install chromium x11-xserver-utils unclutter
```

6. Next, we will modify the LXDE `autostart` script so that Chromium automatically starts and browses to the web application page when the Pi boots:

```
sudo nano /etc/xdg/lxsession/LXDE/autostart
```

7. Comment out the following line. This will disable the default screensaver to ensure that the web application always remains visible:

```
@xscreensaver -no-splash
```

8. Add the following lines at the end of the file. The first three disable the power saving features that would automatically turn the monitor blank and turn it off after a period of inactivity. The final line will start the Chromium browser in a fullscreen kiosk mode and browse to the web application:

```
@xset s off
@xset -dpms
@xset s noblank
@chromium --kiosk --incognito http://localhost
```

By this point, the `autostart` file should look similar to the following screenshot:

```
GNU nano 2.2.6

@lxpanel --profile LXDE
@pcmanfm --desktop --profile LXDE
#@xscreensaver -no-splash

@xset s off
@xset -dpms
@xset s noblank
@chromium --kiosk --incognito http://localhost
```

9. Finally, reboot the Pi to test the setup:

```
sudo reboot
```

All being well, you should see the Pi boot into LXDE (indicated by the Raspberry Pi logo shown on a white background) and shortly after that, Chromium should start and browse to the web application.

Enclosure construction

Now that the electronics and software installation is complete, we can move on to build the plywood enclosure for the mirror. If you do not have access to a router and table for this project, then refer to the *Building the mirror without an enclosure* section described later in the chapter for instructions on how to construct the display without the plywood enclosure.

> When using power tools, proper safety precautions should be taken. Eye and ear protection should always be worn and mains-powered tools should be protected by using a **residual current device** (**RCD**).

First, we need to measure the monitor to determine both the size of the mirrored acrylic sheet that needs to be ordered and the sizes to which the panels for the enclosure should be cut.

The upcoming diagram shows the panels that must be cut out to make the plywood enclosure. Each of the dimensions are given by the following calculations:

- $W = monitor\ width + 24$
- $H = monitor\ height$
- $Wb = W + 10$

- *Hb = H + 10*
- *T = monitor thickness + 9*

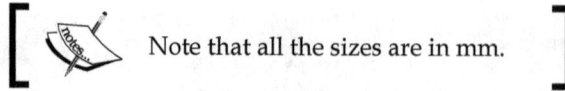

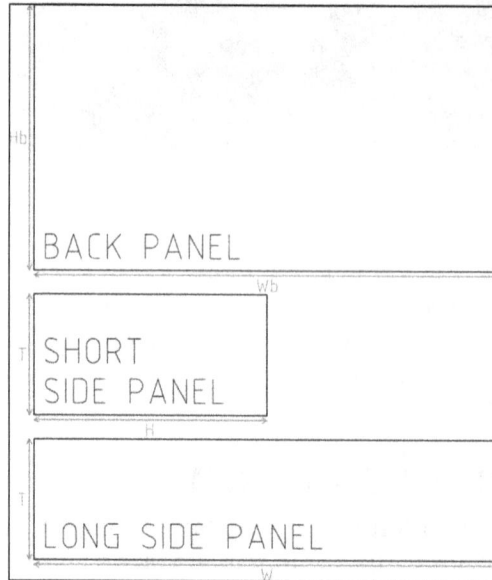

[🖝 Note that all the sizes are in mm.]

To construct the enclosure, perform the following steps:

1. While taking the measurements of the height and width, it is advisable to leave around 2 mm on each side of the monitor, which will allow us to rectify any errors in the measurement while manufacturing.

2. In order to take the next measurement, we must first remove the front plastic bezel from the monitor. This is usually held on with a series of small plastic clips around the edge of the monitor, as shown in the following image. To remove them, use a small, flat screwdriver to prize open the gap between the back of the monitor case and the front bezel. Gradually, work around the monitor until all the clips are released. The front bezel should now lift off with ease.

3. If the monitor has any buttons or LEDs on the front panel, there is likely an additional PCB that must be removed from the front bezel. This usually requires us to unscrew the board.

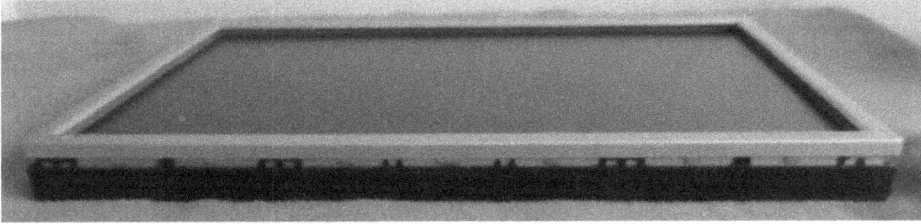

4. Once the bezel is removed, we can now measure the space required inside the box for the monitor. This is the distance from the back of the monitor (specifically the VESA mounting points) to the front (preferably level with the display surface), as shown in the following image. It is advisable to add at least an additional 5 mm to this measurement, as it is easy to add washers to move the monitor forward if the panels are cut too large. However, this is impossible to recover if you cut the panel too small.

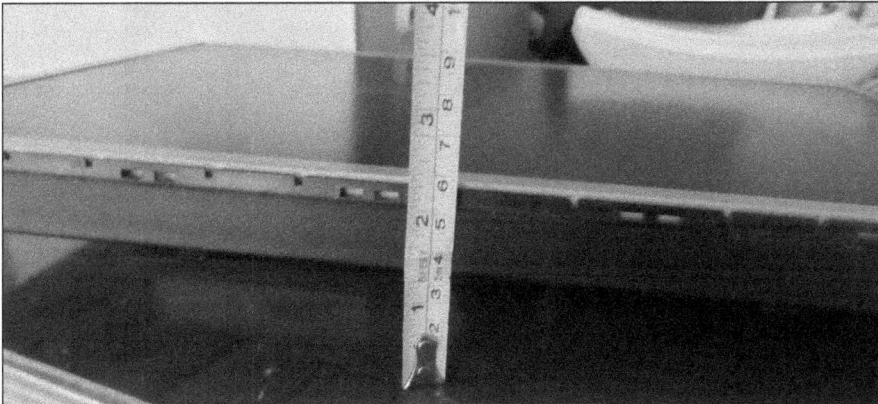

5. Once you have these three measurements, you can substitute them into the calculations shown in the diagram. Using a jigsaw, cut the panels to size. You will need two of both the long and short 12 mm plywood side panels and one of the back 6 mm plywood panel.

6. Once these panels are cut, it is time to cut the slots in them to place the mirrored acrylic. This is done using a 4 mm rebate router bit in a router table, which can be seen in the upcoming image. To do this, perform the following steps:

   1. Firstly, ensure that the router is firmly fixed into the table and the bit is tightened correctly into the router.

2. Next, use the router's depth lock to fix the height of the router, so that the lower edge of the blades are around 4-5 mm above the table.

3. Now, move the fence so that around 5-6 mm of the cutter is exposed on the front of the fence (that is, the cutter can only cut up to 5-6 mm from the material passed along the fence).

7. Once the router and table are set up, it is a good idea to make a few test cuts on a scrap piece of material to ensure that the router is set up correctly. Aim to get a slot that is around 5-6 mm deep into the plywood and around 4 mm away from one edge, as shown in the following image:

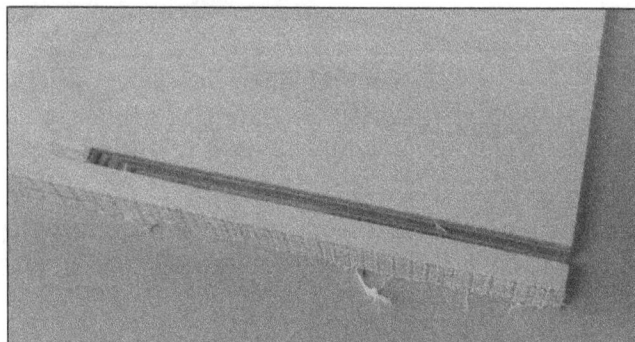

8. Once you are happy that the setup is correct, you can machine the actual panels to end up with a set of panels, as shown in the following photograph. At this stage, it is a good idea to sand the panels with some coarse grit sandpaper to remove any ragged edges left by the router or jigsaw.

9. The next step is to assemble the four side panels that form the outside of the enclosure. This is done using two screws at each end of the long panels that are screwed into the ends of the two short panels. For this, we will use screws that are at least 1 inch in length, but no more than 2 inch. Perform the following steps:

    1. First, we must drill clearance holes into the ends of the two long sides to allow the screw shaft to pass through easily. This hole should be just larger than the shaft of the screw, but smaller than the head.

2. Next, align one of the long panels against a short one, as shown in the following figure, and use the clearance hole as guidance to drill a pilot hole in the end of the short side panel. This hole should be around 0.5-1 mm smaller than the shaft of the screw.

3. Repeat the previous step until all the joints have been fastened, ensuring that the slot for the mirror runs all the way around the inside edge, as shown in the following photograph:

10. The next step is to attach the rear 6 mm plywood panel to the back of the enclosure frame. This can be done using several self-tapping screws around the edge of the enclosure. Note that this panel has intentionally been made larger than what is required.

    1. Firstly, with the enclosure placed on top of the rear panel, draw around the inside of the enclosure to help mark out the positions for the clearance holes so that the screws hold on to the back panel.

    2. Next, using this marking as a guide, drill several clearance holes around the perimeter of the enclosure. Typically, two holes on the short panels and three holes on the long ones should be enough.

    3. Once this is done, drill pilot holes for the screws so that they go into the side panels and attach the back panel to the rest of the enclosure.

11. The next step is to trim the excess material from the back panel (the whole idea here was to remove the need for accuracy while cutting and fitting the back panel). This is done using a straight, bearing guided, router cutter.

    1. Firstly, move the fence toward the back of the router table (we will not use it as a guide here) and fit the straight bit in the router.

    2. Next, using the depth stop, move the router to a position where the bearing is on the same level as the 12 mm side panels, so that there is enough clearance to allow the cutter to remove the excess material on the back panel only.

3. Now, you can machine away the excess material on the back panel by keeping the enclosure tight against the router bit while making a pass along all the edges of the enclosure. Once this is done, the panel should look similar to the following image:

12. The next step is to mark the position of the VESA mounts on the back panel in order to drill the required holes in the back panel. The easiest way to do this is to carefully remove the display assembly from the rear plastic housing, using the following steps as a guide:

1. The display assembly is rarely fixed into the plastic housing by anything other than the fact that it is enclosed by. So, if we give enough force, the display panel and electronics enclosure behind the display panel will be removed.

> Be careful when removing the display assembly as the display panel and electronics enclosure are usually not fixed to each other and excess stress could damage the cables running between the two.
>
> It is also not advised that you apply power to a monitor with the back cover removed as there are potentially dangerous voltages in the rear electronics cabinet.

2. Once this is done, you should be able to place the rear plastic case into the enclosure and easily mark the positions of the four VESA mounting holes.

3. At this stage, it would also be useful to mark the position of the hole that will allow power and video cables to reach the monitor. This hole should be at least 25 mm in diameter so that it accommodates an IEC power connector.

4. Once the holes are marked, you can now put the display assembly back into the rear plastic case.

13. Once the holes in the back panel are marked, the panel can be removed and the holes drilled with the following steps:

1. The four holes for the VESA mount can be drilled using a 4.5 mm drill bit.

2. The 25 mm hole will have to be drilled with either a fairly powerful mains hand drill or, better, a drill press using a Forstner drill bit.

14. Once the back panel has the required holes drilled in it, it is worth giving it a quick sand over by using a coarse grit sandpaper, just to tidy the edge left by the router and Forstner drill bit.

15. Next, reattach the back panel onto the rest of the enclosure using the screw holes made previously.

16. At this point, it is worth powering up the monitor and ensuring that the display is set to fairly high contrast and brightness settings in order to get the best image quality through the mirrored acrylic.

17. Once this is done, feed the cables through the hole previously made for them. Line up the VESA mount with the holes drilled for them and screw the monitor into position.

    If your monitor has buttons mounted on the front panel, you can simply place the PCB they are mounted on behind the monitor within the range of the cable through which they are connected to the monitor.

    Note that if the monitor is too far back in the enclosure (that is, the display surface is more than 1 mm away from the slot for the mirror), then you may need to add some washers and spacers to the screws to move the monitor slightly forward, as shown in the following image:

By this point the enclosure should look something like the following image:

18. The final step is to insert the mirrored acrylic panel into the slot cut for it. This can be easily done by removing one of the short side panels with the following steps:

    1. Firstly, remove the screws that hold the short panel in place on both the long side panels and the back panel and remove the panel.

2. You should now be able to slide the mirrored acrylic panel into the enclosure easily.

3. At this point, you may wish to power on the monitor once more to check whether the display settings leak any light through the mirror panel when the display is black. If so, turn the brightness down slightly.

4. The final step is to reattach the short side panel and the enclosure is complete.

Since the buttons on the monitor are no longer easily accessible from outside the enclosure, it is important to ensure that the monitor will automatically turn on when power is applied to it. This will be the method used to enable and disable the information display on the mirror.

As the enclosure is almost fully enclosed, it is discouraged that you leave the monitor on for a long period of time to avoid excessive build up of heat inside the enclosure. Instead, it is recommended that you only apply power to the monitor when the information display is desired.

If desired, hardware fittings can be used to make the mirror wall mountable. However, for now, we will use ours as a desk mounted mirror only. It is recommended that you place the mirror against a wall to ensure good stability, as its high center of gravity does make it more liable to fall over even if very little force is applied to it. If this is an issue, then you could use it in the landscape mode by changing the display rotation.

Building the mirror without an enclosure

If you do not have access to the tools required to build the plywood enclosure (or would simply prefer a more modern-style mirror) then you can adapt an existing monitor into a mirror relatively simply without any tools. All that is required now is an adhesive.

You may wish to use a temporary adhesive, such as a clear tape or hot glue for this to ensure that the monitor can be reused if you decide to remove the mirror material. Although nothing is stopping you using something like a contact adhesive, such as Araldite, for a more permanent fitting.

1. The first step to construct the display is to measure the size of the mirror material that will be needed. These are essentially the dimensions of the screen that is exposed on the inside of the plastic bezel around the side of the monitor (refer to the following image). Order the mirror material to be cut a few millimeters smaller to ensure that it will definitely fit within the inside of the bezel.

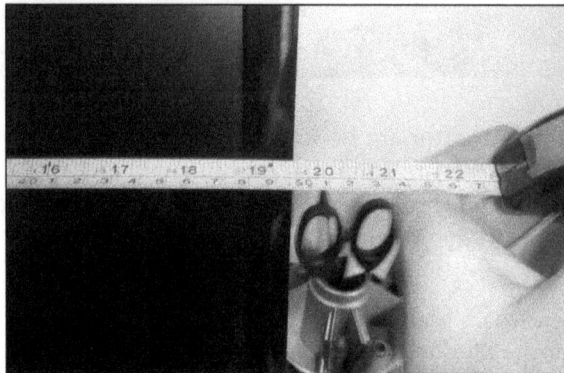

2. Once you have the mirror material, you should find that it simply drops into the bezel with around 1 mm spared on each side.

3. Next, using your adhesive of choice, fix the mirror material into the bezel of the monitor. It is important here to avoid getting adhesive of any type on the display surface, as this can damage the monitor.

The Pi enclosure

Since the Pi is not part of the enclosure we have built, you may wish to keep the Pi in an external enclosure. There are many of these available at online retailers. One of my personal favorites is the Pibow range by Pimoroni (http://shop.pimoroni.com/products/pibow-raspberry-pi-case).

Configuration

Now that the web application has been deployed to the Pi and the display enclosure is constructed, it is time to configure what information is shown and how it is shown on the mirror.

Note that when changing the style sheet, simply reload the page in Chromium by pressing *F5* on a connected keyboard to show the change. Changes to widget configurations will require you to restart the web application by using the following commands:

```
sudo supervisord stop mirror_webapp
sudo supervisord start mirror_webapp
```

Widgets

The widgets are configured using several configuration files in the /home/pi/widget_configs/ directory. Each widget that is displayed on the mirror requires its own configuration file.

The configuration files are divided into several sections: core, ui, position, and widget, each containing several values related to the widget. These options are described as follows:

- core

    ○ class: The name of the widget class

    ○ update_time: The interval at which the UI is refreshed (in seconds; it defaults to 1 minute if the interval not provided)

    ○ title: The title of the widget (can be left blank to hide the title)

- ui

    ○ width: This is the width allocated to the widget (in pixels)

    ○ show_borders: If a border is to be drawn around the widget

- position
  - ° type: This is the type of positioning (top, bottom, left, right, and floating)
  - ° index: This is the number that denotes the position of the widget in a bar (only valid if the type is one of top, bottom, left, and right)
  - ° x: This is the distance between the left-hand side of the widget and the left of the mirror (only valid if type is set to floating)
  - ° y: This is the distance between the top of the widget and the top of the mirror (only valid if type is set to floating)
- widget: This contains configuration information specific to the widget

The effects of the position configuration options are shown in the following diagram:

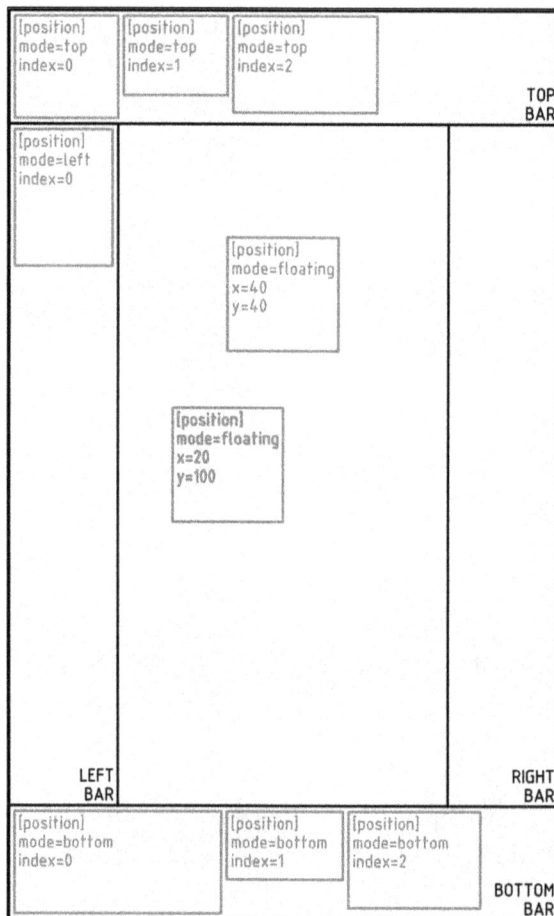

Included widgets

Here is a list of the widgets that come with the mirror web application and a list of their configuration options:

- Digital clock (class: `DigitalClock`)
    - `timezone`: The time zone for which the time is displayed (for example, `US/Eastern`)

- Analog clock (class: `AnalogClock`)
    - `timezone`: The time zone for which the time is displayed (for example, `US/Eastern`)

- Text calendar (class: `TextCalendar`)
    - `timezone`: The time zone for which the date is displayed (for example, `US/Eastern`)

- Current weather (class: `Weather`)
    - `location`: The location for which the current weather conditions are displayed (for example, `Oxford, UK`)

- RSS feed (class: `RSSFeed`)
    - `feed_url`: The URL for the RSS feed
    - `num_items`: This is the number of feed items to be displayed (it defaults to 10 if it is not set)

- RSS headline ticker (class: `RSSTicker`)
    - `feed_url`: The URL for RSS feed
    - `num_items`: Number of feed items to fetch (this defaults to 10 if it is not set)
    - `text_type`: This is the type of text to be displayed (either `title` for a short headline or `summary` for a more detailed description)
    - `ticker_update_time`: This is the time interval shown between new RSS items (in seconds)

Example configurations

Here are a couple of example configuration files with an explanation of what each value does; both are taken from the default widget configuration included in the code for this chapter.

bbc_ticker.conf

The BBC news ticket is shown at the bottom of the mirror using the demo configuration. This widget gives a new headline from the BBC UK news RSS feed every 10 seconds:

```
[core]
class=RSSTicker        #Using the RSSTicker widget
title=BBC UK News      #Give it a title

[ui]
show_borders=true      #Show the rounded borders round the widget
width=450              #Allow the widget to be up to 450 pixels wide

[position]
mode=bottom            #Put the widget in the bottom bar
index=1                #This is the second widget from the corner

[widget]
# This is the BBC UK news RSS feed URL
feed_url=http://feeds.bbci.co.uk/news/uk/rss.xml
text_type=summary        #Just display the short title
ticker_update_time=10  #Give a new headline every 10 seconds
```

clock.conf

The analog clock is shown at the top, in the left-hand corner of the mirror using the demo configuration:

```
[core]
class=AnalogClock      #Using the AnalogClock widget
update_interval=1      #Clocks must have this set to 1 second

[ui]
width=200              #AnalogClock must be set to a width of 200
show_borders=false     #AnalogClock look better with borders disabled

[position]
mode=top               #Put the clock in the top bar
index=0                #This will be the first item

[widget]                #Do not need any configuration here
```

Styles

The global style is configured using the `mirror_webapp/static/style.css` style sheet. This contains the styles that are used in all other widgets and is the easiest way to make alterations to font sizes and layout margins.

> For any configuration that should only affect a single widget, the `style.css` file for that specific widget is a better place to make the change.

The main sections that you may wish to make alterations to are as follows:

- This defines the default style for all the text displayed on the mirror, including the font. If you wish to use an alternative font, this would be the place to make the change (by default, I am using the Roboto font by Christian Robertson):

```
h1, h2, h3, h4, h5, h6, p, li {
    font-family: 'Roboto', sans-serif;;
    margin: 0;
    font-weight: normal;
    color: #FFF;
}
```

- The following set of styles define the size of each of the different levels of text. By default, they use the viewport width CSS size:

```
h1                     { font-size: 5vw; }
h2                     { font-size: 3.75vw; }
h2, h3, h4, h5, h6     { font-size: 3.25vw; }
p                      { font-size: 2.5vw; }
p.small                { font-size: 1.8vw; }
li                     { font-size: 2.5vw; }
```

In `mirror_webapp/templates/mirror.html`, you will also notice the following line at the top of the page. This is used to load the Roboto font from the Google Font service (`www.google.com/fonts`):

```
<link href='http://fonts.googleapis.com/css?family=Roboto:400,100'
rel='stylesheet' type='text/css'>
```

Once the configuration is complete, reboot the Pi and you should be greeted with your customized information display.

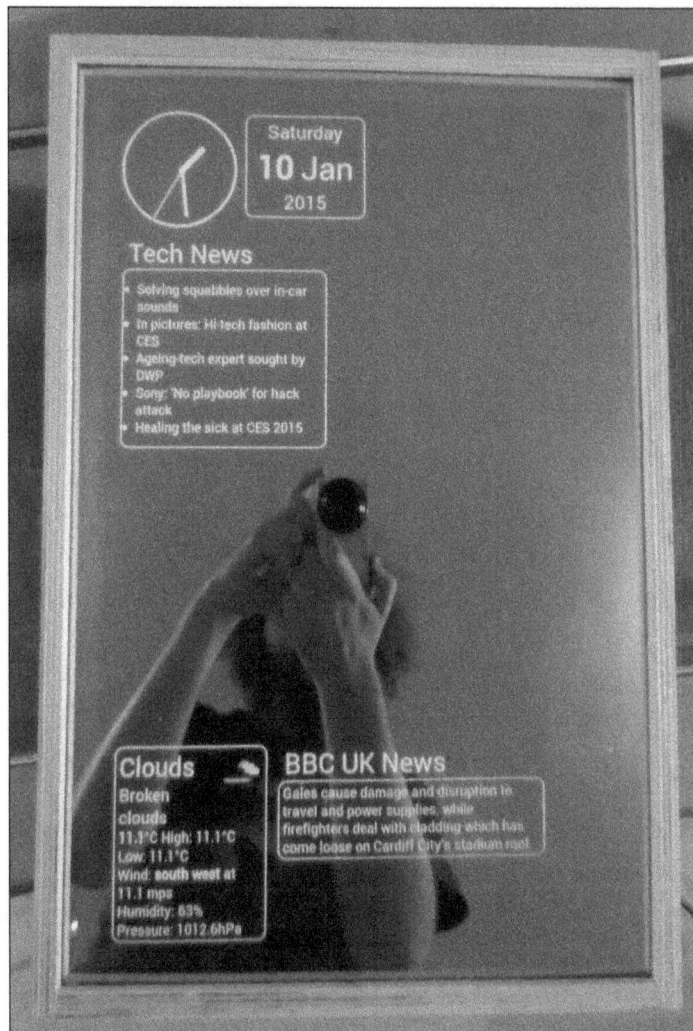

Troubleshooting

This section details some of the common issues you may encounter while building this project and the steps to be taken to resolve them.

For issues not listed here, check either the log files in the /home/pi directory (and its subdirectories) or the Chromium (or Google Chrome) developer console.

The web application fails with the 500 Internal Server Error

This can be caused by a variety of reasons. More information as to the cause of the problem will be available in the `/home/pi/mirror_webapp/mirror_app.log` log file.

Some of the common issues that are likely to cause this are:

- The lack of Internet connection may cause failure to update widgets, such as weather and RSSTicker
- Errors in widget configuration files can cause failure of the server-side Python scripting
- Errors in the widget code itself will also cause this issue; although this is less likely

The display does not work

There can be issues with the usage of certain HDMI to VGA adapters with the Pi. Edit the `/boot/config.txt` file and uncomment the following line:

```
hdmi_force_hotplug=1
```

This forces the Pi to output the video on the HDMI output even if it fails to detect a device connected to it.

If you still have problems after this, then there is likely an issue with the power supply you are using to power the Pi. Since HDMI to VGA adapters also draw power, a larger USB power supply (preferably capable of outputting up to 2 A) is needed to perform stable operations.

Summary

In this chapter, we looked at how to run a web application on the Pi using Flask and Python to create a framework that provides an easy way to add new information displays to the mirror display.

We also had a look at some more advanced techniques to manufacture an enclosure, which can be applied to a wide range of projects you may wish to pursue after this book.

In the next chapter, we will look at yet another example of how the Pi can be used to control electronic devices in real time, when we will build an electronic xylophone that plays music from MIDI files.

10
Bottle Xylophone

In this chapter, we will build a configurable MIDI-controlled xylophone-like instrument made with empty glass bottles and a set of servos. This will make use of almost all of the Pi's GPIO headers to drive the servos.

The servos are controlled using a web application that allows you to upload a MIDI file, set a temp, and allows the Pi to play the file on the bottles using a configuration file to tell it which bottle is tuned to which note. The tuning itself is done by varying the level of water in each bottle.

Since this project requires a lot of GPIO pins, you may wish to opt for a B+ model, which has an additional nine GPIO pins on its 40-pin connector.

What you will need

For this project, you will need the following:

- The Raspberry Pi B+
- A small section of a prototyping board
- USB power supply and a micro USB cable
- High current 5 V power supply
- Several 1000 uF capacitors (www.maplin.co.uk/p/1000f-35v-85c-radial-electrolytic-capacitor-vh51f)
- A breadboard (www.maplin.co.uk/p/ad-100-breadboard-ag08j)
- A strip of 0.1-inch pin headers
- 0.1-inch male-to-female pin jumpers
- M3 nuts and machine screws
- Cable ties
- 15x empty glass bottles

- 15x micro servos
- A 15x servo mount base
- A 15x servo mount

I found that the larger 500 ml bottles are better for this as opposed to the 330 ml ones. Anything larger then 500 ml will still work; however, they may not fit on the servo mount base correctly (this should not stop the servo from working correctly).

To make tuning easier, it is recommended that you use the same size bottles for all the 15 notes.

The amount of capacitors you will need is determined by the power output of the power supply you are using and the number of servos you have; at least five capacitors are recommended for this. The power supply should be rated for at least 2 A to ensure reliable operation.

Assembling a note bottle

The bottle mounts are comprised of two laser cut sections of 3 mm material. This can be any rigid material, such as MDF, plywood, or acrylic. I would recommend you use MDF, as it is less prone to damage under force and can be sanded easily if the joints are too tight.

The base design has two layers, one for the section that is to be cut and a section that shows the rough placement of the bottles. This can be engraved if you would like it as part of the "note bottle" assembly; however, this is not required.

The parts required to assemble one note bottle

The servo arms that actually hit the bottles will be made using a short section of metal bar. This can really be any metal bar as long as all the servos use the same type in order to make tuning easier. To do this, perform the following steps:

1. The first step is to cut 15 lengths of the metal bar. To do this, use a piece of kitchen roll to tightly grip the bar at the edge of a table and cut a section around 10 cm long using a hacksaw.

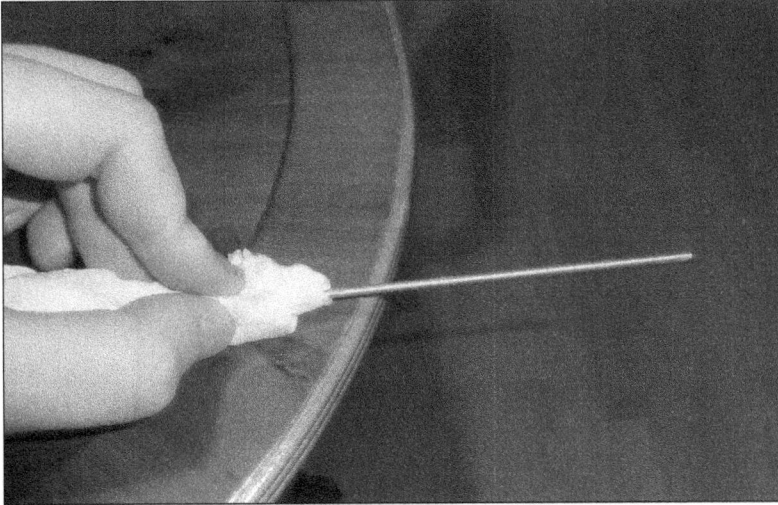

2. Once this is done, you can then attach the bars to the plastic servo arms that came with each servo. To do this, we will use the arm with two large servo arms opposite each other (as shown in the following image) to attach the metal bar to the servo using two cable ties.

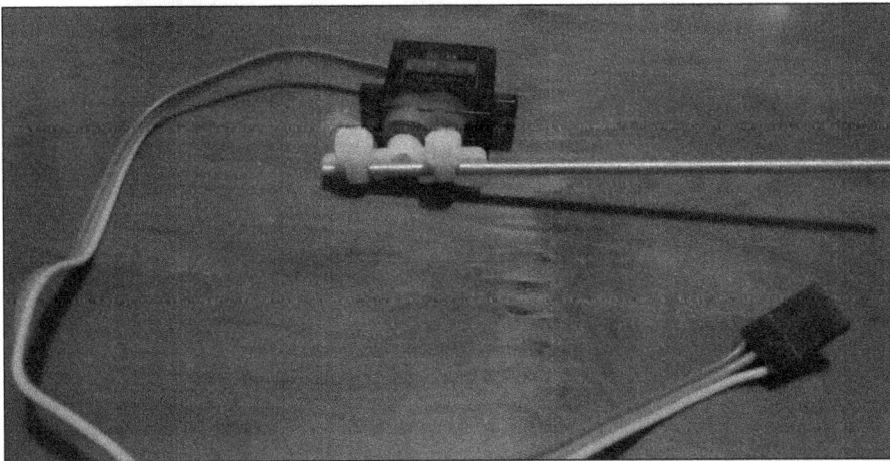

3. The next step is to attach the small servo mount to the larger mount base. You can attach the mount on either of the sets of the mounting holes; however, you only need to attach one servo mount per base.

4. If the joint is slack, then you can use an M3 nut and machine screws to tighten the joint. Whether this is needed or not depends on the resolution of the laser cutter used to machine the parts. If the joint feels fairly tight on its own, then you can skip this step.

5. Now, all that is left is to attach the servo to the servo mount. This can be done using either the small screws that came with the servo or using an adhesive, such as hot glue or Araldite.

Once this is done, you should have a note bottle assembly that looks similar to the one shown in the following image:

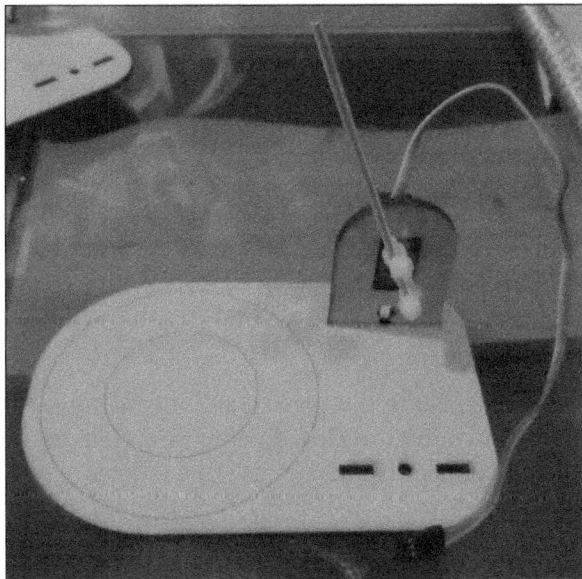

Electronics

Now that the note bottle assembly is built, it is time to build the electronics that will connect the servos to the Pi. This step is relatively simple, as all that you need to do is connect the Pi directly to the signal wire of the servos (usually yellow or white, sometimes orange) and provide power to the servos.

Since this project has the scope to use a lot of GPIO pins, we will use the Pi B+ for this project, which has an additional nine usable GPIO pins on its 40-pin header than on the older Pi model B's 26 pin header.

For reference, the circuit we will construct is laid out similar to the following diagram (note that for simplicity, only one servo is shown here):

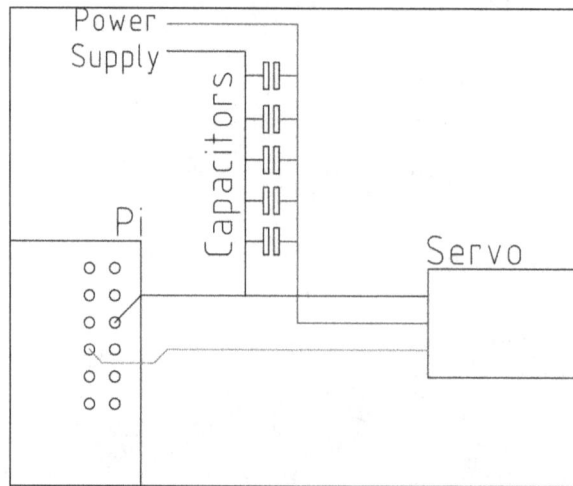

The first step to create the electronic parts of this project is to build a power distribution board that can be connected to all the servos in order to receive power. This board is very similar to the one used for the servos on the robotic arm in *Chapter 8, Remote-operated Robotic Arm*. Perform the following steps to build a power distribution board:

1. Take a section of the prototyping board and 0.1-inch pin headers and solder them, as shown in the following diagram, such that there are two long strips of connected pins:

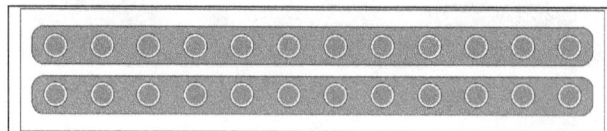

Once this is complete, you should have a board that looks similar to this:

2. If your power supply is rated for 3 A or less, you will most likely need to include a capacitor bank to ensure that there is a constant reliable power supply for the motors. This can be built by simply connecting the capacitors along with one of the power rails of a breadboard. Using two male-to-female jumper wires, connect this to the servo power distribution board.

While building the capacitor bank, ensure that all the capacitors are wired in the correct way. There will be a light strip with several negative (-) symbols next to the leg that must be connected to the ground. This leg is also shorter than the positive leg.

If this type of capacitor is connected in the incorrect way in the circuit, then it can swell, leak, or explode.

3. Next, we will connect each of the servos to the power distribution board such that the signal pin is overhanging on the edge. Note that because of the width of the servo headers, you are better off if you connect them in sets of five, as shown in the following image:

4. Finally, we can connect the servo signal wires to the Pi. The following diagram shows the pins that are available on both the Pi model B (just the pins above the blue line) and the model B+ (the entire connector). In order to use the default configuration supplied with the code, you must have a note bottle on these pins: **4, 17, 18, 27, 22, 23, 24, 10, 9, 25, 11, 8, 7,** and **5.** The following diagram shows the GPIO pins available to connect the servos to and the common ground pin:

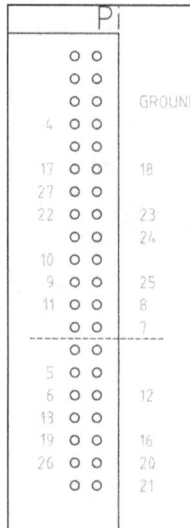

Once this is complete and all the bottles are in place, the finished setup should look something like this:

If you find that you cannot lay out each of the note bottles in a very suitable way due to the short cables on the servos, you can use some extension cables that give around another 30 cm of cable length. Such cables can be found at www.amazon.co.uk/Remote-Control-Servo-Extension-Cable/dp/B007SUKUXM.

The web application

As with the previous chapter, the web application that controls the servos is built using the Flask framework and served using Nginx and Gunicorn. Hence, the deployment procedure will be very similar here:

1. First, we must ensure that the Raspbian installation is up to date and install the packages that we need to deploy on the web application:

```
sudo apt-get update
sudo apt-get upgrade
sudo apt-get install python-pip git python-dev gunicorn supervisor
nginx swig libasound-dev
sudo pip install RPIO
```

2. Next, we will clone the code repository for the MIDI parsing library that will be used to read MIDI files and then install it using Python setup tools:

```
git clone https://github.com/vishnubob/python-midi.git
cd python-midi
sudo python setup.py install
cd
```

3. Next, we will clone the code repository for the Flask framework and install it using Python setup tools:

```
git clone https://github.com/mitsuhiko/flask.git
cd flask
sudo python setup.py install
cd
```

4. Next, we will copy the Nginx configuration files from the project folder to the configuration directories; we will have Nginx verify the configuration and apply the configuration by restarting the Nginx service:

```
sudo cp config_files/nginx/bottle_xylophone.conf /etc/nginx/sites-available/bottle_xylophone.conf
sudo ln -s /etc/nginx/sites-available/bottle_xylophone.conf /etc/nginx/sites-enabled/
sudo rm /etc/nginx/sites-enabled/default
sudo nginx -t
sudo service nginx restart
```

5. Now, we will copy the supervisor configuration and have the supervisor reread its configuration files:

```
sudo cp config_files/supervisor/bottle_xylophone_webapp.conf /etc/supervisor/conf.d/bottle_xylophone_webapp.conf
sudo supervisorctl reread
```

6. Next, we will copy the web application configuration, which will be read by our web application. It contains the configuration for the servo output:

```
cp config_files/bottle_xylophone.conf ~
```

7. Finally, we will update the supervisor and start the web application:

```
sudo supervisorctl update
sudo supervisorctl start bottle_xylophone_webappp
```

Now that the web application has been deployed, you should be able to browse to the application using the IP address of the Pi from a PC on the same network as the Pi. When you do so, you should see a page similar to the following:

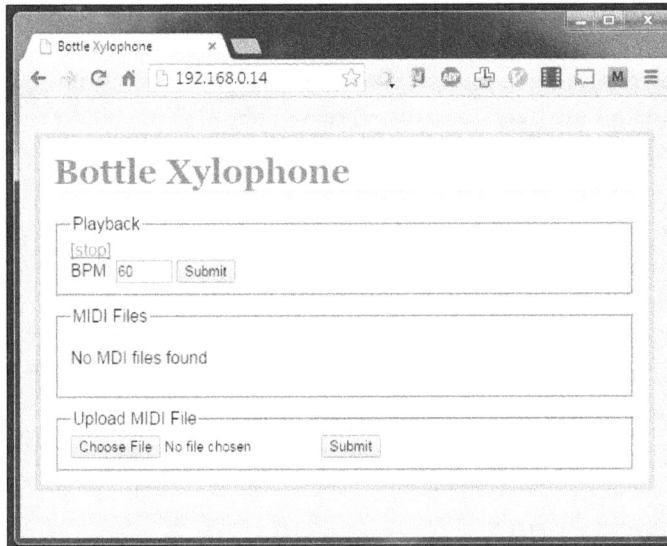

Configuration

Chances are that the Pi and bottles will need to be reconfigured and retuned on a per song basis due to the limited number of notes that can be configured at the same time (if you use the Pi model B+, this may not be a big problem). To help make this process easier, there is a script (midi_note_summary.py) included with this chapter that will take a MIDI file and generate a report of exactly what notes are used in the file. This will make it easier for us to determine which notes have to be configured on the Pi and accordingly, the bottles can be tuned for them.

This script should be used with the following command, where MIDI_FILE is the filename of the MIDI file:

```
python midi_note_summary.py MIDI_FILE.mid
```

Its output is shown in the following screenshot:

Note that this script will work straight away on the Pi without additional configuration, as all the required libraries are installed when the web application is deployed. However, to use the script on a different PC, you will first have to download and install the `python-midi` library (https://github.com/vishnubob/python-midi).

Once you have determined the range of notes that are needed for a particular song, you can then modify the `bottle_xylophone.conf` configuration file to set the GPIO pins that will be used for each MIDI note.

This file must first contain two settings that determine the servo timing output values that correspond to the retracted position (which the servo is in when it is not being used) and hit position (the position at which the servo arm will hit the bottle). These settings will be applied to all the configured servos unless stated otherwise with a servo-specific configuration:

```
DEFAULT_HIT = 1700
DEFAULT_RETRACT = 1500
```

The following section of the configuration file should now contain the mapping between the MIDI note and GPIO number. The general format for this is as follows:

```
MIDI_GPIO_[NOTE] = [GPIO]
```

Here, `[NOTE]` is the MIDI note number and `[GPIO]` is the GPIO number. An example of how notes should be mapped is shown as follows:

```
MIDI_GPIO_49 = 4
MIDI_GPIO_50 = 17
MIDI_GPIO_51 = 18
MIDI_GPIO_53 = 27
```

In the case where a particular servo has different hit and retract positions from the others (for example, because of a different sized bottle or servo arm), this can be configured using the general format:

```
MIDI_HIT_[NOTE] = [SERVO OUTPUT]
MIDI_RETRACT_[NOTE] = [SERVO OUTPUT]
```

Here, `[NOTE]` is the MIDI note number and `[SERVO OUTPUT]` is the servo timing value to the output. An example of this is shown as follows:

```
MIDI_HIT_49 = 1800
MIDI_RETRACT_49 = 1550
MIDI_HIT_50 = 1850
```

Once you have configured the web application, it is worth changing the default log level from DEBUG to either INFO or WARNING to reduce the amount of information that is saved to the log file. This can be done using the following entry in the configuration file:

```
LOG_LEVEL = [LOG LEVEL]
```

Here, [LOG LEVEL] is either INFO or WARNING.

When you are finished making changes to the configuration file, make sure to reload the web application using the following two commands:

```
sudo supervisorctl stop bottle_xylophone_webapp
sudo supervisorctl start bottle_xylophone_webapp
```

Tuning

To get assistance for tuning the bottles, it is best to use a tone generator to get an idea of the sound you are aiming for when you strike the bottles. These are available in many forms; one good website that does this is http://plasticity.szynalski. com/tone-generator.htm, which allows you to select any note and play a sample of it. Audacity (http://audacity.sourceforge.net/) is an example of a piece of desktop software that does a similar thing. There are also many smartphone applications that have similar features.

The first step to tune a set of bottles is to sort the bottles into groups of unique combinations of shapes and sizes. The combination of these two properties will define the pitch of the sound a bottle without any liquid makes when it is struck (the frequency of which is known as the bottle's natural frequency, that is, the frequency at which it will oscillate when not exposed to external dampening). We will then use the bottles with the lowest pitch for the lower-pitched MIDI notes and vice versa.

Once you have a source of the actual note you are aiming for, you simply have to hit each note with one of the servo arms (detached from the servo itself) and change the level of water in the bottle until the note sounds similar to the target note.

Testing

Now that we have finished building the bottle xylophone, it is time to give it a test using a MIDI file. First, browse to the IP address of the Pi and you should be greeted with a page similar to the following:

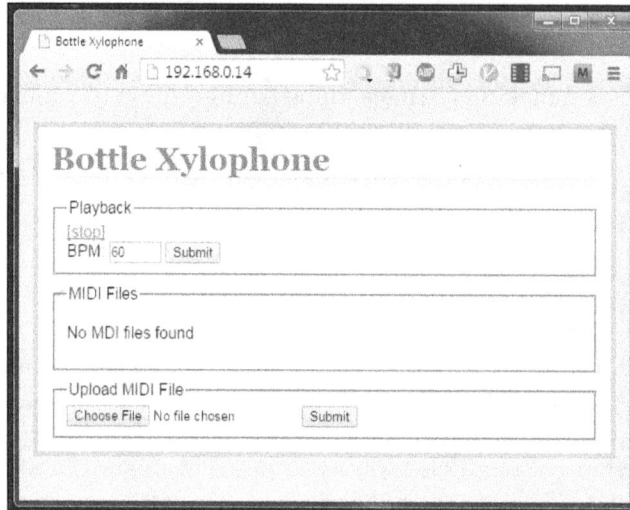

Toward the bottom of the page, you will have the option to browse for a MIDI file (with the .mid file extension) and to upload it. Once you have done so, you will see the file listed in the **MIDI Files** section of the page as well as a confirmation message that the file was successfully uploaded, as shown in the following screenshot:

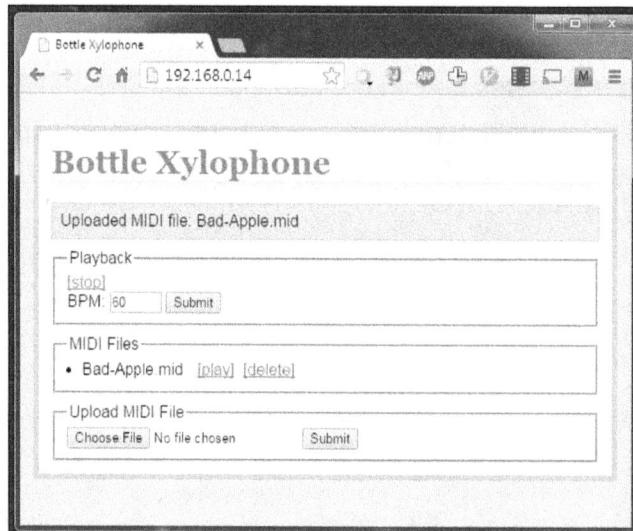

If required, the tempo at which the file will be played can be modified using the tempo setting at the top of the page. This must be set before you select a file to be played by changing the value in the field and by clicking on **Submit**. Once the tempo has been changed, you will see a notification, as shown in the following screenshot:

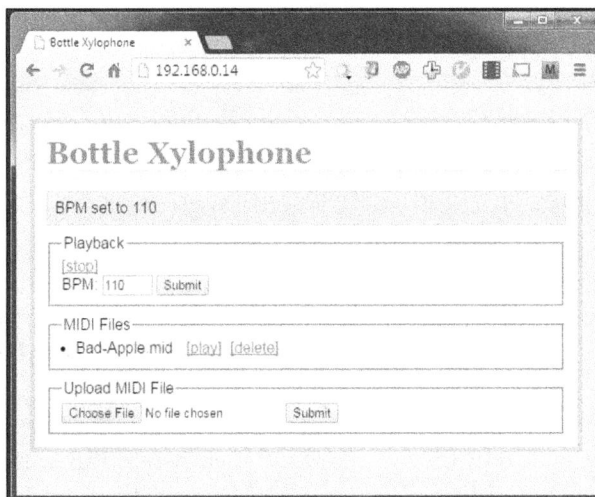

Once you are ready to play a file, simply click on the **[play]** link next to the filename. You should see a notification, as shown in the following screenshot, and the servos should start to move. If you have any issues here, refer to the *Troubleshooting* section later in this chapter.

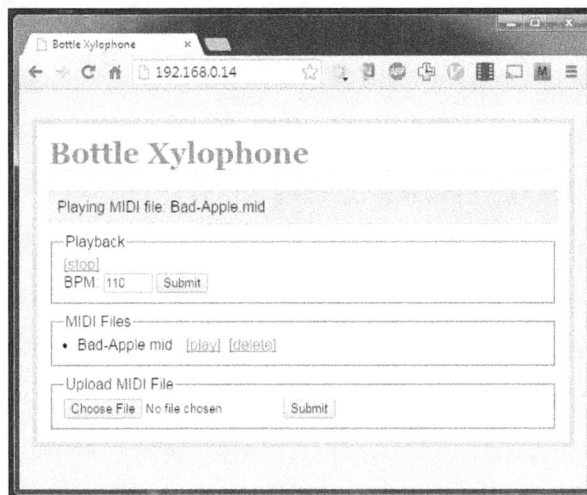

Playback can then be stopped using the **[stop]** link near the top of the page.

Troubleshooting

This section details some of the common issues you may encounter while building this project and steps you can use to resolve them.

Notes are missed

The most common cause of missed notes is the delay between the note on event and note off event in the MIDI file. If the MIDI file is too short, it will not give the servo arm time to extend and retract. This can be rectified using the `midi_note_expand.py` script included in the code for this chapter.

This script can be run using the following command; here, `MIDI_FILE` is the filename of the MIDI file, `DELAY` is the desired minimum delay in milliseconds between note on and note off events, and `TEMPO` is the tempo you intend to play the file at (the delay time will vary depending on the tempo at which the file is played):

```
python midi_note_expand.py -f MIDI_FILE.mid -d DELAY -t TEMPO
```

This script will produce an output similar to that shown in the following screenshot. By default, it saves the modified file as `MIDI_FILE_modified.mid`. By default, the script will only modify the delay between the notes if it is less than the value set using the `-d` parameter. The script can also be used to set the delay between note events for all the notes in the file to the same value by adding the `-s` flag to the end of the command.

```
dan@dannixon-envy-ubuntu ~/R/10-BeerBottleXylophone (master=)>
python midi_note_expand.py -f midi_files/Bad-Apple.mid -d 500
INFO: Ticks per ms for resolution 960.000000 and BPM 60 = 0.960000
INFO: Minumum ticks between note on and off = 481.000000
INFO: Changed 0 notes over track
INFO: Changed 1385 notes over track
INFO: Saved output MIDI file: midi_files/Bad-Apple_modified.mid
```

Servos do not move correctly

If the servos seem to be behaving erratically, then there is almost certainly an issue regarding a lack of sufficient power supply for all the servos. This can be confirmed by measuring the voltage across 5 V and ground connections on the servo power distribution board.

Summary

In this chapter, we continued to look at the possibilities to control hardware using the GPIO ports and had a quick look at the additional features of the Pi model B+.

We also looked at some of the issues caused by driving large numbers of electronic devices that require a large amount of power during their operations. We also looked at how these issues can be overcome.

Now that you have completed all the projects in this book, it is time for you to embark on your own projects using the Raspberry Pi and the vast range of devices that can be used with it to create some impressive projects that can interact with the world around you.

Index

Symbols

7-Zip
  URL 93

A

Adafruit-Retrogame
  URL 66
All Things Pi
  URL 42
Arduino
  setting up, for Maplin sensors 130-132
  setting up, for RF network 169-171
Arduino IDE
  URL 130
Audacity
  URL 249

B

bottle xylophone
  building 237
  configuration 247, 248
  electronics, configuring 242-245
  note bottle, assembling 238-241
  requisites 237, 238
  testing 250, 251
  troubleshooting 252
  tuning 249
  web application, creating 245, 246

C

calibration, robotic arm
  arm 1 servos 198-200
  arm 2 servos 198

chassis motors 197
hand servos 198
camera
  setting up, for robotic arm 181-187
Camera Serial Interface (CSI) 182
captures, GPS-enabled time-lapse recorder
  GPS data, exporting as CSV 88, 89
  time-lapse video, creating 87, 88
  using 87
capture software, GPS-enabled time-lapse recorder
  setting up 84-87
Chromium
  setting up 212-215
closure 208
comma-separated value (CSV) file 88
configuration, magic mirror
  styles 233
  widget 229
Coreutils Viewer
  URL 6

D

Document Object Model (DOM) 208
drive electronics
  configuring, for robotic arm 176-181

E

electronics, portable speaker system
  amplifier circuit, connecting 29-32
  battery, using 33-35
  building 28, 29
enclosure construction, magic mirror
  instructions 215-227
  Pi enclosure 229

URL, for Pi enclosure 229
without plywood enclosure 227, 228
extension cables
reference link 245

F

FileZilla
URL 13
Flask
URL 139

G

**General Purpose Input and
        Output (GPIO) 1**
Google Charts API
URL 139
Google Fonts
URL 233
GPS-enabled time-lapse recorder
capture software, setting up 84-87
captures, using 87
creating 73
hardware, setting up 74
requisites 73, 74
Gunicorn
URL 139

H

hackspaces 92
hardware, GPS-enabled time-lapse recorder
camera board 74
camera module, connecting to
        Raspberry Pi 74, 75
GPS module, setting up 78-83
Raspberry Pi camera, setting up 76, 77
setting up 74
home security system
creating 151
designing 152, 153
requisites 151, 152
RF network 165, 166
sensors, interfacing 163
structure 152
troubleshooting 172
web application, creating 153

home theater PC
assembling 114-119
creating 91
LCD, setting up 104-111
OpenELEC, setting up 92, 93
requisites 91, 92
switches, setting up 111-114

I

installation, Logitech Media Server 42, 43

J

JavaScript
reference link, for development 209
JavaScript Object Notation (JSON) 206
Jinja template language
reference link 208

L

LCD
setting up 104-111
LCD.xml file
reference link 111
LCDproc 106
light-dependent resistor (LDR) 126
Linux
SD card, writing 4-6
Linux distribution
selecting 2
Logitech Media Server
backup image, creating of SD card 40
installing 42, 43
Raspberry Pi, setting up as Wi-Fi access
        point 44, 45
running 40
setting up 21, 22
USB storage device, automounting 41

M

Mac OS
SD card, writing 4-6
magic mirror
configuration 229
creating 203

[PACKT] open source *
PUBLISHING   community experience distilled

Thank you for buying
Raspberry Pi Blueprints

About Packt Publishing

Packt, pronounced 'packed', published its first book, *Mastering phpMyAdmin for Effective MySQL Management,* in April 2004, and subsequently continued to specialize in publishing highly focused books on specific technologies and solutions.

Our books and publications share the experiences of your fellow IT professionals in adapting and customizing today's systems, applications, and frameworks. Our solution-based books give you the knowledge and power to customize the software and technologies you're using to get the job done. Packt books are more specific and less general than the IT books you have seen in the past. Our unique business model allows us to bring you more focused information, giving you more of what you need to know, and less of what you don't.

Packt is a modern yet unique publishing company that focuses on producing quality, cutting-edge books for communities of developers, administrators, and newbies alike. For more information, please visit our website at www.packtpub.com.

About Packt Open Source

In 2010, Packt launched two new brands, Packt Open Source and Packt Enterprise, in order to continue its focus on specialization. This book is part of the Packt Open Source brand, home to books published on software built around open source licenses, and offering information to anybody from advanced developers to budding web designers. The Open Source brand also runs Packt's Open Source Royalty Scheme, by which Packt gives a royalty to each open source project about whose software a book is sold.

Writing for Packt

We welcome all inquiries from people who are interested in authoring. Book proposals should be sent to author@packtpub.com. If your book idea is still at an early stage and you would like to discuss it first before writing a formal book proposal, then please contact us; one of our commissioning editors will get in touch with you.

We're not just looking for published authors; if you have strong technical skills but no writing experience, our experienced editors can help you develop a writing career, or simply get some additional reward for your expertise.

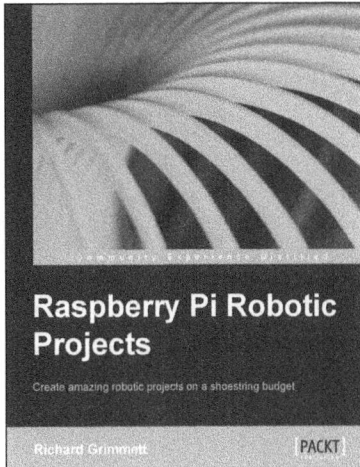

Raspberry Pi Robotic Projects

ISBN: 978-1-84969-432-2   Paperback: 278 pages

Create amazing robotic projects on a shoestring budget

1. Make your projects talk and understand speech with Raspberry Pi.

2. Use standard webcam to make your projects see and enhance vision capabilities.

3. Full of simple, easy-to-understand instructions to bring your Raspberry Pi online for developing robotics projects.

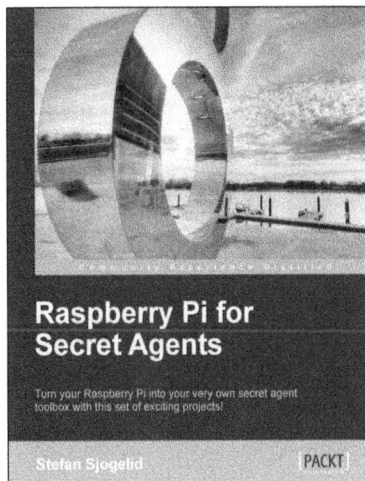

Raspberry Pi for Secret Agents

ISBN: 978-1-84969-578-7   Paperback: 152 pages

Turn your Raspberry Pi into your very own secret agent toolbox with this set of exciting projects!

1. Detect an intruder on a camera and set off an alarm.

2. Listen in or record conversations from a distance.

3. Find out what the other computers on your network are up to.

Please check **www.PacktPub.com** for information on our titles

www.ingramcontent.com/pod-product-compliance
Lightning Source LLC
Chambersburg PA
CBHW082109220326
41598CB00066BA/5930